*The International Series in*

**Guidance and Counseling**


*Consulting Editor*

*the late* **R. Wray Strowig**

*Department of Counselor Education*
*University of Wisconsin*

*Counseling and Values*
A PHILOSOPHICAL EXAMINATION

# Counseling and Values

## A PHILOSOPHICAL EXAMINATION

**James Allan Peterson**

*University of Vermont*

**International Textbook Company**

*An* Intext *Publisher*

*Scranton, Pennsylvania 18515*

*ISBN 0 7002 2276 6*

Material reprinted by permission:

*The Humanity of Man* by Ralph Barton Perry. Copyright © 1956 by George Braziller, Inc. Reprinted with permission of the publisher.

*Psychology and the Human Dilemma* by R. May. Copyright © 1967 by Litton Educational Publishing, Inc. Used by permission of Van Nostrand Reinhold Company.

*The Crisis of Our Age* by P. A. Sorokin. Copyright © 1941 by E. P. Dutton & Co., Inc. Used by permission of the publisher.

*Counseling: Philosophy, Theory, and Practice* by Dugald S. Arbuckle (pp. 15, 275). Copyright © 1965 by Allyn and Bacon, Inc., Boston. Reprinted by permission of the publisher.

Chapter 13 from *Beyond Counseling and Therapy* by Robert R. Carkhuff and Bernard G. Berenson. Copyright © 1967 by Holt, Rinehart and Winston, Inc. Reprinted by permission of Holt, Rinehart and Winston, Inc.

*Science and Human Values* by J. Bronowski. Copyright © 1956 and 1965 by J. Bronowski. Reprinted by permission of Julian Messner, a Division of Simon and Schuster, Inc.

*Mere Christianity* by C. S. Lewis. Copyright © 1943, 1945, 1952, by The Macmillan Company. Reprinted with permission of The Macmillan Company.

*Values in Psychotherapy* by Charlotte Buhler. Copyright © 1962 by The Free Press. Reprinted with permission of The Macmillan Company.

*Existence* by Rollo May, Ernest Angel, and Henri F. Ellenberger (eds.). Basic Books, Inc., Publishers, New York, 1958.

*To Neysa, Sherry, Kathy, and Susie*

# *Preface*

This book is intended for those who are concerned with the development of youth in a society rocked with change and value conflict. It is especially intended for those counselors who by their chosen profession have sought to involve themselves as "helping persons" with those young people who, in such a society, desperately seek an identity and a feeling of significance. This study seeks to clarify that ambiguous word value and then seeks to deal with those conflicting issues that readily surround and plague the counselor who finds himself involved, because of the nature of his work, in value questions and concerns.

These writings are not intended to be, by any means, the final word on the subject. Neither do I claim any special endowment of wisdom. As Byron said, "Words are things, and a small drop of ink, falling like dew upon a thought, produces that which makes thousands, perhaps millions, think." Although I do not pretend such a large body of readers, if the reader is stimulated to think about some of the issues involved, a major goal of this study will have been achieved.

The subject of values is extremely complex. It is not an area of specific, universally agreed upon facts—black and white statements of "truth"—but is rather an area that abounds with controversy. Even though the realm of value theory is complex and difficult, there is a great need to examine it for the understanding it can yield counselors in their daily confrontation with value questions.

> The situation in morals is like that in medicine. You do not stop treating the sick just because there is controversy about basic concepts and underlying theories, even about individual diagnoses. You do your best and keep going. (See Abraham Edel, *Method in Ethical Theory*. New York: Bobbs-Merril, 1963, p. 3.)

I approach the topic of values in counseling with caution and with the realization that the conclusions at which I arrive are offered not as dogmatic and tested "truths" but rather as points for consideration, deliberation, and discussion, to the end that enlightenment may result. With Montaigne I would state, "All I say is by way of discourse and nothing by way of advice. I should not speak so boldly if it were my due to be believed."

A major limitation of this book is that it focuses upon verbal expression of values and not upon actions. Values can operate differently on these two levels. For example, counselors may not do what they say they *ought* to do. This would indicate a difference in value at the action level, perhaps explainable in terms of the *desired* as opposed to the *desirable*. What one *ought* to do, though, serves an important function in measuring the adequacy of what one *is* doing. Regarding his own theory, the counselor must be not only descriptive but prescriptive as well. Of necessity, it is left to others to compare the *action* with the *ought*.

An important assumption made in this study is that counseling and psychotherapy deal essentially with the same value questions. Therefore, learnings concerned with values in psychotherapy are considered to be equally applicable to counseling and have been included.

I am deeply grateful to Dugald Arbuckle for his help throughout this study and to Theodore Brameld, for his timely suggestions and support. Sincere appreciation is also due Paul Nash, who read the manuscript and offered helpful criticism. I would be remiss also not to thank Ruth Barry and Beverly Wolf, without whose encouragement I might never have begun. None of these, of course, are responsible for the final thoughts expressed or any errors that may be found.

Finally, I am especially grateful to my wife Neysa and to our children. They were not only patient but supportive during the several long years this work was in progress.

James Allan Peterson

Burlington, Vermont
May, 1970

# Acknowledgments

The author is grateful for permission to reprint material from:

*The Goals of Psychotherapy* by Alvin R. Mahrer, published by Appleton-Century-Crofts;

*Personality and Social Encounter* by Gordon Allport, published by Beacon Press;

*Method in Ethical Theory* by Abraham Edel and *The Measure of Man* by Joseph Wood Krutch, published by Bobbs-Merrill Co.;

*Essays in Pragmatism* by William James, published by Hafner Publishing Co.;

*The Modern Temper* by Joseph Wood Krutch, published by Harcourt, Brace, and World;

*Counseling and Psychotherapy: Theory and Practice* by C. H. Patterson, *Cultural Foundations of Education* by Theodore Brameld, *Excellence* and *Self-Renewal* by John W. Gardner, *Guidance Policy and Practice* by R. H. Mathewson, *New Knowledge in Human Values* edited by Abraham Maslow, *Reality Therapy* by William Glasser, *Socrates and the Conscience of Man* by Micheline Sauvage, and *The Art of Loving* by Erich Fromm, all published by Harper and Row;

*Realms of Value* by Ralph B. Perry and *Toward a General Theory of Action* edited by Parsons and Shils, published by Harvard University Press;

*An Introduction to Philosophy* by E. S. Brightman, revised by Robert Beck, *Escape from Freedom* by Erich Fromm, *Philosophies of Education in Cultural Perspective* and *Toward A Reconstructed Philosophy of Education* by Theodore Brameld, and *The Modes and Morals of Psychotherapy* by Perry London, published by Holt, Rinehart and Winston;

*The Counselor in the Schools: A Reconceptualization* by Angelo Boy and Gerald Pine and *The School Counselor* by Richard H. Byrne, published by Houghton Mifflin Co.;

*Personality and the Good* by Peter Bertocci and Richard Millard, published by David C. McKay Co.;

*Human Nature and the Human Condition* by Joseph Wood Krutch, and *Culture Against Man* by Jules Henry, published by Random House;

*What Is Value?* by Risieri Frondizi published by Open Court publishing Co.;

*Counseling Points of View* edited by Willis Dugan, published by the University of Minnesota Press;

*The Personnel and Guidance Journal, The School Counselor,* and *Counselor Education and Supervision,* publications of the American Personnel and Guidance Association;

*The American Psychologist, The Journal of Counseling Psychology,* and *The Journal of Personality,* published by the American Psychological Association;

the journals *Human Relations* and *The Humanist;*

and *The Philosophical Forum* published by Boston University Department of Philosophy.

Also to The University of Pennsylvania Press, Columbia University Press, and The University of Chicago Press from whom material has been quoted.

# Contents

# List of Diagrams

# chapter 1

# Counseling and Values:
# A Modern Dilemma

## INTRODUCTION

> The universe revealed by science, especially the sciences of biology and psychology, is one in which the human spirit cannot find a comfortable home. That spirit breathes freely only in a universe where what philosophers call Value Judgments are of supreme importance. It needs to believe, for instance, that right and wrong are real, that Love is more than a biological function, that the human mind is capable of reason rather than merely of rationalization, and that it has the power to will and to choose instead of being compelled merely to react in the fashion predetermined by its conditioning. Since science has proved that none of these beliefs is more than a delusion, mankind will be compelled either to surrender what we call its humanity by adjusting to the real world or to live some kind of tragic existence in a universe alien to the deepest needs of its nature.[1]

Such was the description Joseph Wood Krutch gave of the human dilemma in 1929. Today it appears to be no less true. One has but to pick up the morning newspaper to become aware of the struggle and strife within our society, much of it among the young. The young are no longer willing to accept values merely handed to them. They are asking pertinent questions, and they evidence little remaining patience. Where authority once ruled, violence has erupted, and the young demand a place of significance.

What is the problem? Drastic change. We are living in an age of rapid transition, an age of turbulence and loss of direction. Such times are painful and disruptive. As Eric Hoffer puts it, "Broken habits can be more painful and crippling than broken bones," and "disintegrating values may have as deadly a fallout as disintegrating atoms."[2] We are

---

[1]Joseph W. Krutch, *The Modern Temper* (New York: Harcourt, Brace and Co., 1929), p. xi.

witnessing an increasing movement from scarcity to abundance, from an authoritarian tradition to one that is equalitarian, from work to leisure, from nationalism to internationalism, from the primitive to the modern.

It is not surprising that such a transitional process creates much anxiety and brings about a critical reexamination of meanings and purposes, as well as frenzied efforts to reestablish some sense of integration.

> Now there are times when a whole generation is caught ... between two ages, two modes of life, with the consequence that it loses all power to understand itself and has no standards, no security, no simple acquiesence.[3]

In such periods of history, problems of values come into sharper focus, for man is a valuing being and he dwells in a world of perplexing choices. In such a world, counselors, who by the very nature of their work are involved with individuals in the process of choice-making, cannot afford to neglect the realm of values, for one cannot avoid becoming involved.

## HISTORICAL ASPECTS

To take refuge in a claim of being scientific and thus unbiased is to deceive one's self, and to avoid the issue by claiming neutrality is to take a position of naive realism. Counseling is a process of deep human involvement between subjective valuing beings, and even at the outset of a counseling relationship certain values are presupposed. The counselor becomes a philosopher, often perhaps without recognizing it. Walters states:

> Every psychotherapist is a philosopher of sorts. When the psychologist turns away from his measurements and statistics to deal with troubled individuals on a one-to-one basis, he leaves pure science behind. Becoming a participant in the healing process draws him inescapably into the realm of values.[4]

Allport is in agreement:

[2]Eric Hoffer, *The Temper of Our Time* (New York: Harper and Row, Perennial Library, 1969), p. x.

[3]Herman Hesse, as quoted in Rollo May, *The Meaning of Anxiety* (New York: The Ronald Press, 1950), chapter 1.

[4]Orville S. Walters, "Metaphysics, Religion, and Psychotherapy?," *Journal of Counseling Psychology*, V, 4 (Winter 1958), 248.

Whether he knows it or not, every psychologist gravitates toward an ontological position. Like a satellite he slips into the orbit of positivism, naturalism, idealism, personalism.[5]

Until recently, values in counseling have remained largely implicit. It has been recognized by a number of leaders in the field that it is very important to make values explicit, for only then can they be recognized for the part they play in the counseling process.[6]

The word guidance implies value, for one must ask: Guided toward what end? By whom? On what authority? Everytime he meets a client the counselor is confronted with the value question of whether or not to counsel; if he chooses in the affirmative, he must make some decision as to the goal to follow. In his belief in the counseling process he presupposes certain values regarding the counselee and the counseling relationship. The very quest for counselor role is a value quest.[7] The first task in facing value questions is to make them explicit.

As Sorenson[8] has noted, the willingness of counselors to face philosophical issues is vital to the very survival of counseling as a helping process. Counselors must seek self-renewal in order to survive change. There is a need for the development of a new and more adequate theory based upon ethical and psychological perspectives and the importance of discovering objectives that can be made explicit and thus can be subjected to continuing rigorous examination. Choice-making and the increase of freedom by increasing alternatives is a basic goal. Philosophical issues are involved in better understanding the process of decision-making and in becoming more sophisticated in recognizing and judging ethical assumptions.

The history of the guidance movement in its relationship to values has been largely one of acceptance of assumed values that for the most part remained implicit and thus unexamined in any degree of depth. It is apparent, however, that the early leaders of the guidance movement, in the early 1900's, were concerned with values.

[5]Gordon Allport, "The Psychological Nature of Personality," *Personalist*, XXIV (1953), 347.

[6]Richard Jessor, "Social Values and Psychotherapy," *Journal of Consulting Psychology*, XX, 4 (1956), 264–266.

[7]See C. Gilbert Wrenn, "Philosophical and Psychological Bases of Personnel Services in Education," *Personnel Services in Education*, Fifty-eighth Yearbook of the National Society for the Study of Education, Part II (Chicago: University of Chicago Press, 1959).

[8]Garth Sorenson, "Pterodactyls, Passenger Pigeons, and Personnel Workers," *Personnel and Guidance Journal*, XLIII, 5 (January 1965), 420–437.

Parsons[9] was a utopian social reformer, believing in the perfectibility of mankind. He viewed guidance as a means to a mutualistic society and the counselor's role as one leading to social goals by offering prescriptive advice.

Davis[10] preached the moral values of hard work, ambition, honesty, and the development of good character as assets in the business world. He was an advocate of the then popular "social gospel" and is said to have brought to guidance a touch of the supernatural. In his book *Vocational and Moral Guidance,* published in 1914, he made the following statement:

> From the moral standpoint, the idea of "guidance" is particularly essential in the development of the pupil. Ethical instruction that merely informs the brain does not necessarily produce better character. It is of most value when it is in some way applied to the actual thinking and acting of the pupil. In this connection, guidance means the pupil's better understanding of his own character; it means an awakening of the moral consciousness that will lead him to emulate the character of the good and the great who have gone before; it means a conception of himself as a social being in some future occupation, and *from this viewpoint,* the appreciation of his duty and obligation toward his business associates, toward his neighbors, and toward the law.[11]

Reed and Weaver in their writings emphasized a highly conservative point of view, with adjustment to industrial society a major goal.[12] Hill advocated a prescriptive point of view. He urged that goals should be based upon sound scientific research and should serve to guide youth toward a more perfect society. He further held that society could be improved through the use of education as a tool to cause youth to adjust and to choose the beautiful, the good, and the true.[13]

These leaders reveal the concern over societal and moral values in the beginnings of the guidance movement. At least part of the need for guidance stemmed from shifting values caused by movement from an agrarian to an industrial society.[14] The school had to assume re-

[9]Perry J. Rockwell, Jr., and John W. Rothney, "Some Social Ideas of Pioneers in the Guidance Movement," *Personnel and Guidance Journal,* XL, 4 (December 1961), 349–354.

[10]*Ibid.*

[11]Jesse B. Davis, as quoted by Robert H. Mathewson, *Guidance Policy and Practice* (New York: Harper and Row, 1962), p. 72.

[12]Rockwell and Rothney, "Some Social Ideas."

[13]*Ibid.*

[14]Ruth Barry and Beverly Wolf, *Modern Issues in Guidance-Personnel Work*

sponsibilities in all areas of the child's life rather than in the mere intellectual. In the midst of a growing secularism, college personnel workers assumed responsibility for the spiritual life of the student.

The introduction of the Cardinal Principles of Education in 1918 emphasized the need for more than mere intellectual studies in the schools, and their propositions were heavily value laden; for example, *good* health, *worthy* home membership, vocational *direction,* civic *responsibility, worthy* use of leisure, *ethical* character, as well as command of fundamental processes.[15] Although the Commission on the Reorganization of Secondary Education advocated a narrow guidance role in the schools, dealing with only vocational guidance, some of the leaders in guidance took a broader view; hence, "moral, civic, health, family, social, and even life became popular adjectives for guidance in addition to the older educational and vocational ones."[16] But it appears that throughout the 1930's and 1940's there was more emphasis upon technique than on philosophy, and, although values remained within the guidance framework, they were left unexamined and were assumed to be self-evident. The guidance movement grew with attempts to meet critical, pressing needs in society, and such immediate needs are not likely to leave much room for philosophical examination.

Wrenn in 1959 illustrated in a dramatic way this neglected area in guidance with an analogy to rapid suburban growth.

> If home building is extensive and expansion rapid, the need for streets will be a demanding one. Concrete or asphalt roadways may be laid so rapidly that careful grading and the preparation of foundations is neglected. The streets may carry the traffic and keep people out of the mud, but they will soon break through in spots, or fail to adapt to the runoff in time of heavy rainfall. Such streets may further lack consistency of material and structure—with one block of concrete and another of blacktop, gutters here but no gutters there, street signs on the curb in one block, and on posts in another. . . . An observer viewing this system of streets might cry aloud "expediency," "opportunism," and even "graft," but of course such an observer is not likely to have been present when the pressure was on.[17]

(New York: Bureau of Publications, Teachers College, Columbia University, 1957), chapter 2.

[15]Italics mine. See the Commission on the Reorganization of Secondary Education, *Cardinal Principles of Secondary Education,* Bulletin 35 (Washington: U.S. Govt. Printing Office, 1918).

[16]Barry and Wolf, *Modern Issues,* p. 30.

[17]Wrenn, "Philosophical and Psychological Bases," pp. 47–48.

Guidance, like Topsy, just "growed," with little concern for making explicit any of the value questions or with development of a sound philosophy. This does not mean that philosophical problems were not recognized but that their recognition meant mainly a search for freedom from inadequate frames borrowed from other disciplines. Recently there has been a growing trend toward facing these issues more directly.

> Dominating the philosophical history of guidance has been what we might call a search for a system. This quest was not wanting in the earliest days of the movement but has taken on a more pene-trating, sophisticated, and comprehensive character in recent times when it became increasingly clear that guidance as a profession required a philosophy and conceptual framework in its own right, denoting the meaning of the guidance process, defining the nature of its functions, and providing a rationale for consistent operations.[18]

Although this search for a consistent philosophy has been pre-sent in varying degrees throughout the history of the movement, questions dealing explicitly with individual and social values have been only a recent undertaking.

In a review of articles in the *Personnel and Guidance Journal* over a five-year span from 1952–1957, Barry and Wolf found only 4 articles dealing with values out of a total of 411.[19] Stone and Shertzer[20] examined the next five years (from September 1957, to May 1963) and found 8 articles on values out of a total of 480. This points up the dearth of articles dealing specifically with values. Since 1963 there appears to be a growing interest in philosophical matters, including value issues. This is especially noticeable in new texts, where space is now given to value problems.

Barry and Wolf have stated, "In many ways, the years since World War II resemble the thirty years preceding World War I."[21] Both periods represent rapid change and economic revolution. Where the early periods were a result of the industrial revolution, we are now on the threshold of what may be called the cybernetic revolution, and, although present problems always appear more dramatic than those of

---

[18]Mathewson, *Guidance Policy and Practice*, p. 73.

[19]Barry and Wolf, "Five Years of the *Personnel and Guidance Journal*," *Personnel and Guidance Journal*, XXXVI, 8 (April 1958), 549–555.

[20]Shelley C. Stone and Bruce Shertzer, "Ten Years of the *Personnel and Guidance Journal*," *Personnel and Guidance Journal*, XLII, 10 (June 1964), 958–969.

[21]Barry and Wolf, *Modern Issues*, p. 11.

the past, this new revolution threatens to bring with it an increased value crisis.[22]

Since one is confronted with value problems most directly at the practical level of working with individuals, the counseling process becomes a major source of direct value involvement. Green interprets the history of modern psychotherapy as "an unsuccessful struggle to evaluate the role of social values."

> The existence of social values has been denied; some values have been castigated as baneful to personality development; some therapists have demanded adjustment to some dominant value with an unstinted arbitrariness, some implicitly attempt to inculcate certain values while denying that such is their intention, still others use them as the basis for various schemes to revise the social structure entire.[23]

Counseling in education is not immune to such charges.

Buhler describes the history of psychotherapy in three periods.[24] The first was a period of active techniques where the therapist assumed the responsibility of pressing the client to a new decision. This was the common view of the early psychoanalytic movement, and a "correct" value orientation was assumed by the therapist, who then attempted to shift the client to "wise" and "healthy" decisions. In the second period there was a movement toward techniques of "neutrality, detachment, and noninterference." This was true of the psychoanalysts of this period, and an even greater abstinence from intervention was represented in the nonanalytical orientation of Rogers. In the third period, now present, there appears to be a growing trend toward active techniques once again.

There may be several reasons for this. First, it is now recognized that the counselor cannot be value neutral within the counseling relationship. Second, because he cannot be neutral, he must recognize himself as an influence upon his client. This influence is something he cannot avoid. Third, we live in a time of great disruption of value stability. Therapists are recognizing a shift from neurotic anxiety problems to problems of meaninglessness or valuelessness, that is, to exis-

---

[22]Donald N. Michael, *Cybernation and Social Change,* Seminar on Manpower Policy and Program (Washington: U.S. Dept. of Labor, Manpower Administration, 1964), p. 18.

[23]Arnold W. Green, "Social Values and Psychotherapy," *Journal of Personality,* XIV, 3 (March 1946), 199.

[24]Charlotte Buhler, *Values in Psychotherapy* (New York: The Free Press of Glencoe, 1962), pp. 7, 8.

tential anxiety. As Samler has said, in our current situation "psychologists are no longer defensive about being concerned with values."[25]

Walters seems to be in agreement with Buhler in his perception of this trend toward more active involvement with values.

> In the physical sciences, the swing from a thesis of prescientific speculation to the antithesis of a cocksure empiricism has been followed by a wholesome heuristic humility in a search of a synthesis. The resurgence of an attitude that is willing to acknowledge aspects of reality beyond the reach of science has been recognized both by its opponents and its advocates.[26]

In the same article he quotes Hook:

> In the schools, the churches, and in the literary arts, the tom-tom of theology and the bagpipes of transcendental metaphysics are growing more insistent and shrill. . . . The refurbishing of theological and metaphysical dogmas about the infinite as necessary presuppositions of knowledge about the finite indicates a latter-day "failure of nerve."[27]

The counselor, willingly or unwillingly, is faced with the question of how he will deal with values. The answer he gives is an important one, not only to himself and his profession but, perhaps most of all, to his clients and to the society of which they are a part.

There are two primary areas of value concern upon which we will focus. The first is a concern with goals; the second is a concern with values in the counseling process. To these we shall turn later, but next let us consider the cultural setting from which value problems arise.

## OUR CRISIS CULTURE

As we have said before, we live in troublesome times—in an age of transition. It is no doubt characteristic of each generation to view its particular era as the most troublesome, and we have evidence that points to this. The Egyptians wrote of meaninglessness and alienation. Socrates spoke of his concern for what we today would call juvenile delinquency. And as for transition, someone once said that Adam no doubt looked at Eve and said, "You realize, darling, that we are living

[25]Joseph Samler, "Change in Values: A Goal in Counseling," *Journal of Counseling Psychology*, VII, 1 (Spring 1960), 32–39.

[26]Walters, "Metaphysics, Religion, and Psychotherapy?", pp. 242–252.

[27]*Ibid.*, p. 243.

in an age of transition." All of this may very well be true, but there does seem to be evidence that many problems are more serious today than at any time in history.

My main thesis grows out of such a realization and can be simply stated: *In a time when the quest for purpose, meaning, and identity is a major concern, the counselor must become aware of and concerned with values in the counseling process.* Let us consider some of the problems in our society centering upon questions of value.

First, let us briefly discuss the meaning of the term value. There is no singly agreed upon definition, although there are common principles inherent in the term. (A detailed examination of this area can be found in Chapter II.)

For the purpose of our discussion here, I shall clarify the concept of value thus: a value is a learned conception, explicit or implicit, of what is desirable. It is a hypothetical construct, a criterion upon which choice, either by an individual or a group, is justified and also serves to motivate commitment and action. Value represents more than needs, goals, beliefs, attitudes, interests, or preferences (terms frequently confused with value), although it may be closely related to them.[28]

In the preface to *New Knowledge in Human Values*, a book reporting the proceedings of a 1957 conference at Harvard University on the topic of human values, Maslow stated:

> This volume springs from the belief, first, that the ultimate disease of our time is valuelessness; second, that this state is more crucially dangerous than ever before in history; and finally, that something can be done about it by man's own rational efforts. ... Wealth and prosperity, technological advance, widespread education, democratic political forms, even honestly good intentions and avowals of good will have, by their failure to produce peace, brotherhood, serenity, and happiness, confronted us even more nakedly and unavoidably with the profundities that mankind has been avoiding by its busyness with the superficial.[29]

The use of the word valueless is questionable, as it would seem

---

[28]This concept is a synthesis of the ideas of several writers in the area of values. For a comprehensive discussion of definitive aspects of the term value see Clyde Kluckhohn and others, "Values and Value-Orientations in the Theory of Action," in Talcott Parsons and Edward A. Shils (eds.), *Toward a General Theory of Action* (New York: Harper and Row, 1962). © Harvard University Press, 1951.

[29]Abraham H. Maslow (ed.), *New Knowledge in Human Values* (New York: Harper and Row, 1959), p. vii.

impossible for a person to exist without some values. Barry and Wolf have said:

> Valuelessness is impossible and there is no such thing as a valueless person or a valueless classroom or a valueless society. The word valuelessness serves simply to describe a value judgment about values themselves. When one individual describes another as valueless, he generally means that the other does not subscribe to the same values as he.[30]

The word valuelessness, then, likely refers more to quality of value than presence of value. It appears that Maslow is referring to a lack of clear bases upon which individuals can ground their choices rather than to a lack of values.

Wheelis refers in the same sense to the use of the term collapse of values, which is frequent in the literature.

> "Collapse of values" has become a cliche, used without documentation and without challenge. In some way everyone senses what is meant, but the issue is vague. Values are legion and not all of them are collapsing. The field of value is coextensive with the field of human endeavor, and it is by no means obvious that organized human activity is coming to an end. Tools have value for a mechanic, and food and shelter and friendship have value for everyone. About these things there is no confusion. Values, clearly, cannot be simply lumped together, for they exist on different levels. One can say very little about food and shelter that applies equally well to Christianity and democracy.[31]

Again, the term refers merely to the confusion of valuational bases.

Some writers have referred to ours as a crisis culture. Crisis is a word of suspense. It implies a decisive moment—a turning point. Something crucial is hanging in the balance. In medicine it means the point at which a diseased or injured body moves either toward recovery or toward death. Brameld describes crisis in this sense when he states:

> Crisis connotes a major dislocation—a dislocation of the fundamental institutions, habits, practices, attitudes of any given culture or any section of a culture. When a point is reached in which the major functions, the major structures, the major purposes of a culture

[30]Barry and Wolf, *Values, Motives, and Realities* (New York: Bureau of Publications, Teachers College, Columbia University, 1965), pp. 56, 57.

[31]Allen Wheelis, *The Quest for Identity* (New York: W.W. Norton and Co., Inc., 1958), p. 175.

or subculture are thrown out of joint, then its members often find themselves bewildered, lost, uprooted.[32]

Gruber states:

> We do not have to be a Spengler living in fear of the imminent destruction of Western civilization to realize that we are living in a crisis culture. To be sure, it is not the only or final crisis culture, but the mental and emotional adjustments from a pre-Copernican and a pre-Darwinian world to the atomic age are surely difficult ones. Perhaps Dewey was right when he wrote: "Intellectually speaking the centuries since the fourteenth are the true middle ages."[33]

Few people would deny that we live in such a transitional period today—a period of deep concern to those who understand its implications. To more fully understand just what a value crisis within a society means, it is helpful to understand something of the structure of a culture. The effort here is not to present a comprehensive discussion of our culture today; rather, only sufficient information will be given to indicate some general trends within our society and to provide a basis for assessing and better understanding values within the context of our society.

Culture can be defined as:

> The fabric of ideas, ideals, beliefs, skills, tools, aesthetic objects, methods of thinking, customs, and institutions into which each member of society is born. . . . The culture is that part of his environment which man himself has made.[34]

A society consists of a group of people who hold something in common, whereas culture is the product of that society. "A society is composed of people; a culture consists of the things the people have learned to do, to believe, to value, to enjoy, and so on, in the course of their history."[35]

Linton divides the structure of culture into three categories: universals, specialties, and alternatives. Universals represent all the commonly agreed-upon beliefs, ideas, and ways of acting and behaving, such as common dress, language, and beliefs that certain specific behaviors are right or wrong. Specialities are the skills or knowledge

[32]Theodore Brameld, *Education as Power* (New York: Holt, Rinehart, and Winston, 1965), pp. 10–11.

[33]Frederick C. Gruber (ed.), *Aspects of Value* (Philadelphia: University of Pennsylvania Press, 1959), p. 12.

[34]B. O. Smith, W. O. Stanley, and J. H. Shores, *Social Diagnosis for Education* (New York: World Book Co., 1950), p. 5.

[35]*Ibid.*, p. 6.

that only portions of the society possess and are represented by specific vocations, social class, etc. Alternatives are the elements in society that force choice. They represent any deviation from the commonly accepted way of thinking and acting or any new invention or innovation or ideas that create new possibilities of thinking or behaving. This is the growing edge of the culture.

The universals and specialities make up the enduring and stable core. It is upon these that cohesiveness is based. If people live by the universals, behavior is easily predicted and one can know what to expect from others as well as how to behave in order to be accepted. In a society made up of a firm core of universals there is little choice-making. In any situation there is only one "right" way to act. The general pattern and spirit of a culture are shaped by this core.

Rollo May has indicated that historically in such periods of growing stability therapeutic functions have been a natural part of the enculturation process and have not become distinct functions in themselves. During such periods, individuals have experienced psychological support rather freely, and the educational system has been relatively consistent.[36]

When the alternatives begin to outweigh the universals, the cohesiveness may be momentarily lost and people "shook up." They no longer know what is expected or what to expect. As the alternatives increase, there is greater flux, and this is accompanied by a trend toward disintegration. With this uncertainty comes fear and loss of direction. It is in times such as these that people more eagerly seek to examine meanings and purposes. The frightened individual, in the midst of such instability, lacking clear ideas of how to conduct himself, may surrender himself to a group and seek security by conforming to its fluctuating standards. Or he may become a law unto himself and abandon himself to his own impulse gratification. Or he may by rational examination come to a synthesis of meaning and purpose—discover or create a new identity. These are at least three alternatives faced today.

Historically speaking, in such times of disunity and drastic social change, individuals have received less and less psychological support from the general culture itself, and, as a result, therapeutic functions

---

[36]Rollo May, "Historical and Philosophical Presuppositions for Understanding Therapy," in O. H. Mowrer, *Psychotherapy: Theory and Research* (New York: The Ronald Press, 1953), p. 33.

have become more specific and distinct. In addition, the therapeutic emphasis has been upon relearning as a process of emotional integration as opposed to initial learning.[37]

Change, though always a reality, has reached drastic proportions today. Two factors serve to illustrate this point. In generations past the life span of each generation was shorter in contrast to a long span between climactic cultural changes. In such conditions, several generations would live and die during one period of cultural change. The school in such a period could serve merely to transmit from one generation to the next the necessary knowledge for the continuance of the culture, and change was slow enough so that less emphasis was placed upon innovation. In such a culture the universals were predominant and the alternatives few, thus creating a stable society with a high degree of integration. Today we find the reverse to be true. The life span of man has been increased, and, in contrast to it, the climactic cultural changes have increased so rapidly that today a single generation may live through several climactic changes.[38] Those of us living in the present generation have experienced the tail end of the horse-and-buggy days, have experienced two world wars plus other "lesser" wars, have gone through the Atomic Age and are now in the midst of the Space Age. Who can even begin to imagine the changes yet ahead!

At such a time, the alternatives begin to outnumber the universals, and the society moves ever closer to disintegration. Such a period requires that individuals be able to change too, but each challenge to change is also a challenge to self-esteem.[39] The choices (the alternatives) individuals must face increase, but the bases or criteria for making "good" choices become less tangible. The anxieties of individuals increase in number and intensity.

> When the universals of a culture begin to change significantly, especially if the change reaches down to the fundamental rules of conduct, the picture of society becomes blurred, and individuals find themselves unable to carry on normal activities in a rational way. They are led by the old rules to expect other persons to behave in certain ways. But if these rules are no longer valid, other persons will not conform to these expectations. As this occurs on a wider and

[37] *Ibid.*

[38] These ideas were discussed by Dr. Malcom Knowles at Boston University in May, 1965. He referred to an address by A. N. Whitehead delivered in 1932 in which he spoke of these two ingredients in education.

[39] Eric Hoffer, *The Ordeal of Change* (New York: Harper and Row, 1952), p. 1.

wider scale, the individual becomes bewildered; his sense of common reality vanishes, and with it goes his sense of personal stability and security.[40]

In such times of social insecurity the individual seeks new meanings and a new integration of agreed upon universals.

The quest for direction in our society today is a moral one and involves every man. Individuals are searching for meaning, purpose, and order. Our society needs to discover ends that will unify its members by providing a structure within which self-realization is possible and within which meaning can be sought freely. Whether America as a culture will move toward a higher level of unity and progress or will slide toward complete disintegration will quite possibly depend upon the ability of its citizens to discover meanings and purposes. Education, as both transmitter and modifier of culture, must play a crucial role in this task.

One of the problems young people face in our society today (with such a great number of alternatives) is that they continue to get ambiguous messages about who they are as well as about what is "good." They are constantly bombarded by values that are confusing as well as conflicting. It is difficult for them to find purpose in such chaos, and this lack of purpose has become a focus of attention. Seeley discusses what he calls the "dreadful dearth of purpose." Our youth are growing up in the midst of a

plentitude of means together with a dearth of ends. We have more matter, more power, more techniques, more know-how at our disposal with less sense of what to do with it or about it, I believe, than ever before in history.[41]

But what does all this represent? It represents a clash of values at the very core of our society.

Anthropologists tell us that every society in history has chosen one institution to dominate all others. That is, each society holds to a particular value orientation that serves as its basic foundation, its universal core. As Americans we might be quick to say that above all we value the individual as a being of worth and dignity and respect the freedom of each individual to become all that it is possible for him to become. American ideology is rich with references to freedom. Our

[40]Smith, Stanley, and Shores, *Social Diagnosis*, p. 21.

[41]John R. Seeley, "Guidance and the Youth Culture," *The Personnel and Guidance Journal*, XLI (December 1962), 306.

forefathers came to this country in the name of freedom; they fought to preserve it; they attempted to assure its continuity through the Bill of Rights and the Constitution. It is therefore no accident that American education has stressed freedom or that guidance and counseling from their early beginnings focused upon the dignity and worth of the individual. However, to state it intellectually does not make it so in practice. We find that other alternatives may creep in, at times very subtly, and cause confusion of purposes. In spite of our talk of freedom and our many struggles to maintain it, there are perhaps few who would not admit that our dominating institution is technology, and whenever one institution permeates a culture and dominates to the extent that it causes one-sidedness, then it may carry within it the very seeds of its own disintegration. It is to technology, represented in mathematics and science, that the first and best scholarships go, and it is technology that counselors have been called upon to serve in recent years.[42] Also, draft deferments have been more easily obtained by students in the field of technology than in other areas.[43] It is necessary that counselors understand some of the implications of a value system based on technology as the dominant institution. From a profusion of writing in this area we shall examine only a selection of pertinent works. It is not my intent to thoroughly analyze our current value system, but merely to show how confusion of values grows from it and to draw implications for education.

## A SENSATE CULTURE IN TRANSITION

One of the first prophets of our current crisis age was Pitirim A. Sorokin. In 1937 he wrote:

> Every important aspect of the life, organization, and the culture of Western society is in the extraordinary crisis. . . . Its body and mind are sick and there is hardly a spot on its body which is not sore, nor any nervous fiber which functions soundly. . . . We are seemingly between two epochs: the dying Sensate culture of our magnificent yesterday and the coming Ideational culture of the creative tomorrow. We are living, thinking, and acting at the end of a brilliant six-hundred-year-long Sensate day. The oblique rays of the sun still illumine the glory of the passing epoch. But the light is fading, and in the deepening shadows it becomes more and more difficult to see

---

[42]Consider the National Defense Education Act, 1958.
[43]As attested to during Congressional Labor Committee hearings in March, 1967, regarding the revision of the draft.

clearly and to orient ourselves safely in the confusions of the twilight. The night of the transitory period begins to loom before us, with its nightmares, frightening shadows, and heartrending horrors. Beyond it, however, the dawn of a new great Ideational culture is probably waiting to greet the men of the future.[44]

In a foreword to a 1957 printing of *The Crisis of Our Age* Sorokin wrote:

Since the historical events have been unfolding according to the diagnosis and prognosis of *The Crisis* there is no need for correction of its main propositions.[45]

In general, Sorokin viewed the crisis of our times and other times as a rise or decline of basic value systems. The three basic systems to which he referred are the Ideational, the Sensate, and the Idealistic. These derive from three beliefs about how man can discover or know truth. The Ideational system holds that truth can be known only by supersensory means and is generally based upon belief in a supernatural God as the only true reality. The Sensate is a value system based upon the naturalistic philosophy that the only way of knowing truth and reality is by means of the senses. The Idealistic system forms a transitional view between the Ideational and the Sensate and thus seeks to know truth and reality by a combination of sensory and supersensory means.

Sorokin has described our culture as being a sensate culture in transition. The predominance of this naturalistic epistomology—that truth and reality can be known only by the senses—has borne rich fruit. It has produced by means of science an unprecedented productivity of material goods and comforts and an advancing economy. But it has not been without its bitter fruit. Such a philosophy leads to an inevitable progression of beliefs concerning values. Beginning with a belief that truth and reality can be known only by sensing, everything supersensory is considered to be nonexistent or at least is treated as such. It follows that any intuited idea, any "truth" of faith or religion, any mystic experience, is non-sense or nonsense. The result of this is that the realm of knowing truth and reality becomes dangerously narrowed. All value then must be determined by sense. The next step is to focus only upon the material as the source of all value. This

[44]Pitirim A. Sorokin, *The Crisis of Our Age* (New York: E. P. Dutton and Co., Inc., 1941), p. 13, quoting P. Sorokin, *Social and Cultural Dynamics* (New York, 1937), III, p. 535.
[45]Sorokin, *The Crisis of Our Age*, Foreword to the 1957 edition.

must be so, for the senses can only grasp what is material and particular, and any deeper value is impoverished and given up or reduced to only one of its aspects, that which can be sensed. Man, also, becomes reduced mainly to anatomy and physiology—to those aspects that can be sensed and measured. The door is then open for a radical mechanistic view, for nothing is simpler to sense than mechanical motion. A growing hedonism develops. The criteria of the "good" more and more become pleasure and sensuality, for only these values can be experienced from a sensual point of view. A dominant temporalistic point of view develops. Nothing is viewed as having any stability, and all things are seen in a stage of flux. Nothing is permanent. All things become temporary. Long-range goals become replaced by short-time considerations. Since everything is regarded as transitory, the focus of living is upon getting the most out of the present. As change accelerates, the present ever becomes more fleeting. Time becomes a factor of ever greater importance, and such a society comes to be run by the clock. All things are viewed as relative. Since all is transitory, nothing can be absolute or unchanging. All values, beliefs, and morals vary according to time, place, and group or individual. Relativism sooner or later gives way to skepticism, cynicism, and nihilism. There is nothing left upon which to ground any stability, and so meaninglessness, rootlessness, and moral anarchy increase. As Sorokin stated it:

> The very boundary line between the true and the false, between right and wrong, disappears, and society finds itself in a state of veritable mental, moral, and cultural anarchy. No society can long exist under these conditions.[46]

Under these conditions the deeper things that are involved in what philosophers have referred to as the "good life" but that are difficult to define are replaced by what is tangible and easily defined, such as a high standard of living. But the satisfactions provided by a high standard of living seem to be incomplete. Perhaps it is as Bacon said, "The happiness of the great consists not in feeling that they are happy but in realizing how happy other people think they must be."[47]

The educational system as it reflects the essential beliefs of such a society will focus upon training in skills and crafts and gaining sensory knowledge. Great emphasis will be placed upon developing

---

[46]*Ibid.*, p. 98.
[47]Krutch, *Human Nature and the Human Condition* (New York: Random House, 1959), p. 34, quoting Bacon.

means to manipulate the material world and gain materialistic pleasures. Success is measured in materialistic terms, but with the manipulation of the fleeting and transitory world come fleeting and transitory satisfactions, leaving an increasing vacuum of the more stable values, which are supermaterialistic.

Again to quote Sorokin:

> The society dominated by such an increasingly one-sided truth tends to be led away from reality, from real knowledge, toward ignorance, error, hollowness of values, aridity in creativeness, and poverty of socio-cultural life. This drift leads to an increase of theoretical and practical difficulties for such a society. Its adaptation to reality becomes more and more difficult; its needs less and less fully satisfied; its life, security, order, and creative experience more and more disorganized. Sooner or later the moment comes when it faces the following alternatives; either to continue its dangerous drift and suffer fatal atrophy or else to correct its mistake through the adoption of a different and more adequate system of truth, reality, and cultural values.[48]

The ability of a culture to survive change depends greatly upon the creative forces existent within it and the success of these creative forces to shift to a new form of culture and society that opens up new creative possibilities and new values. In fact, such change is necessary if a culture and society is to remain creative rather than become rigid and uncreative, eventually declining and disintegrating. It is in enhancing creativity as well as in the quest for new unity, that education and counseling can find its most significant role.

Any adequate philosophy must recognize all valid means of discovering truth and reality. Sorokin stated that crises resolve themselves in the following patterns: crisis, ordeal, catharsis, charisma, and resurrection. It is left to the reader to judge the progress of our society on the basis of this continuum.

## A TECHNOLOGICALLY DRIVEN CULTURE

Jules Henry describes our culture as one propelled by "technological drivenness." We are driven to use all potential, human as well as material, to its fullest degree. Such a driven productivity, however, must necessarily have enough consumers or the economy will collapse. To prevent this collapse, new wants must be created in the

[48]Sorokin, *The Crisis of Our Age*, p. 114.

public, and so the first commandment of the new era becomes: "Create more desire!" This is coupled with a second commandment: "Thou shalt consume!" It is the natural complement of the first and requires the loosening and release of impulse—the task of modern advertising. All of this is designed to keep a constantly expanding economy on the rise.

From technological drivenness there develops a new philosophy, referred to by Henry as "pecuniary philosophy." It is the philosophy of the advertiser and by means of the mass media finds ready access into the minds of the American people, with the advertiser becoming the priest of the new order.

Central to any philosophy is its concept of truth, and for pecuniary philosophy:

> Truth is what sells.
> Truth is what you want people to believe.
> Truth is that which is not legally false.[49]

This is a philosophy of the practical man, with success determined on the basis of the amount of consumption propagated. It is a pseudo truth, "a false statement made as if it were true, but not intended to be believed. . . . Its proof is that it sells merchandise; if it does not, it is false."[50] Numerous products all become the "smoothest," "the fastest," "the best money can buy," and on and on to endless claims not meant to really be believed.

Pecuniary psychology attempts to establish beachheads in man's "brain-box" by means of advertising to create new needs and wants. Values become weakened and distorted by becoming materialized, and people are urged to respond to pseudo values as though they were real ones.

> The traditional values are part of traditional philosophy, but pecuniary philosophy, far from being at odds with them appears to embrace them with a fervor. This is the embrace of a grizzly bear, for as it embraces the traditional values, pecuniary philosophy chokes them to death. The specific choking mechanism is monetization.[51]

This process

waters down values, wears them out by a slow attrition, makes them

[49]Jules Henry, *Culture Against Man* (New York: Random House, 1963), p. 50.
[50]*Ibid.*, p. 47.
[51]*Ibid.*, p. 62.

banal and, in the long run, helps Americans to become indifferent to them and even cynical.[52]
Children become virgin territory, and one has only to observe commercials on current children's television programs to be hit by the full force of this drive to consume.

Such a philosophy also has its own view of the nature of man. Man is seen as

> insatiably desiring, infinitely plastic, totally passive, and always a bit sleepy; unpredictably labile and disloyal (to products); basically wooly-minded and non-obsessive about traditional truth; relaxed and undemanding with respect to the canons of traditional philosophy, indifferent to its values, and easily moved to buy whatever at the moment seems to help his underlying personal inadequacies.[53]

Man is valued as consumer and is subtly encouraged to substitute a materialistic, high-rising living standard in place of true self-realization.

What are the results of this philosophy in our society today? There is, first of all, fear and uncertainty, for where markets are uncertain, jobs are equally uncertain. There is the ever present fear of becoming obsolete in a rapidly changing society. With self-denial discouraged and impulse release encouraged, it is an easy jump to make material success substitute for self-realization; man's frustrations can be further escaped through amusement (meaning literally *not to think*), as well as further consumption and impulse release.

> So the consequence of technological driveness is the creation of a people who, though reared to support it—by being trained to heroic feats of consumption—are quietly undermining it by *doing* the least they can rather than the most, not only because it is hard to get anything out of the system but also because they have stayed up so late the night before having fun.[54]

The vicious circle of materialism has started, and values begin to take on pecuniary distortions. The very title of Henry's book, *Culture Against Man*, suggests that man has the capacity to use culture in destructive as well as constructive ways. But whether man will destroy himself or not will likely depend upon whether he commits himself to a continuing driveness of ever increasing wants and unsatisfying goals or to increasing stability by finding anchorage in values based on ideas of good human relations.

[52]*Ibid.*, p. 67.
[53]*Ibid.*, p. 79.
[54]*Ibid.*, p. 44.

Henry felt that in moving from a production economy to a consumption one, Americans are exchanging their real selves for pseudo selves, selves seeking worth in a high-rising standard of living. Superego values (restraint) are descending as Id (self-indulgence) values rise, creating a Midsummer Night's Dream of impulse release and fun.[55]

What effect does this have upon the adolescent today? The school grading system is made the measure of inner worth. Adolescents learn to hate success in others, for that means defeat for themselves and increased negative self-concept. The price of social acceptance becomes conformity and a loss of freedom. People are assumed to be inferior until proven otherwise. Therefore questions such as "What is wrong with me?" and "What can I do to be liked?" become "I am no good!" and "I must change myself so that people will like me." Schooling becomes meaningless except in terms of a distant economic goal. Studying becomes more difficult when training is in impulse release rather than impulse indulgence, for restraint is "the motor of hard work." Adolescents have a tendency to view themselves deterministically in a field of economic forces rather than as autonomous human beings. Pleasure is truth and pain is falsehood. Increasing dishonesty is seen in social relationships. Adolescents live on the periphery of the pseudo self. Fear of failure becomes the motivating force.

## OUR AGE OF ANXIETY

Krutch is another who, in the process of attempting to understand his own feelings as they were caught up in the "modern temper"[56] of the times, has turned to an examination of value questions in our culture. To him our age is an "age of anxiety." "Few ages have been less sure, rightly or wrongly, of what to expect. . . . On one thing only is there almost universal agreement: things can't go on this way much longer."[57]

In *The Measure of Man* he criticizes the inevitable materialism, relativism, and statistical manipulation of man by a dominating behaviorism. He stresses a need to turn from a mechanical and deter-

[55]*Ibid.*, p. 127.
[56]Krutch, *The Modern Temper* (New York: Harcourt, Brace and Co., 1929).
[57]Krutch, *The Measure of Man* (New York: Bobbs-Merrill, 1954), p. 17.

ministic view of man to a recognition that such a view is only partial. Man is not only an "economic man" or an "I.Q. man," he is also a "valuing man," and an empirical science fails to recognize this reality. "The grand paradox of our society is this: we magnify man's rights but we minimize his capacities."[58] One cannot talk of a free society if the individual is merely molded by circumstances beyond his control. We must, according to Krutch, view man in his totality, recognizing both his capabilities as well as his limitations. The realm of values must be recognized apart from and different from mere empiricism.

> Thought about human problems can never get very far without reference to standards of some sort and because many sociologists have renounced all those which seem to them to imply an a priori value judgment, they almost inevitably begin soon to assume that "what is" must be the valid measure of "what ought to be" and that if we desire to find out either how diligently college students *should* study, or what the sexual conduct of the human male *should* be, we have only to find out to what extent the former actually do apply themselves and what the behavior of the latter usually is. This "right behavior" becomes identical with "normal" behavior, and "normal" comes to mean simply "average."[59]

Only by accepting a minimal view of man as at least a partially free being and thus able to make choices as to his destiny, and by coupling this with the continuation of Moral Discourse can man, in Krutch's view, hope to achieve a truly human society.

Although our generation has unprecedented abundance and a hope of an ever increasing standard of living, which comes more and more to represent our idea of the "good life," there is the grim realization that something is amiss and that never before has man had in his control the capabilities of total destruction. "He who rides a tiger does not dare to dismount."[60] There is new interest and a renewed need for true humanity:

> that part of man's consciousness, intellect, and emotion which is neither exclusively interested in nor completely satisfied by either mere animal survival on the one hand, or wealth, power, and speed alone. It is that part of him which is least like a machine and therefore least satisfied by machines. It is the part that would like to know itself and that cherishes values to which nothing in the inanimate

[58] *Ibid.*, pp. 200–201.
[59] *Ibid.*, pp. 222–223.
[60] Krutch, *Human Nature*, p. 13.

world seems to correspond and which the non-human world of living things only dubiously (though none the less comfortingly) seems to encourage.[61]

Krutch also refers to the change of emphasis in our society from production to consumption. We have solved our production problems but now must urge consumption to keep our economy going, and this has of necessity had an effect on our values. " 'Waste not, want not' is a valid injunction only under an economy of scarcity. 'Waste or you will want' is one of the most fundamental truths in the new Rich Richard's Almanac."[62] The "hidden persuaders"[63] become a subtle influence under such a new philosophy. Krutch cites a Yale professor:

> As we shift from a society in which production is the focus of economic attention to one which is oriented to consumption, as we see a new pattern of personality emerging in American life, it seems to me that advertising as an institution moves into a position of influence comparable at least to a degree to such other major institutions for the formation of values as the school and the church.[64]

Man becomes valued as "consuming man." An empirical view would say that the "best" is what exists now; therefore, ends should be established around what is average and an attempt made to adjust man to it. But, if we believe that man has some measure of control over his destiny, we must first choose suitable ends, arbitrarily if necessary. Within our society today "we do not know where we are going; we do not know where we want to go; but we are on our way and we are doing everything possible to accelerate our movement."[65] And so the meaning of life becomes a popular topic.

> Even most of those who are neither Christian nor, in any ordinary sense, mystical do nevertheless feel that there is something lacking in our society and that this lack is not generally acknowledged; do feel that, for all its prosperity and for all its kindliness, generosity, and good will, it is somehow shallow and vulgar; that the vulgarity is superficially evidenced in the tawdriness, the lack of dignity and permanence in the material surroundings of our lives, and more importantly in our aims and standards; that we lack any sense that efficient and equitable systems of production and distribu-

---

[61]*Ibid.*, pp. 15–16.

[62]*Ibid.*, p. 23.

[63]Vance Packard, *The Hidden Persuaders* (New York: David McKay Co., 1957).

[64]Krutch, *Human Nature*, p. 31, quoting a Yale professor.

[65]*Ibid.*, p. 86.

tion are only a beginning, as for that matter, are also our ideal of democracy and our struggle for social justice. You may, as a few do, attribute this alienation to a "lack of religion." But perhaps even that term is not broad enough. It is a lack of any sense of what life is *for* beyond comfort and security, and it would still be so even if all these good things were conferred upon all. At best life would still remain, in Yeat's phrase, "an immense preparation for something which never happens."[66]

Krutch suggests grounding our idea of the "good life" in our understanding of the nature of man. We must recognize that man is first a valuing being, and that he is "not by nature a pure materialist." If we hold to these statements, an idea of the "good life" based solely upon a high standard of living runs contrary to man's nature. We have too often "forgotten that know-how is a dubious endowment unless it is accompanied by other 'knows'—by 'know what,' 'know why,' and —most important of all at the present moment—'know whether!' "[67]

## AMERICAN SOCIETY AND THE MARKETING ORIENTATION

Fromm, a psychoanalyst, is another who has spoken out on current problems of man in present day society. He recognizes in man's very existence an inborn problem that must be handled in some manner by man. This is the problem of freedom. Man either uses his freedom for productivity or he tries to escape from it.[68] But man must work out his problems within the society of which he is a product. The influence of society upon man can be positive or negative depending upon whether it is in harmony with his nature or opposed to it.

Fromm has criticized current American society through discussion of what he calls its "marketing orientation." The danger he recognizes is that man becomes a "thing," a commodity, and is dependent upon the market value of his "personality package" for his feelings of worth. Due to the materialistic orientation of our technology, man turns his worship upon the product and in the process experiences alienation, a ceasing to be his true self, in turn living a determined sort of existence much like that of an automaton. He no longer thinks his own thoughts, but rather the thoughts that he thinks others would want him to think. He becomes a slave to conformity and develops and

[66] *Ibid.*, p. 115.
[67] *Ibid.*, p. 210.
[68] Erich Fromm, *Escape from Freedom* (New York: Farrar and Rinehart, 1941).

maintains his sense of identity solely according to others' expectations of him. This can happen so subtly because of the social pressures involved that he can be induced to think in a certain way and yet experience such thoughts subjectively as his own.

This also carries over into decision-making. The individual decides what he thinks others would want or expect him to decide. He becomes interested not in life and happiness, but in how he can become "saleable" on the personality market. He must discover the sort of personality that happens to be the current vogue and then conform to this image. If he is successful in so doing, he is considered valuable. If he is unsuccessful, however, he becomes a failure and is worthless. Such people are relentlessly driven toward success in these terms and as such are not free. They may live in what is referred to as a "free society," but within themselves they are psychologically in chains, for comformity is sought at the cost of one's own freedom to be one's self. Men are automatons and as such are needed by the technological structure as it now exists. Fromm describes it thus:

> Vastly centralized enterprises with a radical division of labor lead to an organization of work where the individual loses his individuality, where he becomes an expendable cog in the machine. The human problem of modern capitalism can be formulated in this way:
>
> Modern capitalism needs men who cooperate smoothly and in large numbers; who want to consume more and more; and whose tastes are standardized and can be easily influenced and anticipated. It needs men who feel free and independent, not subject to any authority or principle or conscience—yet willing to be commanded, to do what is expected of them, to fit into the social machine without friction; who can be guided without force, led without leaders, prompted without aim—except the one to make good, to be on the move, to function, to go ahead.
>
> What is the outcome? Modern man is alienated from himself, from his fellow men, and from nature. He has been transformed into a commodity, experiences his life forces as an investment which must bring him the maximum profit obtainable under existing market conditions. Human relations are essentially those close to the herd and not being different in thought, feeling, or action. While everyone tries to be as close as possible to the rest, everybody remains utterly alone, pervaded by the deep sense of insecurity, anxiety, and guilt which always results when human separateness cannot be overcome.[69]

[69]Fromm, *The Art of Loving* (New York: Harper and Row, 1962), p. 72.

For Fromm the only answer is to structure a society that can provide the end of the "good life" based upon an understanding of the needs of man that grow out of his nature. In such a humanistic society, man will truly be able to become the productive self that is his nature.

## VALUES AND THE QUEST FOR IDENTITY

Numerous other writers have also concerned themselves with the problems of our culture. Riesman has written about the "other-directedness" of individuals in our society.[70] Goodman has spoken out against the loss of individual freedom.[71] Michael has warned of coming problems stemming from automation, many of which we are already facing, and has stated a major concern that we must somehow learn how to help people to find meaning in their lives. He found this task a difficult one when people give themselves up to what they see as a determined existence. He stated that those who are going to have some kind of significant job in our society

> will have to be taught values which allow them to cope comfortably with change, to be flexible, to be committed, to be responsible, to have integrity, to be concerned with their rights as members of a democracy. Now, these aren't mere platitudes. We use these words idly, and in fact we do a bad job of educating people to express them, as you well know. I am suggesting that we are going to have to do a much better job of inculcating these values if life is going to be satisfying in a cybernated society.[72]

Many existentialists have commented upon these issues of our times, but it is not possible here to elaborate on all discussions of our culture and problems.

Such is the cultural setting in which young people today attempt to discover themselves, and it is characteristic of youth to attempt to make order of the chaos confronting them. It is characteristic of human beings in general that they seek order as a means of survival in all realms of their experience. They fight a perpetual battle against chaos. In the biological realm man seeks survival of his body—the ordered pattern we refer to as health. In the psychological realm he

---

[70] David Riesman, *The Lonely Crowd* (New Haven: Yale University Press, 1950).

[71] Paul Goodman, *Growing Up Absurd* (New York: Alfred A. Knopf, Inc, & Random House, Inc., 1956).

[72] Donald N. Michael, *Cybernation and Social Change*, Seminar on Manpower Policy and Program (Washington: U.S. Dept. of Labor, Manpower Administration, 1964), p. 18.

fights chaos in an attempt to establish order between his needs and his environment. Bertocci states it thus:

> It is clear that if a person is going to avoid fruitless, unnecessary conflicts he must have the clearest conception possible of his own motives, of his abilities, and of the real environment in which he lives. *The psychological situation, then, is one in which there can be conscious or mental awareness of conflict between motives, abilities, and environment, or any combination of these. The human problem* is to know as much as possible about each factor in the human situation and to keep motive (need or want), ability, and environment together, reducing *needless* conflict.[73]

Traditionally, counseling has concerned itself for the most part with this psychological realm of experience. It has dealt with preferences, interests, impulses—concepts all bordering on values, but primarily ignoring the concept or realm of value itself. This is not to say that value elements were not present. Rather it is to say that value elements remained primarily implicit. Dealing with this psychological realm of behavior, it is perhaps correct to say that the counselor deals more with the raw materials of choice than with the quality of choice itself. In so doing, he is attempting to free the counselee to become a better chooser by assisting him to improve his raw materials of choice—that is, his interests, feelings, impulses, and the like—by eliminating distortions and clarifying his perceptions. This is perhaps adequate and not too serious within a society that has a stable value orientation and where many of the problems faced are mere psychological conflicts, for the values inherent are then assumed to be self-evident. However, in a society such as ours today, rocked with change and with rapidly shifting value patterns, one might question whether this is enough.

To confront the realm of choice itself in a normative manner is to enter another mode of man's existence, that of the moral. Man seeks not only physical and psychological order, but moral as well. One enters the moral realm as soon as he begins to reflect upon the desirable—as soon as he deliberately decides which of at least two conflicting experiences he is to prefer in a given instance. This is the realm of value, when a man chooses from alternatives on the basis of his deliberations of how he hopes to get the most from life. When a man so chooses

[73]Peter A. Bertocci and Richard M. Millard, *Personality and the Good* (New York: David McKay Co., 1963), p. 17.

> he is not concerned with survival or even quality of physical survival;
> neither is he concerned with the moment-to-moment and day-to-day
> struggle to relieve needless tension and gratify his wants. Having
> reflected on the problem of *how to get the most from his physiological*
> *and psychological orders of existence in this kind of world, he acts*
> *from policy.*[74]

This, then, is not mere reflection upon interests, preferences, or
feelings, but it is evaluation of them, of self, and of the world upon the
basis of some criterion of the desirable, which itself is a product of
continued reflection.

Buhler has referred to this as the "constructive intent" of the
individual, "an active directedness toward the accomplishing of the
most beneficial future; beneficial in whatever sense the persons engaged in the process may understand."[75] A constructive intent, then,
is a matter of perception of what comprises the "good life." Within this
moral realm of choice one is confronted with the problem of meaning,
for to seek order in morality is to seek meaning in life. To have moral
order is to have a personally validated conception of the "good life"
and to have some satisfaction in the attainment of it to some degree.
To have moral chaos and anarchy is to have rootlessness, anomie,
meaninglessness, and emptiness. There appears to be an increasing
recognition, as evidenced by the professional literature, that counselors can no longer afford to neglect this third realm of human experience.

Morality, then, is involved in man's choosing and acting on the
basis of his choices (commitment). As such, it touches upon three
areas: one, an individual's relationship with himself—his internal organization; two, an individual's relationships to other individuals; and
three, the purpose or meaning of life. Lewis described these three in
vivid terms.

> There are two ways in which the human machine goes wrong.
> One is when human individuals drift apart from one another, or else
> collide with one another and do one another damage, by cheating or
> bullying. The other is when things go wrong inside the individual—
> when the different parts of him (his different faculties and desires and
> so on) either drift apart or interfere with one another. You can get
> the idea plain if you think of us as a fleet of ships sailing in formation.
> The voyage will be a success only, in the first place, if the ships do

[74] *Ibid.*, p. 19.
[75] Buhler, *Values in Psychotherapy*, p. 36.

not collide and get in one another's way; and, secondly, if each ship is seaworthy and has her engines in good order. As a matter of fact, you cannot have either of these two things without the other. If the ships keep on having collisions they will not remain seaworthy very long. On the other hand, if their steering gears are out of order they will not be able to avoid collisions. ...

But there is one thing we have not yet taken into account. We have not asked where the fleet is trying to get to. ... However well the fleet sailed, its voyage would be a failure if it were meant to reach New York and actually arrived at Calcutta.[76]

The questions of the young, "Who am I?" "What can I do?" "Where am I going?" "What is the Meaning of life?," receive no final answers, and uncertainty persists. The period of being uncommitted is longer and choices become more tentative. The sense of self remains unstable, checked only according to conformity to a fluctuating group. The sense of alienation, that one is not in control of one's life, is prevalent. Commitments are temporary and long-range goals appear too risky before such an uncertain future—a future made even more uncertain by the threat of war and anihilation. Yet, in the midst of such uncertainties, the questions remain, and the individual is confronted by them.

To the counselor who listens—who is able to tune in to the correct wave length of youth—such questions regarding the quest for identity loom large, are at the very heart of the counseling process. To discover one's identity is to recognize that meaning, purpose, and commitment are inseparable. To find an answer to "Who am I?" is also to find an answer to "What must I live up to?" "What are my obligations?" and "To what must I commit myself?"[77] Such a search is deeply personal and is a search for values. "We may even *define* therapy as a search for values, because ultimately the search for identity is, in essence, the search for one's own intrinsic, authentic values."[78]

Allen Wheelis has defined identity thus:

Identity is a coherent sense of self. It depends upon the awareness that one's endeavors and one's life make sense, that they are meaningful in the context in which life is lived. It depends also upon

---

[76]C. S. Lewis, *Mere Christianity* (New York: The Macmillan Co., 1952), pp. 70–71.

[77]John Gardner, *Self-Renewal* (New York: Harper and Row, 1963), p. 103.

[78]Maslow, *Toward a Psychology of Being* (Princeton: D. Van Nostrand, 1962), p. 166.

stable values, and upon the conviction that one's actions and values are harmoniously related. It is a sense of wholeness, of integration, of knowing what is right and what is wrong and of being able to choose.[79]

It is my assumption that assistance in the quest for identity is at the very heart of the counseling process. Such a quest is no simple undertaking and involves areas of great ambiguity and perplexity.

## THE SEARCH FOR SIGNIFICANCE

There is a new concern that one must also consider in an examination of our current cultural dilemma. This is the concern with the rebellion of youth. Student rebellion, within American culture at least, is not new. Where there are no clear rituals that usher individuals into adulthood it is natural that challenge of adult authority would be a part of the process of asserting one's autonomy and independence. One can find ample evidence that throughout our history as a nation we have not been without campus turmoil resulting from disorder brought about or at least initiated by the young. Even in regard to dress one finds the following declaration made by a Massachusetts official on November 3, 1675:

> Whereas there is manifest pride openly appearing amongst us in that long haire, like woemen's haire, is worne by some men, either their oune or others haire made into perewigs, and by some woemens wearing borders of haire, and theire curlings, and immodest laying out theire haire, which practise doeth prevayle especially amongst the younger set. . . .
> This court doeth declare against this ill custome as offencious to them, and divers sober christians amongst us, and therefore doe hereby exhort and advise all persons to use moderation in this respect.[80]

When one looks into our immediate history one finds a similarity between the current trend of student activism and a similar period occuring in the thirties. Both periods were preceded by a time of apathy, conformity, and emphasis on security.[81] Following World War I and during the depression, large numbers of students were involved

---

[79]Wheelis, *Quest for Identity*, p. 29.

[80]"Perspective U.S.A.," *This Week Magazine*, April 7, 1968.

[81]Jeanne H. Block, Norma Haan, and M. Brewster Smith, "Activism and Apathy in Contemporary Adolescents," in James F. Adams (ed.), *Understanding Adolescence: Current Developments in Adolescent Psychology* (Boston: Allyn and Bacon, Inc., 1968).

in protest movements and joined radical organizations. The main issues were pacifism and demanded changes in the social and economic order. Students

> organized associations of the unemployed, they picketed, demonstrated, signed the Oxford Pledge refusing to bear arms for the United States, designated Army Day as an annual day of protest on which rallies were held and strikes conducted in the cause of peace.[82]

One can easily recognize the similarities to student revolution today.

But are there differences, and if so, what are they? Block, Haan, and Smith have noted that student movements differ today in that they are less doctrinaire, and thus separate groups tend to cooperate more easily; they operate autonomously rather than through affiliation with some adult organization; protest now occurs in a time of unprecedented national abundance; and finally, strategy has centered in civil disobedience.[83]

Rollo May has indicated a difference in the current state of affairs in our society, especially in regard to psychological development. Whereas the chief problem of the fifties was a search for identity, he sees it now as a loss of a sense of significance, which seems to be one step beyond loss of identity.

> It is possible to lack a sense of identity and still preserve the hope of having influence— "I may not know who I am, but at least I can make them notice me." In our present stage of loss of sense of significance, the feeling tends to be, "Even if I did know who I am, I couldn't make any difference as an individual anyway."[84]

Revolt, during such a time and to the extent that one feels quite insignificant, becomes a means of gaining recognition.

> It is, indeed, one of the clear values of being a rebel, as Camus and countless others in human history have said . . . that by the act of rebelling I force the impersonal authorities or the too systematic system to look at me, to recognize me, to admit that I *am*, to take account of my *power*.[85]

One of the frightening aspects of this development is that when individuals lose their sense of significance they also lose their sense of

---

[82] *Ibid.*, p. 199.

[83] *Ibid.*, pp. 200, 201.

[84] Rollo May, *Psychology and the Human Dilemma* (Princeton, N.J.: D. Van Nostrand, 1967), p. 26.

[85] *Ibid.*, p. 27.

being responsible, for why bother to burden one's self with responsibility if in the face of a "factory-like" existence what one does does not matter anyway. According to May, such feelings stem from a general feeling of anxiety. Such anxiety is also relevant to a discussion of values, for *"a person can meet anxiety to the extent that his values are stronger than the threat."*[86] The task of meeting anxiety is complicated by a culture in which the disintegration of values is a characteristic description. It is only as the student experiences a meaningful inner core of values (has moral order) that he has a base from which to face anxiety courageously. Crucial to human development, then, in our day, is a recognition of the importance of values and also a recognition that values can not be merely handed to students or placed within a fixed curriculum with the expectation that students will experience them automatically as meaningful. It rather demands that we give attention to the *process* of valuing, which includes the process of choosing, of owning one's own values as his own, and of commitment. This means that we must be willing to question and, having questioned, to act in behalf of what is held to be constructively purposeful.

[86] *Ibid.*, p. 51.

*chapter* 2

# Values: A Realm of Complexity

## PHILOSOPHY: A TOOL FOR UNDERSTANDING VALUES

In a universe dominated by the "scientific," not only has the human spirit met with difficulty in finding a comfortable home, philosophy itself has been met by hostile skepticism. Within the mood of "scientism" the philosopher has been viewed as one with his head in the clouds, a mystic with no desire to contaminate himself with the mundane practicalities of everyday living. There no doubt have been so-called philosophers who have earned themselves such a reputation, but such a picture does not speak for philosophy as the term is used here. It is important that we grasp the full meaning of what philosophy can contribute to our understanding of the contemporary world.

Philosophy, first of all, means love *(philia)* of wisdom *(sophia)*, but this definition is not complete. There are many who would claim to be philosophers while clinging loosely to theories or basic principles of almost anything. Although philosophy is the love of wisdom, our definition must be more precise than this, for philosophy demands a rigor in the search for wisdom.

The following definition of philosophy helps to further clarify the meaning of the concept: "Philosophy . . . may be defined as thinking that seeks to discover connected truth about all available experience."[1] Philosophy is concerned with the whole of being, whereas science specializes and becomes concerned with parts. It is the task of philosophy to understand the relationships between parts that makes for connectedness in experience.

> The philosopher is the geographer—or, better, the astronomer —of all experience. His search for a view of the whole imposes on

[1]Edgar S. Brightman, *An Introduction to Philosophy*, 3d ed., revised by Robert N. Beck (New York: Holt, Rinehart, and Winston, 1963), p. 7.

him the duty of systematic, as well as of critical, thinking. He seeks a place for everything, with everything in its place. Creative imagination is required to construct, or even to grasp, the meaning of such an inclusive system.[2]

The student of philosophy, therefore, is not one who commits to memory unchanging answers to all possible questions. He is rather one who is learning how to grow in a growing world; in particular, he is one who is learning how to think in the process of growth.[3]

Philosophy is also a method for attempting to understand the crucial problems of our day and how to deal with them in an effective way. Philosophy is a means of analyzing, of criticizing, of synthesizing, and of evaluating. As Brameld has stated:

> Philosophy . . . is most properly defined as the effort of any culture to become conscious of itself—to face honestly and stubbornly its own weaknesses as well as strengths, failures as well as achievements, vices as well as virtues. . . . It is the supreme instrument man has fashioned by which, through the ages, he comes to terms with himself as he struggles to organize his existence within culture.[4]

Philosophy, thus understood, is crucial as an instrument for understanding the role of values in counseling. Also, the knowledge that philosophers have gleaned in their study of values can aid us in building a bridge between the process of counseling on the one hand and axiology, the study of values, on the other. In the building of such a bridge, our focus is upon connectedness and upon relating the whole of human experience to an understanding of value issues in whatever way they come to play in the counseling process.

To become aware that as a counselor one cannot avoid becoming or acting as a philosopher should also make us aware of our responsibility to then philosophize as effectively as we can. To be committed to this means that we must give up the easy and shallow kind of acceptance of what is and replace it with a keenly scrutinizing attention, questioning not only those beliefs that we hold explicitly but also those beliefs that we may hold as self-evident, which, when held as such, seldom emerge in awareness.

> Philosophy is the art not merely of *having* beliefs regarding life, or even of *articulating* them, but of deliberately inquiring into

[2] *Ibid.*, p. 8.
[3] *Ibid.*, p. 9.
[4] Theodore Brameld, *Philosophies of Education in Cultural Perspective* (New York: Dryden Press, 1955), p. 4.

the nature of beliefs and thus of *judging* them in order to determine whether they are worth holding.[5]

Although it is beyond the scope of this chapter to fully discuss the various branches of philosophy, it is necessary that the reader be familiar with the three most common broad branches. The reader who is not familiar with the basic principles of philosophy is encouraged to do further reading in an introductory text in philosophy.[6] We will give most emphasis here to the third branch, that of axiology, since it is the main area of concern in this work.

The first branch of philosophy is ontology. The term is derived from the Greek *on*, meaning being, plus *logos*, meaning logic or theory.[7] Thus, ontology is the theory of being or the study of beliefs about reality. "This is the task of ontology: to determine what is real about any and all aspects of the world."[8]

The second branch of philosophy is epistemology, derived from the Greek *episteme*, meaning knowledge, and *logos*, meaning theory or logic.[9] Thus, epistemology is the theory of knowledge or the study of beliefs about knowledge. This is the "branch of philosophy which investigates the origin, structure, methods and validity of knowledge."[10]

The third branch, axiology, from the Greek *axios*, meaning of like value or worth, plus *logos*, refers to the study of beliefs about value.[11] Axiology raises the question about what is "good" and consists of the investigation of the nature of the "good," its criteria, and also its ontological status.

> The problem of axiology is to clarify the criteria or principles by which we determine what is good in human conduct, what is beautiful in art, what is right in social organization, and, finally, what these have in common as well as what distinguishes them from one another. The significance of axiology for education is, then, *to examine and integrate these values as they enter into the lives of people through the channels of the school.*[12]

[5] *Ibid.*, p. 5.

[6] See Brightman, *Introduction to Philosophy.*

[7] Dagobert D. Runes (ed.), *Dictionary of Philosophy* (Paterson, N. J.: Littlefield, Adams, and Co., 1966), p. 219.

[8] Brameld, *Philosophies of Education*, p. 28.

[9] Runes, *Dictionary of Philosophy*, p. 94.

[10] *Ibid.*

[11] *Ibid.*, p. 32.

[12] Brameld, *Philosophies of Education*, p. 33.

This statement defines not only the broad field of value theory but also the three common subbranches of ethics (the study of moral conduct), esthetics (the study of the taste and value standards for judging art), and sociopolitical philosophy (the study of social order).

Let us turn now to see what the axiologists have to offer in clarifying the term value.

## HISTORICAL ASPECTS

In any discussion of values, the first logical question to ask is "What is value?" In seeking a definition it was discovered that here is a concept that does not belong strictly to one field of study, for various disciplines have staked their claim, a factor that has not added to simplicity of definition. The axiologist, the specialist in values, thus finds himself in unfamiliar areas. Perry expresses feelings of humility because of this fact when he states:

> Theory of value so conceived is a bold and far-flung program which cannot be undertaken without a humble awareness of its immense complexity. It requires the philosopher to enter fields in which specialists have already staked their special claims, and where the philosopher finds himself an amateur among professionals. He cannot hope to do their special work better than they do it, but only to incorporate their results and add items and relationships. The philosopher is accustomed to this somewhat shameless role. He does not, however, undertake the task arrogantly or overconfidently. For it is the philosopher who, having undertaken the task, is most acutely aware of its difficulty.[13]

The philosopher who undertakes this task provides an important service to all fields of knowledge, for his task is to assemble knowledge into meaningful wholes. Where the specialist seeks narrow understanding, the philosopher seeks broader understanding and, in so doing, serves the important function of unifying knowledge, thus adding to its meaning. This task is of special importance concerning value, for value represents a common element in all of the social sciences and thus can represent a unifying base.

> The concept "value" supplies a point of convergence for the various specialized social sciences, and is a key concept for the

[13]Ralph B. Perry, *Realms of Value* (Cambridge, Mass.: Harvard University Press, 1954), p. 1.

integration with studies in the humanities. Value is potentially a bridging concept which can link together many diverse specialized studies—from the experimental psychology of perception to the analysis of political ideologies, from budget studies in economics to aesthetic theory and philosophy of language, from literature to race riots. . . .

Sophisticated use of value-theory can help to correct the widespread static-descriptive bias of the social sciences.[14]

The naive realist assumes that everyone is in agreement with his particular definition, an assumption that is prevalent and that adds to confusion of communication. Such assumptions add difficulty to an already difficult field. Edel, in reference to the definition of ethical terms, states: "Here there is sufficient difficulty to make us pause. In fact the history of ethical theory shows that the greater part of theoretical controversy is often cast as a conflict of such definitions."[15]

At least at the level of practice, man has always been concerned with values, for the capacity to value and to evaluate is a unique part of man's existential nature. Man, being faced with making choices, has constantly been faced with a search for criteria, something that would make choice meaningful and also simplify it. It is possible, therefore, to trace the history of values in Western thought to beginnings in Plato's theory of forms or ideas and further in work by Aristotle, the Stoics, and the Epicureans.

From the times of Plato, Aristotle, Augustine, and St. Thomas Aquinas, to the middle of the nineteenth century, specific values were viewed as separate entities in an isolated manner. They considered such ideas as love, justice, goodness, and beauty.

Western philosophy began with the Ionian concern over the external or physical world. The Ionians viewed reality in terms of material substance and things. The Pythagoreans, Socrates, and Plato directed their attention to the realm of ideas, essences, and ideal objects. Thought then gradually focused upon inner subjective experiences such as perception, memory, joy, and grief.

The study of values, which we term axiology, arising with Lotze (1817–1881), Windelband (1848–1915), and Rickert (1863–1936) in the early nineteenth century and continuing with Hartman

---

[14]Clyde Kluckhohn and others, "Values and Value-Orientations in the Theory of Action," in Talcott Parsons and Edward Shils (eds.), *Toward a General Theory of Action* (New York: Harper and Row, 1962), p. 389. ©Harvard University Press.

[15]Abraham Edel, *Ethical Judgment* (New York: The Free Press of Glencoe, 1955), p. 76.

(1882–    ) and Perry (1876–1957), is relatively new and views values not as separate and atomistic but as interrelated and subsumed under a broader category. In this sense specific values take on new meaning, for they are recognized as an important part of a broader total concept of value.

There is considerable flux within the field of axiology to warrant considerable breadth of definition of the concept value. Brameld has stated, "Few if any fields of scholarship, inside or outside of philosophy, have become so involved in disputation, confusion, and cross purposes."[16]

Perry has observed (correctly, I think) that "one can generally tell a man's special field of investigation by the words which he uses carefully and the words he uses carelessly."[17] For example, the theologian is careful with the word God, the biologist with heredity and environment, and the mathematician with number. Other people will assume a common sense meaning for such words and banter them back and forth in an ambiguous and unexamined manner.

> Reading the voluminous, and often vague and diffuse literature on the subject in the various fields of learning, one finds values considered as attitudes, motivations, objects, measurable quantities, substantive areas of behavior, affect-laden customs or traditions, and relationships such as those of individuals, groups, objects, events. The only general agreement is that values somehow have to do with normative as opposed to existential propositions.[18]

Such is the dilemma also in counseling literature. With few exceptions one must conclude that value is not one of the "careful words." Its use is frequent in the literature, but its meaning is largely assumed to be self-evident and is therefore seldom clarified.

Even to axiologists to whom value is a "careful word," it is a source of disagreement and a word that does not have one closed definition.

The guidance and counseling field is one that is immersed in value concepts and questions, and one can ill afford to leave the word value unexamined. Although it is impossible at present to arrive at a conclusive understanding of the term, it is possible with the help of value theorists to proceed to greater clarity and to discover generally

---

[16]Brameld, "Book Review," *The Philosophical Forum*, XXI (1963–1964), 112.
[17]Perry, *Realms of Value*, p. 1.
[18]Kluckhohn and others, "Values and Value Orientations," p. 390.

agreed upon principles within the term. It is the purpose of this chapter to seek this clarification.

Parker, in his book *The Philosophy of Value*, suggests several reasons why the nature of value is so complex and has been "hidden as by a veil."[19] First are endless varieties of values. Second is the matter of relativity—"One man's meat is another man's poison." The third reason suggested is that there is a multiplicity of already existing theories. One can attempt to better understand the greater variety of values by more clearly understanding their functions. The problems of relativity can be clarified by a more thorough understanding of the relationship between subjectivism and objectivism, and the great multiplicity of existing theories and definitions can perhaps yield at least some common elements.

The word value itself does not contribute to clarity of understanding, for it is one of those words in the English language that has several usages without change in the word itself.[20] For example, it is used sometimes as an abstract noun, sometimes as a concrete noun, and sometimes as a verb. As abstract noun, value refers to the property of value or of being valuable. As concrete noun (a *value*, singular, or *values*, plural), value refers primarily to things that carry the property of value or to things that are valued. As a verb, value *(to value, valuing, or valuation)* refers to a process or a mental action of experiencing or feeling value. Value theory is concerned with both the property aspect (noun) of value as well as the process aspect (verb), and in seeking definition one must deal with several pertinent questions.

In considering value as property we ask:

> What is its nature? Is it a quality or a relation? Is it objective or subjective? Is it a single property, or is it several properties, value being an ambiguous term? Is its presence in a thing dependent on or reducible to the fact that the thing is valued by someone?[21]

In considering value as process:

> Is it a mere feeling or desire? Or does it involve judgment and cognition? And if so, is this a cognition of a value already there independently of the act of valuing or of knowing?[22]

One can find inherent in these questions the polarities of the classical

---

[19]Dewitt H. Parker, *The Philosophy of Value* (Ann Arbor: University of Michigan Press, 1957), pp. 3–5.

[20]Runes, *Dictionary of Philosophy*, p. 330.

[21]*Ibid.*

[22]*Ibid.*

objective-subjective controversy among value theorists, a problem to which we shall give more detailed attention later. For the present, historically, this conflict has centered in the question, "Do men value objects because they are valuable, or are they valuable because men value them?" The group known as the objectivists has attempted to reduce values to essences or absolute ideas inherent in the object itself, independent of man's desires. The subjectivists have attempted to reduce value to a psychological condition, such as desire, which gives the object its value. About reducing value to things, Frondizi has stated, "If, indeed, no one has tried to reduce values to the status of things, there is no doubt that the former have been confused with the material objects which enfold them, that is, with their depositories or carriers."[23]

## CHARACTERISTICS AND CLASSIFICATION

Now let us examine some characteristics of values. Values have the characteristic of polarity. They always have a corresponding opposite, i.e., good-bad, beautiful-ugly, and the corresponding disvalue or negative value exists by itself and is not merely the absence of positive value.[24] This makes an attitude of indifference to a value impossible, for even a statement of neutrality implies a judgment one way or the other, depending upon the situation.

Another characteristic of values is that they arrange themselves in a hierarchy from inferior to superior.[25] Hierarchy is not the same as classification, for classification does not imply degree of importance or worth, whereas hierarchy does. Every individual establishes some form of hierarchy of values based upon preference, which then serves as a guide in the process of choice. For example, if a person is faced by a choice between two alternatives, both of which he would like to do, the one he chooses will reveal itself to be at a higher position in his hierarchy, at least for the moment. It is easier to point to the existence of a hierarchy than it is to indicate its structure. One can infer a hierarchy from behavioral choices, but one could also hypothesize that there would be a considerable shifting of position within it. One could also hypothesize that there exists in the individual a hierarchy of "desires" and also a hierarchy of "oughts" and that they may be in conflict. The constant evaluation of such hierarchies is an impor-

[23] Risieri Frondizi, *What Is Value?* (LaSalle, Ill.: Open Court, 1963), p. 4.
[24] *Ibid.*, p. 9.
[25] *Ibid.*

tant aspect of the developmental process of the individual.

Classification of values must also be considered, for classification can help to narrow the great variety of values and aid one in better understanding similarities and differences between various characteristics of specific values and their categories. There is no comprehensive and agreed upon value classification. This is a cause of confusion when discussing values, for individuals may fail to communicate clearly the dimension of value of which they speak. In any classification system one must be cautioned against rigidity and use the system rather flexibly as a mere tool of understanding.

Perhaps the best known of the content classifications is Spranger's theoretical, economic, aesthetic, social, political, and religious.[26] This is the classification used in the Allport-Vernon Scale of Values. Kluckhohn felt that this classification is limited by cultural bias.

Understanding some of the dimensions of value can help one to see the broad diversity of values. Brightman and Beck list the following categories—a contrasting of opposites.[27] The first category is intrinsic and instrumental values. Intrinsic values are valuable as ends in themselves. Instrumental values are values as means to achieving a valued end or intrinsic value. The second category, permanent and transient, contains values such as truth and moral goodness, which exist through any adverse conditions and are thus permanent. Others, such as good health, may vanish and thus are called transient. The third category is termed catholic and exclusive. A prized statue could be possessed only by a single person or a specific group at one time and so would be an exclusive value. Catholic values are those that may be shared by all, such as truth. The fourth category is higher and lower values. Generally speaking, the intrinsic values can be considered to exist in a hierarchy, but one that may change, depending upon contributions of values to the whole of life as well as their complexity.

Kluckhohn offers an elaborate discussion of dimensions of value based upon work done by Whiting. For our purpose we shall mention only a few of these dimensions. There is a dimension of intensity of value under which one can refer to categorical values, namely, the *musts* of a particular culture, such as respect for property; preferential values, values strongly preferred (such as achievement in our Western culture); and utopian values, idealistic goals beyond immediate attainment but which nevertheless exert strong influences upon behavior.

[26]Kluckhohn and others, "Values and Value Orientations," p. 412.
[27]Brightman, *Introduction to Philosophy*, pp. 191–193.

There is also the dimension of explicitness. Explicit values are those that are given lip service by the actors, whereas implicit values must be inferred by an observer either from actions or from verbalizations. The dimension of extent includes idiosyncratic values (values held by only one person within a group), and group values (an abstraction based upon values commonly agreed upon by the majority of the group). Personal values grow out of a background of group values. As Kluckhohn states, personal value is "the private form of a group value or a universal value."[28] Each individual's value system is unique, but there will usually be much common value among members of any group. However, this is a fluctuating variable, and in times of cultural crisis and social upheaval commonalities will tend to decrease and differences will increase. Within the dimension of intent falls the question of cultural values as relative or universal. This also is a question of considerable importance to which we shall turn later in our discussion.

Kluckhohn also refers to the importance of hierarchical thinking concerning values. Values are discriminating ("better than," "more useful than," "more beautiful than"). Within this notion that values tend to become organized into hierarchical patterns is the important characteristic that they are interpenetrating. Values occur in relationship to other values involving an interconnected pattern of meanings. The fact that "values do appear to occur in clusters rather than alone," is a factor that "makes them both interesting and difficult to deal with."[29]

Brightman and Beck also refer to this complexity when they state that "no values can be fully appreciated without taking all other values—indeed the whole personal consciousness—into account. . . . No one has the right, rationally speaking, to say, 'This is of value,' unless he has related it to everything he knows."[30]

One becomes aware of the relationship between value and philosophy when one talks in terms of relationships to wholes. "Thus the study of value leads to metaphysics. If one wishes to think truly about value, he must seek to think about reality as a whole in which value is experienced."[31] This involves looking at the unique and whole individual in his whole or total context.

[28]Kluckhohn and others, "Values and Value Orientations," p. 412.
[29]*Ibid.*, p. 416.
[30]Brightman, *Introduction to Philosophy*, p. 194.
[31]*Ibid.*

## DEFINITIONS

Lepley, approaching the meaning of value from a historical point of view, has suggested three primary meanings that value or value theory may have. First, when used in the least inclusive way, the terms refer to an interest in morals, ethics, and ethical theory, which developed early in the history of human thought and in this sense is as old as philosophy itself. Second, the terms may refer to a "distinction between facts and values and between judgments of fact and judgments of value."[32] This meaning involves questions of what *is* in relation to what *ought to be*. The third, and most inclusive meaning of the terms, "has resulted from increased attention to the similarities, differences, and inter-relations of interests such as truth, beauty, and goodness and of activities such as business, science, art, politics, and religion."[33]

Let us consider for a moment Lepley's second primary meaning, the most widely recognized distinction between different types of values, that between factual or descriptive values and normative or prescriptive values. This has been a point of confusion.

> The term "value" has a wide range of current usage in philosophy and the sciences. Descriptively, a man's "values" may refer to all of his attitudes for or against anything. His values include his preferences and avoidances, his desire-objects and aversion-objects, his pleasure and pain tendencies, his goals, ideals, interests and disinterests, what he takes to be right and wrong, good and evil, beautiful and ugly, useful and useless, his approvals and disapprovals, his criteria of taste and standards of judgment, and so forth.
>
> Parallel to this *descriptive* usage lies the realm of *normative* usage. Men do not merely have values; they also make value judgments assessing their values. For in every self-conscious choice that the individual makes, in every creative act as well as every criticism, whether economic, moral, aesthetic, or any other, there are assumptions about what is desirable as well as desired, preferable as well as preferred, appropriate standards as well as functioning standards, and so forth. The same is true of social decisions, even as embedded in the normal functioning of social institutions and agencies.[34]

[32] Ray Lepley, *Verifiability of Value* (New York: Columbia University Press, 1944), p. 2.

[33] *Ibid.*

[34] Edel, *Method in Ethical Theory* (New York: Bobs-Merrill, 1963), p. 185. Italics mine.

Margenau also points to this distinction. Beginning with the definition of value as "the measure of satisfaction of a human want," a definition he recognizes as being inadequate, he states that

> the loose complex covered by our definition is pervaded by a deep fissure which separates beyond possibility of comparison two kinds of value, one called factual, the other normative. Crudely stated the difference is this: Factual values are observable preferences, appraisals, and desires of concrete people at a given time; normative values are the ratings which people *ought* to give to value objects.[35]

This difference is also acknowledged by a large body of philosophic writing.

The main distinction here appears to be in the approach to the problem. Factual value is most easily determined because it is empirical, a measure of what men do in fact value. Those factual values are not right or wrong but rather are mere facts of observation. Because factual values are easiest to establish and work with, it is not surprising that most value studies are concerned with factual values. Although this approach is useful in establishing a base for normative judgments, it cannot replace such judgments. To remain strictly empirical is to assume that the best life is what now exists. It is to be satisfied with the *is* rather than the *ought*. One cannot afford to neglect normative values on the basis that they are too complex and difficult to grasp, for as Edel has pointed out, there are normative judgments and assumptions present in all choices that the individual makes. Such normative aspects of value make a more profound claim of validity.[36] They further "point to and receive their value from a *command* or a *directive* to which a person is committed."[37] But a system of ethics requires both command plus validation.[38]

Morris, in an empirical study of preferences for various concepts of the good life, found the meaning of value to be multiple and complex and chose not to presuppose a definition of the term. Rather, he referred to three common usages of the term. The first is "the tendencies or dispositions of living beings to prefer one kind of object rather

[35] Henry Margenau, "The Scientific Basis of Value Theory," in Abraham Maslow (ed.), *New Knowledge in Human Values* (New York: Harper and Row, 1959), pp. 38–39.

[36] *Ibid.*, p. 39.

[37] *Ibid.*, p. 42.

[38] *Ibid.*, p. 50.

than another."[39] He called this first definition "operative values." This definition seems to be more closely related to need and implies less conscious deliberation. It also implies "a subjectivist view of value in that its primary focus is upon the inner tendencies of individuals in the process of assigning value to objects."[40] The second common usage of the term value is "preferential behavior directed by an anticipation or foresight of the outcome of such behavior."[41] This is the definition of Dewey and implies reflection concerning the outcomes of choices—not mere preference alone. It requires some justification for the choice made, some criterion of valuation. Morris called these "conceived values." The third common usage is "what is preferable (or "desirable") regardless of whether it is in fact preferred or conceived as preferable."[42] He called these "object values" and the objectivist orientation is apparent.

Morris has noted the similarities of the three definitions in the word preference and views this as the key link to the scientific study of value behavior.

Perhaps the most popular definition of value in the behavioral sciences is that of the Harvard Study Group: "A value is a conception, explicit or implicit, distinctive of an individual or characteristic of a group, of the desirable which influences the selection from available modes, means, and ends of action."[43]

Kluckhohn emphasizes that this quite comprehensive definition includes the affective ("desirable"), the cognitive ("conception"), and the conative ("selection") as all being essential elements within the concept of value. Also, according to his further elaboration of this definition, value is a logical construct; it includes justification of a preference by what is deemed desirable; it involves choice of action commitments; all values can be verbalized; value is primarily a cultural product (values are learned) although each individual gives the value his own meaning; they influence behavior; and they involve selection from a plurality of alternatives.

Opler[44] objected to the Kluckhohn definition on the basis that

[39]Charles Morris, *Varieties of Human Value* (Chicago: University of Chicago Press, 1956), p. 10.

[40]*Ibid.*

[41]*Ibid.*

[42]*Ibid.*, p. 11.

[43]Kluckhohn and others, "Values and Value Orientations," p. 395.

[44]Morris Opler, "Values and Education in Cultural Perspective," *Values in American Education*, Theodore Brameld and Stanley Elam (eds.), (Bloomington, Ind.: Phi Delta Kappa, Inc., 1964), p. 65.

it does not limit values to what he felt was really important and that it confuses value with mere preference. It seems clear to this writer that this was not Kluckhohn's intent, but it does point up the confusion between what is "desired" and the "desirable" which does seem prevalent.

Lippitt's definition is similar to that of Kluckhohn. He describes value as "a criterion of judgment being used by an individual or group to choose between alternatives in decision and action situations, or used by the participants to explain the reason for making a particular choice."[45]

Some definitions seem to focus only upon the desired. For example: "Values are felt desires, and value-judgments are ideas or hypotheses about what we need to satisfy or harmonize these desires."[46]

Smith couches his definition in more psychological terms as he refers to value system:

> The *value system* of the individual is best described as a multifactor spiral or behavioral bias which molds and dominates the decision making power of the particular person.[47]
> Values seem to depend for stability or instability on beliefs. Individual beliefs are of two origins: in reference to what is or was; and to what ought to be or ought to have been. The first of these is usually referred to as *facts;* the second as valuations, judgments, or opinions.[48]

Barry and Wolf define value as "a learned belief so thoroughly internalized that it colors the actions and thoughts of the individual and produces a strong emotional-intellectual response when anything runs counter to it."[49]

Williams, a sociologist, relates his definition to self-perception or self-concept when he defines values as "affectively charged conceptual structures registered by the individual which act as directives. They form an important part of the apprehension of self and act as direc-

---

[45]Ronald Lippitt, "Values Issues for a Classroom Change-Agent," in Brameld and Elam (eds.), *Values in American Education*, p. 34.

[46]Philip P. Wiener, "Values in the History of Ideas," *Aspects of Value*, Frederick C. Gruber (ed.), (Philadelphia: University of Pennsylvania Press, 1959), p. 56.

[47]David W. Smith, "Value Systems and the Therapeutic Interview," *Counseling: Selected Readings*, Herman J. Peters and others (eds.), (Columbus: Charles E. Merrill, 1962), p. 372.

[48]*Ibid.*, p. 373.

[49]Ruth Barry and Beverly Wolf, *Motives, Values, and Realities* (New York: Bureau of Publications, Teachers College, Columbia University, 1965), p. 40.

tional factors in the organization of behavior."[50]

The relation of value to self-concept is recognized by Ginzburg in his definition of value as "a criterion which helps us to distinguish between alternatives and affords us a base for recognizing ourselves in relation to the rest of the world."[51]

Albert, an anthropologist, separates values from the actualities of conduct.

> Values are by definition criteria, that is, ideals, goals, norms, and standards. Accessible principally through analysis of verbal behavior, values are not the same as the actualities of conduct. Actualization may reveal that values in the fact are not so elegant as they seemed when they were theoretic, shining ideals; that performance does not measure up to intentions; that practice does not vindicate theory.[52]

She seems to equate value more closely to the ideal and the normative as opposed to how men do in fact act.

## RELATED CONCEPTS

When the word value in its usage becomes a "careless word," it is likely to become confused with related, but nevertheless different, terms. The meaning of value can be further clarified by showing how it differs from such related concepts. This can be done by referring to what value is not.

1. *Value is **not** the same as need.* Motivation theories based upon need have grown out of a medical base using the concepts of homeostasis and equilibrium. In this context, need refers primarily to a lack of something, which pushes the individual toward tension-reduction by restoration of equilibrium. For example, the hungry man satisfies himself by eating food to fulfill his lack of, or need for, food. Value may be involved in such tension-reduction, but it cannot be reduced to it. Value is more comprehensive in that it is often tension-producing. When one values something, he may be creating a new need or discovering a new goal. He is thus pulled by it rather than pushed by a mere physiological drive. This, however, is not a simple

---

[50] C. H. Patterson, *Counseling and Psychotherapy: Theory and Practice* (New York: Harper and Brothers, 1959), p. 55.

[51] *Ibid.*

[52] Ethel M. Albert, "Conflict and Change in American Values," *Ethics,* LXXIV, 2 (October 1963), 20.

process. Kluckhohn summarizes the relationship of value and need thus:

> Since a value is a complex proposition involving cognition, approval, selection, and affect, then the relationship between a value system and a need or goal system is necessarily complex. Values *both* rise from and create needs. A value serves several needs partially, inhibits others partially, half meets and half blocks still others.[53]

Patterson also summarizes this relationship:

> Values are thus not simply derived from needs, appetites, or interests, which include valuation but are not values, but come into play when a choice must be made which is *not* decided simply on the basis of a need, but is influenced by the ego ideal. ... Values reflect needs and interests, but are neither of these.[54]

Values involve some criteria of justification of the desirable and the good, an element missing in mere need or desire.

It appears to this writer that within much of the psychological literature, needs are commonly confused with values. A case in point is found in Maslow's hierarchy of needs. When he speaks of deficit needs he is no doubt referring to needs, for these imply a lack of something, a deficit or need that must be filled to maintain equilibrium. However, when he speaks in terms of growth needs and growth motivations, he appears to be moving into the realm of values, that is, choices based upon criteria of the desirable. Maslow indicates a dislike for the term value and suggests that the term will eventually become obsolete. "It includes too much, means too many diverse things and has too long a history. Furthermore, these varied usages are not usually conscious. They therefore create confusion and I am tempted often to give up the word altogether."[55] This would no doubt add to reduction of ambiguity, but words that have lived long do not die easily.

2. *Values are* **not** *the same as goals.* Values are more than the goals themselves, although they may at times serve as goals. They are criteria by which goals are chosen.[56] "Values are not the concrete goals of behavior, but rather are aspects of these goals. Values appear as the *criteria* against which goals are chosen, and as the *impli-*

[53]Kluckhohn and others, "Values and Value Orientations," p. 428.

[54]Patterson, *Counseling and Psychotherapy,* p. 55.

[55]Abraham Maslow, *Toward A Psychology of Being* (Princeton, N.J.: D. Van Nostrand, 1962), p. 158.

[56]Patterson, *Counseling and Psychotherapy,* p. 55.

*cations* which these goals have in the situation."[57]

3. *Value is* **not** *the same as belief.* Value involves beliefs concerning one's self and the context in which he lives but is not reducible to belief alone. Value involves more than mere belief alone and necessitates some degree of commitment to the belief. A person may have numerous beliefs that do not really involve him actively. Belief, then, as defined here is a mere affirmation of possibility, whereas value involves commitment to action. Opler implies this definition when he states:

> Value, properly conceived, really reduces choice; that is, if you reserve the term "value", as I think it should be reserved, for directives that are really important, that are a basic part of the character structure, there really is a minimum of choice in situations where strongly held values are involved.
>
> If a person feels deeply about matters of honesty—pecuniary honesty—it isn't a choice of "Shall I take a little money that doesn't belong to me or a lot?" He just isn't going to take money that doesn't belong to him. And if he does, something catastrophic has happened that gnaws at him that makes life extremely uncomfortable for him.[58]

There is a value element involved when one is *committed* to act upon a belief. Kluckhohn suggests the following schematization.

> (1) This is real or possible (belief); (2) This concerns me or us (interest); (3) This is good for me or us, this is better than something else that is possible (value). *Belief* refers primarily to the categories, "true" and "false"; "correct" and "incorrect." *Value* refers primarily to "good" and "bad"; "right" and "wrong."[59]

In Margenau's breakdown of values into the factual and the normative, he includes the idea of commitment primarily under the normative. He defines "normative values" as ratings "which people *ought* to give to value objects."[60] He further states: "honesty, veracity, friendship, love of mankind, and all the rest: they point to and receive their value from a *command* or *directive* to which a person is committed."[61]

Buhler[62] recognizes the element of commitment as being the

[57]Kluckhohn and others, "Values and Value Orientations," p. 429.

[58]Opler, "Values and Education," p. 64.

[59]Kluckhohn and others, "Values and Value Orientations," p. 432.

[60]Margenau, "The Scientific Basis of Value Theory," p. 39.

[61]*Ibid.*, p. 42.

[62]Charlotte Buhler, *Values in Psychotherapy* (New York: The Free Press of Glencoe, 1962), p. 33.

main difference between normative and factual values. Factual values are merely "observable preferences, appraisals, and desires of concrete people at a given time,"[63] and thus are of a looser category of mere descriptiveness—relative and particular. They lack the authority and directiveness of the normative, which tend to be viewed as universal by the valuing individual. The normative involve right and wrong, whereas factual values are neither right nor wrong but are merely facts of observation.[64]

Buhler also recognizes within normative values what she calls a "constructive intent." This involves "an active directedness toward the accomplishing of the most beneficial future; beneficial to whatever sense the persons engaged in the process may understand."[65] *"We seem to set up these beliefs as something which we hold on to and they become something that holds us up."*[66] Because these beliefs to which people become committed vary and even conflict within our pluralistic society, individuals are forced to make their own decisions as to what is "truth" by their own deliberation over the alternatives. "Many different value systems seem to prevail, and all we can see as their common denominator is what we call their constructive intent."[67]

4. *Value is **not** the same as attitude.* Using Allport's definition of attitude, "a mental and neural state of readiness, organized through experience, exerting a directive or dynamic influence upon the individual's response to all objects and situations with which it is related,"[68] one can see the similarities to the valuing process. Attitude is an organizing and directing influence upon behavior, but value is more than mere attitude, for attitude lacks primarily the imputation of the desirable and is exclusively referable to the individual.[69] Values, as criteria by which choice is justified, may affect attitudes or attitudes may affect value choice; nevertheless, the two are different.

5. *Value is **not** the same as mere preference.* Preference is surely a part of the value experience. Morris refers to preference as a common element of various definitions of value and views this as the key link to the scientific study of value behavior.[70] However, mere prefer-

---

[63]Margenau, "The Scientific Basis of Value Theory," p. 39.

[64]*Ibid.*

[65]Buhler, *Values in Psychotherapy,* p. 36.

[66]*Ibid.,* p. 35.

[67]*Ibid.,* p. 40.

[68]Kluckhohn and others, "Values and Value Orientations," p. 423, quoting Gordon Allport.

[69]*Ibid.*

[70]See Morris, *Varieties of Human Values.*

ence alone is of a lower order than value experience itself. The limitation here is that one may experience felt preferences without any conception of the desirable.

> Value is more than preference; it is limited to those types of preferential behavior based upon conceptions of the desirable.[71]
>
> A value is not just a preference but is a preference which is felt and/or considered to be justified—"morally" or by reasoning or by aesthetic judgments, usually by two or all three of these.[72]
>
> To say, following certain contemporary usage, "Eating spinach is a value for Smith," because Smith likes spinach or prefers spinach to broccoli is to confuse the desired with the desirable. This practice both negates one of the few constant differentia of value (that of approval-disapproval) and makes the category value so broad as to be useless. It is much more convenient to separate "value" and "preference," restricting "preference" to those selections which are neutral (i.e., do not require justification or reference to sanctions) from the point of view of the individual and/or the culture. Of course, if Smith justified his preference for spinach in rational or pseudo-rational terms of vitamins, mineral content, and the like, it then becomes by definition one of his values. If, however, he simply says, "I like spinach better than broccoli," it remains a mere preference.[73]

Kluckhohn further differentiates value from other related concepts such as culture, configuration, motivation, cathexis, drives and learning, utility functions, sanctions, and ideology. It would be beyond the scope of this book to elaborate further upon these terms.

## COMMON PRINCIPLES

If a simple and generally agreed upon definition of value is difficult to formulate, we can at least outline some of the common principles of value. Such common principles seem to be generally agreed upon.

1. *Values are hypothetical constructs.* They must be inferred.[74] They are unreal qualities[75] that appear as mere qualities of value

---

[71]Kluckhohn and others, "Values and Value Orientations," p. 422.

[72]*Ibid.*, p. 396.

[73]*Ibid.*, p. 397.

[74]Patterson, *Counseling and Psychotherapy*, p. 55.

[75]Frondizi, *What Is Value?*, p. 5.

carriers as viewed objectively. Viewed in this sense they are criteria by which choice of objects or goals are justified. Viewed subjectively, they are responses involving elements of belief, interest, wants, and desires, both cognitive and affective in nature, and involving commitment to what is experienced as contributing to constructive intent as perceived by the individual.

2. *Values represent the desirable in the sense of what one "ought" to do or what he perceives is the "right" thing to do in any given circumstance.* Once again values are criteria by which action choice is justified. It is necessary to understand the distinction between the "desired" and the "desirable," for many have fallen into confusing these two terms. The desired is tied more closely to physiological needs, whereas the desirable transcends the mere physiological. The desired may be supressed, even though strongly wanted, by the authority of the desirable, which changes the desired into the not-desired.[76] In this way, values also become what Kluckhohn calls "more or less stable ways of resolving ambivalence," and "actors perhaps most often think about and refer to values when they are in doubt about alternative courses of conduct."[77]

3. *Values are motivational forces.* Frankl has recognized the motivational power of values. Holding a somewhat objectivist orientation of values, he views them as not "pushing" man but rather "pulling him."[78] Values are independent of man and confront him in existence. Thus values are not created but are rather detected, and the "striving to find meaning is the primary motivational force in man."[79] Mental health is based, he feels, "on a certain degree of tension, the tension between what one has already achieved and what one still ought to accomplish."[80]

Values as motivators are also inherent in Allport's concept of propriate striving. Barry and Wolf recognize values as subsidiary motives "with which each person embroiders the universals."[81] They list universal motives as striving to live, to internalize a culture, to perpetuate internalized learnings, to express one's self within a culture,

[76]Kluckhohn and others, "Values and Value Orientations," p. 395.
[77]*Ibid.*
[78]Viktor Frankl, *Man's Search for Meaning* (New York: Washington Square Press, 1963), p. 157.
[79]*Ibid.*, p. 154.
[80]*Ibid.*, pp. 165, 166.
[81]Barry and Wolf, *Motives, Values, and Realities*, p. 39.

and to achieve positive experiences. All of these are heavily involved with values.

Kluckhohn clarifies the relationship between values and motivation.

> Values and motivation are linked, but only rarely do they coincide completely. Values are only an element in motivation and in determining action; they invariably have implications for motivation because a standard is not a value unless internalized. . . . Values canalize motivation.[82]

When one deals with value from a psychological orientation, as a counselor does, one is led to emphasize the motivational aspects, namely, this definition: "Value may be defined as that aspect of motivation which is referable to standards, personal or cultural, that do not arise solely out of immediate tensions or immediate situation."[83] "The value component in motivation is a factor both in the instigation to action and in setting the direction of the act."[84]

The importance to the counselor of the motivational elements in value can be seen in this statement by Buhler:

> The therapeutic relationship becomes an effective *human* impact through the undercurrent of human values that both the therapist and the patient feel to be of the essence in their lives, while the therapeutic relationship becomes an effective *emotional* impact through the analysis of motivation.[85]

## SUBJECT OR OBJECT: A PERSISTENT PROBLEM

Now let us examine what has been one of the most persistent problems in axiology. Known historically as the subjective-objective controversy, it also includes within its scope many of the other important value questions. Frondizi states that this controversy "was born together with axiology itself, and the history of the theory of values could be written, considering this problem as the axis and outlining the various solutions which have been proposed in order to resolve it."[86] It is felt by this writer that recent developments in this controversy have implications for philosophical issues in counseling. The question, simply restated, is this: "Do objects possess value because we desire

---

[82]Kluckhohn and others, "Values and Value Orientations," p. 400.

[83]*Ibid.*, p. 425.

[84]*Ibid.*

[85]Buhler, *Values in Psychotherapy*, p. 4.

[86]Frondizi, *What Is Value?*, p. 13.

them or do we desire them because they possess value?"[87]

In the use of the terms objective and subjective, it is important to clarify their meanings. In the consideration of values we have previously pointed to two levels of value. First, one can focus upon what is *desired*. At this level one observes values empirically. They can be described as the interests, desires, or preferences that an individual or group of individuals actually experience. It is in reference to this level that one refers to values as subjective. The second level focuses upon the *desirable*. These are prescriptive and represent what men *ought* to desire. They establish or represent criteria for judging what is the right or best action to take. They are to the experiencing subject "out there," that is, independent of him; they are objective in nature, although this objectivity may be a mere construct—something that *pulls* the individual toward it because of its "rightness" for him. This "rightness" may or may not be pleasurable. It is because it is "right" as perceived by the individual that it is desirable. Objective values also represent some sort of authority, which validates them to the individual.

As with many technical definitions, the terms subjective and objective have become fuzzy with common usage. One is likely to think of subjective in terms of the product of one person's thought and feeling and as untrustworthy because relative and unverified by "truth." One may inversely view anything objective as being "truth" because a number of people have agreed upon it. As one examines more deeply such common usages, one can see inconsistencies; any person's reaction is always subjective because it comes from the person, the subject, and any agreement arrived upon by a group may in actuality be a group distortion of what is real.[88] The difficulty here rests in a confusion of the focus of these terms. Reference in correct usage is to the process of perception and judgment and not to persons, opinions, and factual validation. The difference between subjective and objective judgments depends on whether the judgment pertains to subject or object. All judgments of objects are made by subjects, but if reference is to an object—something independent of the perceiver—it is objective. If, however, the reference is to the experience of the subject, it is a subjective judgment. In value experience one is subjective in his experience of desiring but is objective in the act of choosing

---

[87] *Ibid.*

[88] See Erich Fromm, *The Sane Society* (New York: Holt, Rinehart and Winston, 1955), especially chapter 2.

what is desirable, which involves some criteria of "rightness." Thus, "an objective judgment is one made by testing in all ways possible one's subjective impressions, so as to arrive at a knowledge of objects,"[89] or, one could say, value objects. Value is "objective if it is independent of a subject or a valuating consciousness; conversely, it is subjective if it owes its existence, its sense, or its validity to the reactions of the subject who does the valuating, regardless of whether these be physiological or psychological."[90]

When one reads either the position of the subjectivist or the objectivist, one is impressed by the emphatic assertions of both groups and also by the logic of either position *for particular value situations.* Both positions make statements that are seemingly true, yet when opposed to one another the controversy continues to rage. What is the solution to such a dilemma?

This writer is in agreement with Frondizi when he formulates the question thus:

> This going around in circles, from one position to the opposite one, and then back again to the first, makes us think that perhaps the difficulty is derived from the fact that the problem has been poorly stated. Does value necessarily have to be objective or subjective? ...
> The difficulty originates in the complexity of the problem, and the confusion is due to the fact that both doctrines make statements which are actually true; the error in both positions consists in taking into consideration only one aspect of the question. ... The original error in both schools of thought is to be found in the fallacy of false opposition.[91]

The error, then, may be due to rigid adherence to a dualism that in actuality does not exist. Rather than viewing subjectivism and objectivism as separate and contradictory, perhaps they are complementary—two sides of the same coin. If one desires an object, must not this imply that the object exists? And, if the object exists, how is one to comprehend it but by his subjective experience? Our experience then becomes relational, a dynamic dialectic between our subjective experience and our objective world. Zen Buddhism and recent existential writings lend support to this view and will be discussed in a later chapter.

It is possible, for example, that the psychological states of

---

[89]Jacques Barzun and Henry F. Graff, *The Modern Researcher* (New York: Harcourt, Brace and World, 1957), p. 146.

[90]Frondizi, *What Is Value?*, p. 14.

[91]*Ibid.*, pp. 21, 103, 124.

pleasure, desire, or interest, are a necessary but not a sufficient condition, and that these states do not exclude objective elements, but on the contrary, assume them. This is to say that value may be the result of a tension between the subject and the object, and therefore presents a subjective as well as an objective aspect, deceiving those who stake their all on only one of these.[92]

If value were merely a matter of personal desire, we would indeed live in a chaotic world. Moral education would not make sense, nor could there be such a thing as erroneous valuation. Normative or objective value is a necessary element in the stabilization of value experience, for it focuses upon the *quality* of desire, the *desirable*.

On the other hand, if value is totally objective without regard for the relationship to man, the question of value experience is left up in the air. The value theorist then may soon find himself so heavenly minded that he becomes no earthly good. Value experience must be recognized to be a great complexity of dynamically related subjective and objective factors that not only exert influence but also may in turn change in the process. Let us consider one more related aspect.

Frondizi raises the question of whether or not all values have the same character.[93] Perhaps some values are more subjective in nature than others. This appears to be so if one examines possible hierarchies. For example, let us take Maslow's hierarchy of needs, which to this writer represents a continuum moving from lower needs (deficiency motivation) upward to normative values (growth motivation). Maslow lists these needs as physiological, safety, belongingness and love, importance, self-respect, self-esteem, independence, information, understanding, beauty, and self-actualization. The lower needs are physiological and psychological in nature, stem from a deficit, and imply pleasure in their fulfillment. The experiences described here are most closely described as desire, preference.

When one examines the lower values, derived mainly from a pleasure-pain criterion, one finds a strong element of the subjective, with the objective or normative being less apparent. To one man coffee is better than tea; to another tea is better than coffee. The subject here seems to be the source of the pleasantness in response to the coffee, for men have different tastes. At this level, one is also closest to what has been referred to as factual value. Preference apparently is a strong element here.

However, as we ascend the scale to the higher values, the ethical

[92] *Ibid.*, p. 21.
[93] *Ibid.*

values such as truth or beauty or honesty, we find the objective element becoming stronger. We do not judge truth upon the basis of our feeling or whether or not it is pleasant to us. Truth, rather, becomes an objective criterion that is to be accepted in spite of our feelings. As Frondizi puts it, one could hardly trust a judge who allowed his verdicts to be conditioned by the function of his stomach or liver or by his quarrels with his wife.[94]

Value experience, then, is a dynamic relationship between subjective and objective elements, but these elements vary in their strength according to a hierarchical arrangement. The lower values are composed more of the subjective element and the higher ethical values are composed more of the objective, with a tendency toward equal balancing in between. One might diagram it thus:

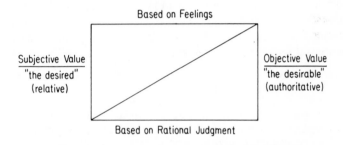

Diagram 1. Schematic presentation of subjective and objective values.

Buhler has added to the categories of factual and normative value a third category of value that she calls "consensus value" because she finds an overlap between factual and normative values. By consensus value she refers to a "type of value that to certain groups represents a norm, while for others the belief in this value is only factual evidence of what some people believe in."[95] Many religious norms are of this kind. "They represent normative values to the adherent of a particular religion and only factual values to others."[96] Buhler views consensus as growing out of factual values, becoming doctrine, and then gradually becoming norms. She diagrams[97] it thus:

[94] *Ibid.*, pp. 22-23.
[95] Buhler, *Values in Psychotherapy*, p. 45.
[96] *Ibid.*
[97] *Ibid.*, p. 48. Reprinted by permission of the MacMillan Co.

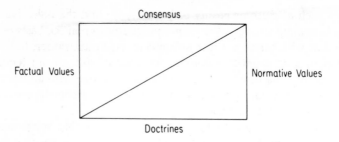

Consensus

Factual Values    Normative Values

Doctrines

One must keep in mind the dynamic relationship between the subjective and objective elements of value experience. Although objective elements place more demand upon the individual in the service of the "desirable," it is also possible that the subjective element may serve to weaken the objective in the service of pleasure. This may be particularly true in times of stress, fatigue, anger, and other such physiological and psychological states.

> Whatever be the case under examination or the position of the value in the scale, we shall always be faced with two aspects of the question: subjective and objective. Of course, it should not be supposed that both elements are always fixed, and that the only thing that varies is the relationship between simple, permanent or homogeneous entities, but rather a complex and variable interrelationship of objects which are also complex and dynamic.[98]

The subjective element of value experience may be influenced by one's physiological or psychological condition at a particular time. One is influenced by his perception, by his self-concept, and in general by a vast number of past experiences. One's immediate sense experiences and one's ideas as they are associated with the value object will be of influence, as will all of one's learning regarding the object.

The objective aspect also has its influences. There may be specific qualities in the object that set up certain reactions in the individual. The objective conditions surrounding the object will be of influence. The value carrier plays an important part—it matters whether a statue is made of marble or concrete. Other values interpenetrate with the value object. A statue of a man, for example, may arouse feelings of patriotism.

The relationship between subject and object also happens within

[98]Frondizi, *What Is Value?*, pp. 131–132.

a particular culture at a particular time, involving many other societal influences. Value experience must thus be recognized for the interaction that it is between these two elements, the subjective and the objective. One can never assume a simple hierarchy or categorization of values for any individual, for in each individual there will be a continuing dynamic interaction between the subjective and the objective.

## ABSOLUTE OR RELATIVE: A RELATED PROBLEM

Related to the problem of subject and object is the question of absolutism (or universalism) and relativism. One could construct a continuum with extreme absolutism on one end and extreme relativism on the other, and all ethical theories could be placed somewhere along this continuum. The traditional values stemming from a theistic value orientation have assumed an absolute position, and these have been prominent throughout history, but primarily during periods such as the Middle Ages, when theism was the dominant orientation. Since the Rennaisance, science, based upon a naturalistic orientation, has pushed these values back and has slowly undermined them with an emphasis on relativism. Positivistic science, based upon an epistomology of the senses, can know only particulars, and any absolutes are all but impossible to find in a world of rapidly changing particulars. Such a view has left a vacuum—people are clamoring for science to replace the structure it tore down.

> We are no longer inhibited by the rigidities of nineteenth-century morality. Zealous wreckers have torn that house down. The question is not one of further pulverizing the fragments but of asking what we intend to do to protect ourselves from the elements.[99]

The problem of finding a value core remains, which in large part is a search for principles approaching universality upon which men could ground their choices. Significant work is being done in this area, and although it is beyond the scope of this book to elaborate upon this in great detail, it is important to understand some of the implications for counseling theory.

Edel has been one of the leaders in philosophy in a search for a valuational base. Science and ethics have been traditionally opposed to one another. It has been a common assumption that science can

[99]John Gardner, *Self-Renewal* (New York: Harper and Row, 1963), p. 121.

determine only what *is* (fact and description), whereas ethics attempts to deal with what *should be* (value and prescription), and never the twain shall meet. Edel has taken opposition to this view and has urged a cooperative venture of the two in separating out the strands of relativism. The essence of relativism is indeterminacy, and science and ethics can work cooperatively toward greater determinacy. Only as one approaches determinacy can one begin to formulate an ethical base. Edel describes an evaluational base as a crystallization of determinate elements that have been discovered for the purpose of utilizing them in the process of evaluation. The process of counseling is largely a process of individual evaluation, and one can anticipate the usefulness of such a base to the client in the helping relationship. Edel further describes the valuational base as consisting of a blend of universal and local elements.

> The universal are the fundamental human needs, the perennial aspirations and strivings, and the discovered high values that are deeply grounded in these needs and aspirations. ... The local elements will be the central conditions and special contingent elements (not necessarily values themselves) which may press heavily upon men's pursuit of values in the given age.[100]

We might raise the question in passing as to what use could be made of a well-formulated valuational base for counselors. Let me suggest a few ways.

1. It could serve as a guideline for professional social policies, aims, and objectives of the desirable in working with people.

2. It could serve as a general thermometer of the current status of a society—a diagnostic tool in the measure of freedom.

3. It could be used as a tool in counseling to assist the counselee to become aware of his value orientation in relation to the valuational base and to thus evaluate it in terms of future probabilities by use of phase rules ("break-only-with-regret rules").[101]

4. It could also be used broadly in examination of any current society or of any society in history where data is available.

Such a valuational base is based upon the assumption that "growing human knowledge does provide a standpoint for evaluation."[102] This knowledge is always open to examination, refinement,

---

[100]Edel, *Ethical Judgment,* p. 297.
[101]*Ibid.,* pp. 46–48.
[102]*Ibid.,* p. 299.

and further growth and change. A valuational base must, of necessity, focus upon a middle level of values. One cannot, in a pluralistic society, impose higher (for example, religious) values upon individuals; nor should one be especially concerned with lower relative and particular values based predominantly upon preference. It is at a middle level that most agreement should be found, for such values are humanistically based. Each choice has a probable outcome, and the client would do well to consider the logical consequences of his choices.

# chapter 3

# Counseling: An Expression
# of Social Philosophy

That philosophy should be rather fanned than extinguished by times of decadence is not surprising, since it is precisely the unacceptable which sets the reflective conscience in motion. Philosophy is in fact nothing but the reflective conscience of mankind.[1]

## THE COUNSELOR AS PHILOSOPHER

Counselors must begin by first recognizing that everyone philosophizes, for we do so any time we express ourselves regarding what life is all about. Our style of living represents a philosophy of life. It is in those moments when we are jarred from our complacency that we are most likely to examine or reexamine the beliefs that we hold.[2] Such examination is likely to come either when our own beliefs conflict with someone else's or when our own beliefs are recognized to be in conflict with one another. This is likely to occur frequently in a crisis culture.[3] When such is the case, we are compelled to make some kind of choice.

Brameld lists nine different possible reactions—choices—to a disturbance in one's beliefs.

1. *The complacent choice.* One ignores the disturbance and continues as before.

2. *The negative choice.* One merely examines his beliefs but does nothing toward resolution of the conflict.

---

[1]Micheline Sauvage, *Socrates and the Conscience of Man* (New York: Harper and Brothers, 1960), p. 19.
[2]See Theodore Brameld, *Philosophies of Education in Cultural Perspective* (New York: Dryden Press, 1958), especially chapter 2, and Edgar S. Brightman, *An Introduction to Philosophy,* revised by Robert Beck (New York: Holt, Rinehart, and Winston, 1963), chapter 1.
[3]Brameld, *Philosophies of Education,* p. 21.

3. *The skeptical choice.* Following examination of one's beliefs, one definitely disbelieves them and ends by doubting them.

4. *The agnostic choice.* One decides through examination that it is impossible to know the truth or falsehood of one's beliefs and so the individual remains uncommitted.

5. *The eclectic choice.* One keeps the "best" of varying beliefs and holds them separately, ready to shift them when the situation demands.

6. *The conservative choice.* After thorough examination of one's beliefs one decides that in general they are sound and worth upholding even in the midst of change.

7. *The liberal choice.* One chooses to test out some possible changes in beliefs for the purpose of gradual modification and progress.

8. *The regressive choice.* One decides that it is best to give up his present beliefs in favor of some more satisfying ones found to have been prominent at some time in the historical past.

9. *The radical choice.* One decides to give up his present beliefs in favor of a new set, completely different not only from his own but also from those of any other time in history.[4]

The choice the counselor makes reflects his social philosophy. Because he works in a social setting and is aware of social and economic pressures, he cannot avoid becoming involved. Even to assume that these concerns are not important is to assume a social philosophy, implicit though it may be. For example, Karl Mannheim has shown that there are always those whose ideology is intended to maintain the status quo and those whose ideology is to change it.[5]

This does not mean that the school counselor is an active agitator or that he gives vast amounts of his time to demonstrate or to lobby for needed legislation, although for some counselors at some times these activities might seem to be important. The fact remains that, within the confines of the counseling office while working with individuals either on a one-to-one or on a group basis, the counselor becomes a subtle influence either as a change agent in terms of a future goal or ideal or as an advocate for the status quo in the service of a present economic and social system. This he may do, for example, by

[4] *Ibid.*, pp. 22, 23.

[5] Karl Mannheim, *Ideology and Utopia* (New York: Harcourt, Brace and Co., 1936).

restricting the choices of the individual and influencing him to conform or adjust to a present pattern or future goal not his own by choice; or he may work toward the goal of freeing the individual to be himself, to live his own life spontaneously, to throw his weight into the future in the direction that *he* feels is important and that he has chosen freely.

The counseling program, if effective, should be the growing edge of the school and can be an important influence. It is here that vital issues of the educational process come to focus upon the individual. It is in counseling that many of the school system's weaknesses become apparent. The counselor is one who is close to the pulse beat of the school. If he is a serious student of education he can offer leadership and recognize the vital needs, if any, for reconstruction.

Becoming aware of one's own implicit philosophy and seeing clearly the possible outcomes of it puts one in a better position to commit himself to justified intent. This does not mean that it is possible to discover all answers for all time. It does mean that we can be as Allport has stated it, "Half-sure and whole hearted." One's philosophy should represent a balance of tentativeness and commitment.[6]

Counseling, as a part of education, is an agency designed to carry out the values of the society it serves. The counselor should examine, though, who chooses and evaluates such values. Who decides upon the nature of the "good life"? One of the tendencies of the past in guidance has been to operate within the status quo patterns of values. In a crisis age the counselor cannot afford to unquestioningly serve values that are merely handed to him. Nor can he afford to run his guidance program as though it were a bureaucracy.

## THE ASSUMPTIONS OF A SOCIAL ORDER

Philosophy, once again, is important as a tool for examining assumptions inherent in what we believe. Such assumptions play an important part both in the selection and acceptance of goals for a counseling program, even though the choices themselves may be made unconsciously. The important value question is what kind of counseling program "ought" we to have, or what "ought" the counseling process be like? Such questions are answered upon the basis of what we believe

---

[6]See Gordon Allport, "Psychological Models for Guidance," *Harvard Educational Review*, XXXII, 4 (Fall 1962), 373–381.

about reality (ontology) as well as what we believe about how one comes to know (epistemology). In choosing the values to which we will commit ourselves we thus base our choices upon certain key philosophical questions.

In general, there are four questions that must be considered, first as basic concepts, and then as they pertain specifically to counseling.

1. What is the nature of man?
2. What is the nature of the world and its constituents?
3. What is the nature of community?
4. To what degree can one know the answers to the above, and what is the process involved?

In addition, the counselor should attempt to understand the culture in which he lives and the major problems of the contemporary situation. It is upon one's answers to these questions that one's philosophy, whether explicit or implicit, will be based.

## THE NATURE OF MAN

To do a good job of philosophizing, one is first compelled to make his beliefs explicit. Let us examine, then, some basic concepts relative to the assumptions underlying one's choices. One may begin by looking for "givens" in human existence. Such "givens" refer to those experiences of man that are contextual and evident to him in his experiencing.[7]

### Man Exists in Space

Man possesses a body and therefore exists in a cultural or environmental context. The environment is external to him and to a degree exerts a determining force upon him. For example, man cannot choose the family into which he will be born. The environment is what it is objectively and, though man can alter it, it still determines the context of space in which man dwells and also to some extent the kind of interaction he can have with it. Man can influence his environment, but his environment also bears an influence upon him. Man's space includes "self" and "other" as he experiences them, and for him this makes up "reality."

[7]Material partially taken from notes of lectures by Irizim Kohak. The writer is here indebted to Professor Kohak for ideas that clarified and simplified for this writer the meaning of social philosophy. Professor Kohak, of course, is not responsible for interpretations by this writer.

### Man Exists in Time

The existentialists say that "existence preceeds essence." Such a concept may be useful here in that man is a dynamic being in process. He is never complete at any one moment and is always in movement and change within time. He is born without choice and he must die without choice, although he may choose to hasten his death. Thus he is finite. He is an experiencing being that lives in a continually moving "razor-edge" present, which leaves past behind it and presses continually into the future. He cannot escape the present, although he can bring either the past into the present by means of memory or the future by means of anticipation of possibility. The following diagram illustrates man and his place in time.

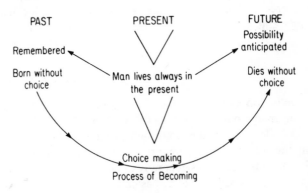

Diagram 3. Man and his place in time.

### Man Is Free and Finite

Because man is finite, order is necessary, and because he is free to choose how he will act out his motivations, order is problematic. Because man is free, it is possible for differing social orders to be chosen in similar circumstances. Man can act out his goals in varying ways. Man experiences choice phenomenologically, that is, he experiences himself as making choices and can choose how he will influence his environment and also can choose his reaction to environmental influence upon him. Because man is free and finite, the question of which social order is the "best" order becomes problematic.

### Man Is Imperfect or "Fallen"

This is not meant here as a theological concept but rather as a descriptive term. That man is imperfect refers to his present situation of being in some sense less than perfect. Man is in some way deficient. He is not what he should be, but he has possibility of becoming more than he is in the present. Thus this presents a social problem as to his nature and also as to what sort of order is necessary to move him toward completeness. Three views of the nature of man have been popularly enumerated: Man is basically good; man is basically evil; or man is neutral but has potential for either good or evil. Included in this third view are the possibilities that either man is basically good but is corrupted by society or, on the other hand, that man is corrupted by natural indolence but can become good by process of reason. Which of these three beliefs one assumes will greatly influence his social philosophy and, for the counselor, his counseling theory.

## THE NATURE OF ORDER

One's beliefs concerning order will be closely related to his beliefs concerning man's nature. Here again we can refer to three possible views: (1) Order can be taken for granted and is natural. This requires belief in the innocence and uncorruptability of man. This point of view, for obvious reasons, is generally rejected. (2) Order is arbitrary. In this view man is believed to be basically evil and must therefore be controlled. (3) Order is neither natural nor arbitrary. This is based upon a view of man as neither totally evil nor totally good, but having potential for either good or evil and in the process of becoming. For example, if one believes that man's basic nature is to become good but that he has been corrupted by society, then the chosen order must return him to his natural state. This belief advocates a return to nature and the natural good impulses within man. It is empirical and past oriented. If one believes that man is basically corrupted by his own sloth, an order will be sought that will help him overcome such sloth by education or some other means. This indicates a need to look by reason to the future, to what "should be" or "ought to be," to the development of a social order that will allow man to develop his goodness over his potential for evil. This view is normative (that is, in the meaning of a model or ideal type rather than in the common meaning of average) and is future oriented.

### Choices of Order Based on Time Orientation

Man's choices will be based upon which time orientation is preeminent in his assumptions: the past, based on memory, custom, habit, tradition; or the future, based upon possibility, goals, intentions, ideals. The orientation one chooses, though, must be lived out in the present. In determining what is "best," if the orientation is to the past —to history and fact—then the approach will be empirical. If, on the other hand, the orientation is toward the future, the approach will be by the molding of possibility by reason.

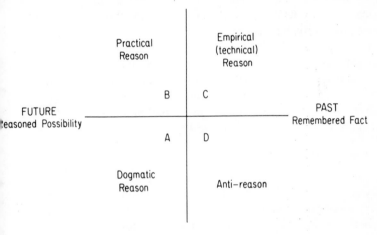

Diagram 4. Assumptions of a social order: time orientation.

It is necessary to define what is meant by reason as here used. In Quadrants A and B of the accompanying diagram,[8] reason refers to man's ability to be conscious of himself in process and to take "others" into account. It is the ability of man to experience himself both as subject and as object. It is the individual's consciousness that he is a "being-in-the-world." It is not only a state of "awareness" but also a state of "being aware that one is aware." Because man can experience "self" and "other" he can also make judgments as to what the "ideal" order would be and thus act into the future on this basis and so structure his existence.

In Quadrant C of the diagram the word reason is used more narrowly. Here one finds a distrust of man's consciousness as de-

[8]Diagram adapted from notes of lecture by Professor Kohak of Boston University.

scribed above. Reason becomes a survival tool in the process of discovering or "uncovering" nature. Man's consciousness is to be distrusted, but his rational powers can be used to discover the truth to be found in the existent order of the world. The approach then is empirical and "scientific." In Quadrant D reason is distrusted altogether. Here the recourse is to feelings and instinct, impulse, etc.

In Quadrant A dogmatic reason refers to a formulation of what is the "best" social order as a future possibility followed by an imposition of this order with little regard for the context. This view would tend to advocate that the end justifies the means. In Quadrant B practical reason refers to a formulation of what is the "best" order as a future possibility, but also considering the best means of implementation, taking into consideration the context. In Quadrant C the "best" social order is formulated by factual, empirical means—what already exists—and adjusting to it. One describes what is, to discover what is "normal," that is, normal in the empirical sense of "average." In Quadrant D there is complete distrust of reason, an irrational falling back upon instinct unguided by reason.

### Choices of Order Based on Space Orientation

Not only will man's choices be based upon his time orientation, they will also be based upon his space orientation; that is, whether primary emphasis is placed upon a self that molds the environment or on a self that is primarily concerned with accommodating itself or adjusting to the environment. We are thus concerned with the context of man's existence. There exists self and there exists world, including other people, and each is in interaction with the other. The question here is one of whether the self or others is the final court of appeal in social decisions. Does the individual determine the design and structure of the community or does he submit to a sovereign other? Does the individual rule or does the group? We can now add to Diagram 4, with emphasis above the line on the individual and below the line on the group.

In Quadrant A of Diagram 5[9] the group or individuals speaking for the group would interpret by reasoned possibility what is "best" for the individual and then impose it upon him. In Quadrant B the individual is sovereign and by reasoned possibility plays a part in the

---

[9]Diagram adapted from notes of lecture by Professor Kohak of Boston University.

determination of what is "best" and also in the implementation of it. In Quadrant C the individual plays a part in interpreting nature empirically and thus determines what is "best." In Quadrant D the group determines what is "best" by interpreting the demands of nature or of instinct.

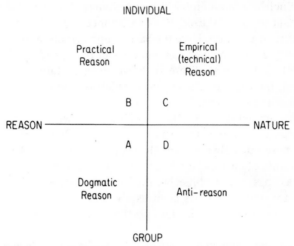

Diagram 5. Assumptions of a social order: space orientation.

### The Nature of Community

The view one holds of the nature of the group and the place of the individual within it also plays an important part in one's social philosophy or counseling theory. To be defined as a community, a group must have a capacity for channeling action, for directing action in purposive directions. In short, it must have organization and not be chaotic like a mob. Also a community must have the capacity for both internal and external self-preservation. Internally it must be capable of enforcing law to prevent disintegration from within, and externally it must be able to protect itself from outsiders; for example, by membership requirements or by an army, depending upon the level to which one is referring.

The word community carries within it the idea of commonality. It is the commonality within a community that is the basis for cohesiveness, and this cohesiveness can have its orientation in emphasis upon either the past or the future. Focus upon the past offers strong bonds of cohesiveness through common memory. For example, common geographical origin, common language, folk customs and traditions all serve to bind members on a common ground, and this is a fairly safe existence, though it produces little change. Tradition offers a stable base for a community, provided outside conflicts are not too great. Such a community will resist change, for the new is always bought at the cost of the old. But a basis for commonality can also exist in a future orientation. Here the basis is upon a commonly held possibility or goal, and change can come about by agreed upon actions in terms of such a goal. There is, however, a certain amount of risk involved, for when one opens up possibilities, he can never be quite certain of the outcome.

A community offers the possibility of power by directing itself to a purpose. However, the group is only the context of the power, and the purpose must always come through the individual. A group based upon tradition, custom, and habit can function smoothly without leadership as cogs in a machine, but the locus of possibility for change lies within the individual. As soon as an individual breaks conformity he becomes a potential leader and then becomes the locus of possibility.

Another important question to consider is the emergence of the individual. Does the individual owe his existence as an individual to the group or does the group owe its existence to the individuals? There are two possible views. First, the individual is merely a member of the class, man. He thus owes his individuality to the group and is an individual only by his acceptance in a particular group. In this view, the group is prior to the individual. Second, the individual may be viewed as unique, as a private consciousness and as existing as an individual even apart from a particular group. It is from this belief that the concept of the brotherhood of man is derived.

We can now summarize by listing the assumptions within each quadrant of Diagram 5.

**Quadrant A**

1. Reason is sovereign.
2. Man structures his existence by reason.
3. Nature is completely plastic and can be shaped by reason.
4. The rational community is prior to the individual.
5. The individual articulates himself within the rational community.
6. The individual is of the class, man.

**Quadrant B**

1. Reason functions within incoercibles or limiting factors.
2. Man as reason in existence. He chooses who and what he shall become.
3. Nature is shaped by reason but is resistant.
4. The individual is defined by reason and exists prior to the group.
5. The community is the product of the individual by reason through common goals.
6. The individual is valued as unique and sovereign.

**Quadrant C**

1. Man is viewed as a thinking animal and is unique in that he does think.
2. Nature is merely understood and described by reason.
3. Nature is not plastic. Man accommodates himself to it.
4. The individual is defined by his nature, his essence.
5. Community is the product of the individual in terms of custom and tradition.
6. The individual is the locus of value.

**Quadrant D**

1. Man is viewed as nature (instinct, impulse, etc.).
2. Nature cannot be understood by reason.
3. This view is anti-reason. Reason is viewed as a disease.
4. Nature molds man.
5. The natural community is the reality in which the individual is distinct only as a unit.
6. The individual is real only to the extent that he participates in the group as defined by the natural community, "the folk."

## COUNSELING PHILOSOPHY AS EXPRESSION OF A SOCIAL ORDER

On the basis of Diagram 5 we can illustrate the types of guidance programs that would follow. In Quadrant A dogmatic reason, the counselor, through deliberation of future possibility, would make certain value judgments, decide upon what guidance "ought" to be, and then dogmatically impose it without consideration for any possible resistance on the part of the individuals being imposed upon. He would make certain judgments as to what the end products of the program would be and would work toward the end of producing such products. The individual would not be the main focus; rather, the group would be the important factor. Individuals would be valued in terms of their usefulness to the group—society. The group would be considered to know what is best for the individual. Such a model best fits a society that is autocratic and one that values the group over the individual. In such a system it is believed that through wise planning and the use of the correct means the "Good Life" can be brought about through rational efforts. Man is expendable in this system, and the end tends to justify the means. This type of system would be anti-guidance as we know and define the term and so would not be an important consideration within a democratically oriented society.

Plato's Republic is an example of dogmatic reason. By reason Plato structured a social order based upon justice—an ideal where every individual is serving a function best suited to him, thus bringing about a balanced and interdependent society. He structured this norm by use of a rationalistic epistomology—he looked for universal needs inherent in the nature of man. If he could discover the universal needs in man and of society he could then prescribe an ideal society as future possibility and then seek to bring it about.

In looking for the "built in" needs of man and of society Plato discovered that every society must be (1) nourished, (2) defended (both internally and externally), and (3) administered. He also discovered that the capacities of men seemed to fit these same needs and that men tended to fall into one of three categories.

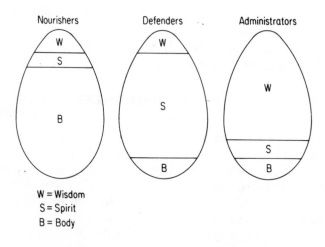

W = Wisdom
S = Spirit
B = Body

Diagram 6. Plato's three categories of human types.

First of all, there were those in the society who were more body oriented, with less spirit or wisdom. These individuals tended to be somewhat slow and lethargic but happy-go-lucky and content to do manual labor. They were strong and muscular and would enjoy working in the fields.

The second type formed a group of people who were strong and wiry, frequently getting into trouble and fights, and who were rather explosive in their natures. According to Plato, these individuals would be the ideal defenders of the society. However, since this group would also likely cause the most difficulty because of their selfishness, he would make them the landholders of the society. This group was strong of spirit, with fewer body oriented characteristics and less wisdom.

The third group, the philosopher kings, were the academically talented of the society, being strong in wisdom, with less body orientation or spirit. Its members would serve ideally as administrators for the society.

Plato believed that if one could structure a society with every man functioning happily within the realm for which he is best suited, then one could have an ideal, just society. But how could one implement such a plan? Plato decided that this could be done by instituting a ladderlike school system, which could serve as a screening device to place every man in his proper place. The students would thus begin school en mass and would progress up the ladder. The first to begin to fall by the wayside would be "counseled out" and sent to work in the fields where they could best fulfill their obligations to the state. The rest would continue to the next level, at which time the defenders would be screened out and then drafted into the army. This left the wisest group of the society, the elite, who, by continued lengthy training, were to receive the education necessary to develop them into philosopher kings. Such a system would by reason conquer and reverse the results of the fall of man.

Plato was later given a rare opportunity to implement his plan at Syracuse, but the result was failure and he had to flee, barely escaping with his life. Even the ideal can fall before the recalcitrance of human nature.

In Quadrant D, anti-reason, we would find hostility to an organized conception of guidance or counseling. A guidance function would rather be a natural process of selection on the part of the society itself. The "good" would be tested and found "pure" within the crucible of the natural society. The individual would be important only after he has been discovered to be one of the "in" group, this group being based upon custom, tradition, etc. There would be little hope for change of a preplanned sort; "Whatever will be will be." The following excerpt of an editorial from the *Chicago Tribune,* August 4, 1963, entitled "Protest! Keep the Slobs Out of the Schools," reveals that such a philosophy does exist within our society and, though hostile to organized guidance, nevertheless must be taken into consideration.

Upon entering the classroom the first day of school, the experienced teacher can tell, almost by instinct, which are the "A" students and which are not. He may be wrong occasionally; a head cold will throw him off his stride, a mosquito bite may lower his perceptive qualities somewhat. But one thing even an attack of yellow jaundice or black death will not hide, and that is which students are the dissatisfied, the misfits, the illiterate, undeserving, *non compos,* nincompoops. No teacher, no intelligent observor of human nature can miss them. They are an open sore on the flank of education. Their clothes are usually black, as are their finger nails. Their hair is usually long and oiled with a glutinous grease. But strip them of costume and shave them of hair, the teacher will know them still. They are inescapable; there is one in every class; at least one. . . .

Where these boobs tread, the flowers die; where they sit, learning expires. They throttle a class and provoke the teacher; yet they are tolerated, even given special privileges which more deserving students do not receive. They forget their books, cut their classes, fail to do their assignments, and then come whining to the desk with a lie on their lips to cajole a minimum passing grade so that they can "get outta this place." This is the password and the dream of the ignoramus and his sister, the ignoramazon. . . .

The ignoramuses have had their chance. It is time to make them responsible for their actions. A general housecleaning is called for. Sweep through the schoolhouse with a fiery broom. Remove the dead wood, the troublemakers, the no-goods, the thugs. Let them get out into the world; let them be free. Many will return in six months sober students, many will remain successfully where they have always wanted to be. The few others who fail to meet the challenge will end up in jails, asylums, and morgues, but they would be better off, and so would the nation. The money to pay for the slightly increased use of these institutions could come from the savings made by firing hundreds of school guidance counselors who would no longer be needed. Actually the number who fail in the outside world would be the same as always; they would just fail sooner. . . .

Thoreau "came into this world not chiefly to make this a good place to live in . . ." yet by being firm, by remaining resolute, he made the world a better place. We can follow suit. We must follow suit soon. Sweep out the schools. Speak back to the ignoramus. Say to him, "Be savage or citizen—the choice is yours, the responsibility yours. Take it or leave it." The world will profit, the nation will profit, even the ignoramus will profit.[10]

Our major concern in this book is with Quadrants B and C, as these are highly representative of the major political and social views within our culture. On the one hand we have a liberal tradition, which advocates a positive attitude toward change, represented in Quadrant B, and on the other hand, a conservative tradition, which advocates adjustment or adaptation to what already exists, Quadrant C. Concentrating now upon these two upper quadrants of the diagrams, let us attempt to relate them to current educational philosophies and hence to guidance and counseling as they fit within these philosophical frameworks.

It is important to view these as cultural interpretations and as a means to finding answers for the many cultural problems that now face us. Each system promotes goals set upon the basic assumptions underlying each. In answer to the perplexing problems that have served to force reexamination of beliefs, the philosophies represented within Quadrants B and C have gravitated toward the four following choices: the regressive, the conservative, the liberal, and the radical. In American culture these four choices result in four main educational philosophies: perennialism, essentialism, progressivism, and reconstructionism. These schools may be placed as indicated in Diagram 7.

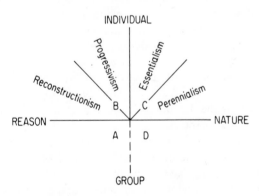

Diagram 7. Assumptions of a social order:
educational philosophies.

[10] *Chicago Tribune Magazine* (August 4, 1963). Also in Joseph Bentley (ed.), *The Counselor's Role: Commentary and Readings* (Boston: Houghton Mifflin Co., 1968), pp. 291–294.

It is important to recognize that these categories, as well as the preceding diagrams, are not fixed and rigid but at points blend into one another and are to an extent interrelated. The main value of categorizing lies in helping one to understand the basic assumptions upon which each rests.[11]

For our purposes we shall consider the philosophies as two contrasting pairs, perennialism and essentialism, forming a pair resting on the assumptions of Quadrant C, and progressivism and reconstructionism, resting on the assumptions of Quadrant B. In Quadrant C the emphasis is on transmission of the cultural heritage of the past, and in Quadrant B emphasis is upon innovation.[12]

Philosophies of education grow from and are the expression of a particular culture. A philosophy of education is an expression of how education can best function in meeting the needs of current society. But if one anchors philosophy within culture, where it rightly must be anchored, the possibility of lag comes in; for cultures are dynamic and moving—change today is one certainty that cannot be denied. It then stands to reason that one must continue to examine his beliefs to make certain that they are "up-to-date" and not lagging behind in the present cultural situation. This is especially so in times of drastic change, and it is on this point that the conservative transmitting point of view must be rejected. Such philosophies, based upon a more static view of reality, have served their purpose in more stable times, but that such a system can stand up within a transitional culture is questionable. Individuals who are merely handed the ways of thinking, the values, the customs, of the past are likely to experience them as obsolete. In order for individuals to transcend current cultural difficulties and rapid change, they must above all learn to be flexible, to create, to learn. It is this writer's contention that the innovative point of view is the only defensible one for the day in which we live, an argument that will be developed in later chapters.

This innovative point of view is based upon the assumptions that man is capable of considering himself in a world of "others" and that upon this basis he is capable of structuring a social order; that although the environment does influence him and is determining to a degree,

---

[11]See Brameld, *Philosophies of Education*, and Brameld, *Toward a Reconstructed Philosophy of Education* (New York: Dryden Press, 1956).

[12]Brameld, *Education as Power* (New York: Holt, Rinehart, and Winston, 1965), p. 28.

within these limits man is free to choose and, by choosing, to influence his environment; that he becomes more free as he recognizes the ways in which the environment is determined and determining; that because man freely chooses and can also take others into consideration in his choices, he is responsible, and chooses what he becomes; that the individual is valued as a unique and dignified person worthy of love and respect, who exists over and above the group, but who finds fulfillment within it; that, because the individual is responsible, he bears responsibility to the kind of community produced, one that can be united in the common purpose of bettering human existence in all respects, keeping in mind the supreme value of the individual.

The key words in the innovative point of view are freedom and creativity, and these go hand in hand with knowledge, for they make possible the processing of knowledge in meaningful ways. Edel, after discussing the quest for values in education, has this to say:

> I should like to suggest that if you really want some keynote values in the valuational base for education today, values that combine the qualities of perennial ideals, that may correspond to basic needs, that are becoming urgent as great instrumentalities in the modern world, and that offer a more abiding approach to the solution of critical contingent problems than any narrow subset of virtues or national goals, your best candidates are the advancement of knowledge on all fronts and the promotion of creativity, especially in the form of originality, inventiveness, and independent thought. Platitudes they may be, but what power they contain, and how little we would recognize our contemporary schools if we really acted upon them.[13]

There also appears to be general agreement, at least among writers in the counseling field, concerning the innovative point of view. Richmond, utilizing the definition of freedom as the spontaneous expression of an authentic self, set out to determine whether or not freedom was an accepted current objective of counseling and guidance by writers in the field. Upon examination of writings during the years 1959 through 1963 he concluded that, although writers vary in degree of emphasis, they were committed to freedom as a goal in counseling and urged that this could serve as a more definite basis for

[13]Abraham Edel, "Education and the Quest for Values," *The Philosophical Forum*, XX (1962–1963), Department of Philosophy and the Philosophical Club, Boston University, 34.

evaluational purposes.[14] Freedom is, of course, an ambiguous word, and individuals use it in differing ways. We shall attempt clarification of the concept in Chapter VII.

Beck, who in his study of the philosophical foundations of guidance found that predominating models of guidance have been built upon a framework of realism and idealism (or in our terms, essentialism) with some advocates for progressivism, judged these inadequate and urged the acceptance of existentialism as an acceptable framework or basis for guidance philosophy. Counselors who unquestioningly accept the prevalent essentialistic philosophy to be found in many schools may unknowingly be serving such a faulty framework.[15]

Let us turn now to a brief examination of the assumptions behind essentialism and the emphasis upon transmission of culture, especially in reference to counseling. It is important to recognize that to transmit cultural heritage is important. The weakness of essentialism lies not in its acceptance of that premise but in not going beyond it. In times of stability each generation can live effectively by merely being taught the content of the past, but in a rapidly changing world content quickly loses validity. In such times, process—learning to learn, creativity, etc.—becomes increasingly important.

## ESSENTIALIST GUIDANCE: A CRITICAL VIEW

Guidance programs growing from Quadrant C reflect these presuppositions. Man is thought of primarily as a rational being—a being who can think—and, qualitatively, this is the main way in which he differs from the animals. This ability to think, however, is different from the trust in man's consciousness found in Quadrants A and B of Diagram 5. In Quadrant C man's existence is structured by "technical or empirical reason," which refers to the use of man's thinking powers to uncover the realities of nature. Man's consciousness is distrusted, for it is subjective and relative. The emphasis, then, is upon empirical data and objectivity. Only when agreement can be reached by a number of "consciousnesses" can one be certain that he has truly discovered "reality." Nature can thus be understood and described only by tech-

---

[14]Bert O. Richmond, *A Concept of Freedom Related to Recent Pronouncements in Counseling and Guidance,* unpublished doctoral dissertation, Indiana University, 1964.

[15]Carlton Beck, *Philosophical Foundations of Guidance* (New York: Prentice-Hall, Inc., 1963).

nical reason. Nature is not easily changed, but when the underlying order is understood man can more easily accommodate himself to it. The "scientific" method is the key means of understanding nature, and even man is defined by the use of it. Measurement becomes an important tool for discovering "reality." Man is viewed as a "nature," and through empirical investigation one can come to know what "human nature" is really like. Man is only as he should be—that is, "normal" in the sense of average—when he expresses his true nature as defined empirically. The individual is the locus of value, and the community is made up of individuals bound together on the basis of common past —history, custom, language, ideology. The "good" is also defined empirically and is based upon what is now in existence, for one cannot describe by empirical means what does not yet exist. There follows from this a tendency to give up ideals and to focus pragmatically upon the business of living, accommodating one's self to those incoercibles which seem impossible to change, accepting them as a part of the nature of things. Emphasis is placed upon the practical aspects of living, such as vocation and the technological, reflecting the values of a technological society.

It has been stated that the educational philosophies of both perennialism and essentialism fit into Quadrant C and these assumptions. Because essentialism—realism and idealism—has played a prominent role in the history of the public school and thus of guidance, we will focus upon it here. One must recognize that philosophies of guidance are changing and that there appears to be a growing tendency to favor the presuppositions of Quadrant B, the innovative point of view. One would do well then to view this critique of essentialism as an illustration of how presuppositions do underly actions of any group within any historical setting. We turn first to the historical development of guidance with focus upon the essentialist presuppositions.

The history of the guidance movement has grown primarily from the essentialist point of view and the presuppositions previously mentioned. Whereas technology advanced rapidly as a result of the "scientific" approach to knowledge it was assumed that human nature could be known by similar methods and could be objectively understood, thus leading to an objective science of human behavior. It is interesting that although physical science appears to be discarding this point of view, many behavioral scientists still cling to it.[16] The psychology

---

[16]Rudolf Dreikurs, "The Scientific Revolution," in C. E. Smith and O. G. Mink

of individual differences, a product of the "scientific" approach of technical reason, contributed greatly to the beginnings of the guidance movement. In 1908 Frank Parsons, often referred to as the father of the guidance movement, published *Choosing A Vocation*, which set forth what he called "three broad factors" that are necessary to vocational choice:

> (1) ... a clear understanding of yourself, your aptitudes, abilities, interests, ambitions, resources, limitations, and their causes;
> (2) a knowledge of the requirements and conditions of success, advantages and disadvantages, compensations, opportunities, and prospects in different lines of work;
> (3) true reasoning on the relations of these two groups of facts.[17]

This model became a popular pattern for vocational guidance. But how could one avoid the pitfalls of mere subjective opinion regarding either the nature of the particular individual or of the nature of specific occupations in the world of work? The answer was provided by the objective approach offered by the scientific point of view and specifically by the testing movement. The testing movement offered a means of understanding just what the nature of the individual was and also of where he would best "fit in" to the world of work by revealing the qualifications and characteristics necessary to be successful in specific occupations. The role of the counselor involved being skilled in successfully using objective information about the individual and about the world of work within the counseling relationship. The counselor in this approach is viewed as the expert who helps the individual to face empirical reality and then to make "realistic" choices. Such practice grows from the essentialist ontology

> that the universe and all its elements are governed by encompassing law and pre-established order and that therefore the chief task of men is to understand this law and order so that they may appreciate and adjust to it.[18]

From such a view of reality it follows that the counselor is only doing his duty when he, as the expert, helps the novice student to understand the objective order. Popular here is the medical model, the

---

(eds.), *Foundations of Guidance and Counseling: Multidisciplinary Readings* (New York: J. B. Lippincott Co., 1969), pp. 59–69.

[17]Frank Parsons, *Choosing a Vocation* (Boston: Houghton Mifflin Co., 1908), p. 5.

[18]Brameld, *Toward a Reconstructed Philosophy*, p. 8.

expert doctor who diagnoses and prescribes according to the patient's needs. The emphasis is upon adjustment to the existing order, which is usually unquestioned, and the counselor may be quite unaware that he is making a value judgment. Realism may be used as a mask to cover the counselor's values. If the counselor approves the choice—if it fits the natural order as perceived by the counselor—then it is a realistic choice; if he disapproves—if it does not conform to the natural order as perceived by the counselor—then the choice is unrealistic and unwise. The counselor bases his judgment upon his collection of objective facts from varying sources: tests, occupational information, cumulative records, interviews.

> The enforcement of realism on students is simply another weapon in the long battle to produce conforming adults out of nonconforming children.[19]

The view of order is also static. The view of man is in reference to states of being or of contents. One measures intelligence or aptitude or anxiety as though they were objective quantities somehow existing as contents within the person. To measure something requires that it be tangible in some form. The product of measurement becomes static, for measurement must necessarily be taken at a point in time. The empirical becomes factual, and facts are always static. To base prediction upon such "facts" demands that the object be fairly stable and not change much in its real nature. If prediction is based upon an intelligence quotient, a static number, one assumes that the quantity of intelligence will not change.[20] If man is not static, then test scores, as soon as they are stated, are no longer representative of the individual, for he has moved beyond that point in time. It is like judging the nature of a river by analyzing and describing a bucket of water scooped from its shallows. While it may give clues as to the character of the river, it does not represent its flowing, changing aspects.

This is true of "facts" gathered from the world of work also. Can a sample of the characteristics of a particular occupation remain valid for a very long period in times of drastic change?

If one views nature objectively and approaches the problem of understanding the individual from the "scientific" point of view, he is .

---

[19]Ruth Barry and Beverly Wolf, *Epitaph for Vocational Guidance* (New York: Bureau of Publications, Teachers College, Columbia University, 1962), p. 100.

[20]See Robert Rosenthal and Lenore Jacobson, *Pygmalion in the Classroom* (New York: Holt, Rinehart, and Winston, 1968).

likely also to view the individual as an object. Like the contemplating scientist he will describe the individual from an external and objective point of view. In this he comes to know *about* the person but is not likely to know *the person*. And the person is likely to be indignant, for who likes to be treated like an object.

Evaluation is also likely to be more externally and quantitatively oriented in the essentialist view. A material universe lends itself to quantitative measurement, but the quantitative is always limited to the tangible. Can one assume that quantity means quality? There is a tendency to evaluate on the basis of quantitative enumeration alone. How many services does the school offer? How many students see the counselor each year? How many students get into college? How many former students are not in the vocation they chose as the result of counseling? How much information is available? We must ask instead whether or not such measures are justifiable. Do services in themselves guarantee that students' needs are being met? Cannot counseling be detrimental as well as helpful? Is a student in college but unmotivated to learn and uncommitted an asset to himself or to society if he is there only to conform to others' demands? Is the matter of choosing a vocation to be considered successful if this person becomes just a cog in the machine or surrenders his happiness for material gain and amusement?

One can recognize within the essentialist philosophy the emphasis upon conformity. There exist objective facts, events, and laws, and the individual fulfills his responsibility by fitting in, by becoming a "productive" member of society. Productivity is generally measured in terms of the technical—What does he do? How much does he earn? How successful is he in his occupation?—which is an expression of the ideology of the system, success being measured in terms of material aspects. College then may become the main route to success, justified on the basis that "the college graduate will earn so many more dollars in his lifetime than will the noncollege person." It is small wonder that youth would look for shortcuts on such a road, for in such a view a college education is nothing but a painful necessity on the road to materialistic gain. With the pressure of such a journey one also is likely to miss the discovery that learning can be a joyful and fulfilling experience of itself. It is no wonder that students are rebelling against this "marketing orientation." Again, as Fromm describes it:

> Modern capitalism needs men who cooperate smoothly and in large numbers; who want to consume more and more; and whose

tastes are standardized and can be easily influenced and anticipated. It needs men who feel free and independent, yet willing to be commanded, to do what is expected of them, to fit into the social machine without friction; who can be guided without force, led without leaders, prompted without aim—except the one to make good, to be on the move, to function, to go ahead.[21]

Many youths see through such shallowness and seek desperately the "something more" of existence.

The epistemology of essentialism rests

upon one or another variation of the correspondence theory of knowledge—the theory that the truth of any idea is determined by its correspondence with, or representation of, objective facts, events, and laws.[22]

In this epistemology truth is determined by agreement with what is *objectively* known. This objective truth is held by the "more mature," whose task it is to *transmit* such knowledge to the "immature." The test of their having "learned" it is the ability to "re-present" it. In this view it becomes easy to ignore the importance of "experiencing" to the process of learning. The tendency, then, is for learning, either in the classroom or in the counseling office, to be viewed as mere intellectual "assent" to external facts. The emphasis is upon the teacher's or counselor's doing something "to" or "for" the "immature" student. Emphasis is on the cognitive and informational aspects, with some counselors even warning that one should not "meddle in personality." Can meaning be experienced solely in an intellectual way apart from the emotional? The following quote from Jersild has equal application for counselors:

Much of what teachers have to learn, much of what they have to teach, and much of what the millions of pupils who attend our schools are compelled to study is not meaningful, but meaningless, largely because we have assumed that knowledge has value apart from its meaning for the one who acquired it.[23]

Must not the whole experience of the individual be recognized as important to personally relevant and meaningful learning?

---

[21]Erich Fromm, *The Art of Loving* (New York: Harper and Row, 1962), p. 72.
[22]Brameld, *Toward A Reconstructed Philosophy,* p. 8.
[23]Arthur T. Jersild, *When Teachers Face Themselves* (New York: Bureau of Publications, Teachers College, Columbia University, 1955), p. 81.

Where there is meaning, there is involvement. When something has meaning, one is committed to it. Where there is meaning there is conviction. Such commitment and conviction is something different from conformity, or merely playing a part, or living as a cog in the machine, or losing one's individuality in what Kierkegaard has called the "featureless crowd." Where meaning is lacking in one's work as a teacher [or counselor], the self is uninvolved. The substance is lacking, and teaching [counseling] is just an empty formality.[24]

Along this same line of thought, students of essentialist schools generally find themselves submitted to an *external* discipline. The "expert" assumes most of the responsibility for decision making, direction, content, and method, and the student finds little alternative other than to conform or rebel. Does such external discipline produce internal self-discipline or does it rather produce dependency? It is likely to produce the latter, and the standards are forever increased to which students are expected to conform. Students must get "better" grades in classes that are continually "beefed up" to insure college admission. The student no longer is allowed to fail. His opportunities to take risks based upon his own decisions, and to experience the possible failure—an important learning experience in itself—are more and more narrow.

One could ask what is being done to the mental health of such students when they are forced into such perfectionist standards? And what are the implications for the counselor? Also, because of the stress placed upon material gain to the neglect of art, beauty, and creativity it also creates a lack of patience. One is forced to move as rapidly as possible into a "useful" position.

Another tendency in the essentialist view is to be reductionistic. The individual is understood in terms of traits, interests, abilities, and cognitive capacities or in terms of narrow vocational aspects. Objective realism runs strong here, and the emphasis is more upon man as a reactive organism. The tendency in counseling may be to focus upon the past in terms of causes or empirical "fact." As Allport put it:

> One would think that the client seated opposite would protest, for the language of response negates the subject's immediate certainty that his life lies in the future.[25]

---

[24] *Ibid.*, pp. 78–79. I have taken the liberty to insert the word counselor after the word teacher because I feel it is applicable.

[25] Allport, "Psychological Models," p. 375.

The essentialist axiology proceeds from

> the basic belief that values of art or conduct are preexistent to indi-
> vidual experience—that they are provided for in the orderly universe
> of which man, too, is an element.[26]

This belief concerning values opens the door to a strong objectivist approach. Again, the counselor, who is more "mature," may
assume that he knows what the objective values are and that it is his
responsibility to "guide" the client toward them. The very term guidance seems to have originated from this point of view—a steering of
someone or something along a predesignated path. An assumption
that values are solely objective coupled with an emphasis upon an
external or narrowly cognitive learning process opens the door to
indoctrination. The counselor may feel responsible to mold individuals to the needs of society and justify this by the feeling that he is truly
"helping" the individual. After all, these are the values that the client
"ought" to hold, and are they not justifiable in terms of the "success"
the client will experience?

These essentialist values tend to be accepted as self-evident and
thus are not likely to be critically examined. The individual assumes
that his approach is true reality. The history of the guidance movement, as much of the literature attests, has been characterized by little
philosophical analysis. It is perhaps natural that the neglect of self-
criticism and philosophical analysis would characterize essentialist
guidance, for

> an individual whose strongest motive is to adjust by complying with
> the demands of his environment is unlikely to probe deeply into the
> cultural forces that affect him.[27]

Perhaps of greatest importance is the need for each counselor to
look honestly at himself and ask the question: "To what degree have
I become a cog in the educational machine and surrendered my individuality to conformity to unquestioned practices?" In spite of the
current emphasis upon counselor role and the explication of role
statements, the counselor must make clear to himself what he really
believes.

> Guidance-personnel work needs secure, confident, knowledge-
> able practitioners in order to be a contributing factor in the lives of

---

[26]Brameld, *Toward a Reconstructed Philosophy*, p. 8.
[27]Brameld, *Philosophies of Education*, p. 261.

students. The work needs understandable purposes providing clear indications of what to do, sound theory explaining why, practices stemming from and implementing theory and purposes, and effective training. With these four requisites, guidance-personnel workers can develop a feeling of confidence and faith in the value and future of their work. Then they can face students with the realization that their work entails a reciprocal relationship—if students are to have faith in them, they must believe in students.[28]

A counselor who is aware of his presuppositions, even if they be of the essentialist philosophy, is less likely to subtly impose them upon his clients. The counselor who frees himself from conformity to what naively seems self-evident must then continually be in a process of analyzing the culture of which he is a part, determining its strengths, needs, and weaknesses, and then on the basis of his integrated knowledge constructing a program that will serve the needs of each unique student. As Barry and Wolf have put it:

> Planners of programs would do well to adopt as a space age maxim: "Guidance is for missles; Counseling is for people!"[29]

[28]Barry and Wolf, *Modern Issues in Guidance-Personnel Work* (New York: Bureau of Publications, Teachers College, Columbia University, 1963), p. 242.
[29]Barry and Wolf, "Should Vocational Guidance Be Junked?" *National Education Association Journal*, LII, 9 (December 1963), 31.

# chapter 4

# Goals in Counseling

Someone has said that any road will do just fine if you don't care where you are going.[1]

## THE IMPORTANCE OF GOALS

The question is, Which road are counselors traveling, and from whence have they come? Will any road do or are they trying to get "somewhere" in particular? Such questions lead us to consider the goals of counseling. As Arbuckle and others have recognized, the counselor's behavior in counseling is shaped by his goals and objectives and reflects a philosophy of life rather than a mere set of techniques.[2]

The topic of goals in either counseling, psychotherapy, or guidance, seldom appears in the literature as a specific topic, and when it does it is almost always (if not always) accompanied by a reference to the complexity involved and with an air of humility. Walker and Peiffer in one such article,[3] after admitting that "the problems of goals in counseling are many and difficult," stated that it was their intent to

> elicit a keener appreciation of the extent of the many issues we present. Perhaps it is our hope, also, to substitute a certain seemly humility concerning the problems of the goals of counseling in the place of an inchoate and pious hope that everything will somehow turn out right, where such feelings exist in the minds of counselors.[4]

[1]Ben Strickland, "The Philosophy-Theory-Practice Continuum: A Point of View," *Counselor Education and Supervision*, VIII, 3 (Spring 1969), 167.
[2]Dugald S. Arbuckle, "Five Philosophical Issues in Counseling," *Journal of Counseling Psychology*, V, 3 (Fall 1958), 211–215.
[3]Donald E. Walker and Herbert C. Peiffer, Jr., "The Goals of Counseling," *Journal of Counseling Psychology*, IV, 3 (Fall 1957), 204–209.
[4]*Ibid.*, p. 209.

**89**

Mahrer, as editor of a forum on the goals of psychotherapy,[5] also acknowledged the difficulty of studying goals and offered his presentation as "catalytic rather than final," and to "provide a stimulus rather than a solution to resolving the problem of psychotherapeutic goals."[6]

The emphasis of the literature most often falls upon either techniques and methods or upon indices of improvement.[7] But focus upon these areas is of little help in regard to goal problems, for as Mahrer has suggested:

> The methods and techniques are only working subgoals which point the way toward the ultimate goals without telling us a great deal about them. Nor is the understanding of goals furthered by progress in identifying indices of improvement, for the study of indices is tangential to the study of the ultimate goals themselves. The essential goals of psychotherapy remain inadequately explored.[8]

Historically, though there has been early recognition of the need for goals in counseling and guidance, there have been only two serious attempts at definition.[9] The first attempt was by Jones in 1929 and was geared to defining the role of the counselor,[10] which met with little success. The second was by Super in 1958. Currently there has been a renewed effort toward the definition of counselor role and the establishment of goals in policy statements by the American School Counselor Association and the Association for Counselor Education and Supervision. It has been recognized that firm goal statements can serve as important guides to choice of means in the midst of a turbulent society when plagued by societal pressures. When the National Defense Education Act of 1958 presented a threat to the individual through manipulation and loss of freedom in the name of national defense, guidance workers, recognizing the rights of the individual to his own choice, used the benefits of such an act *for* the individual in spite of societal pressure to the contrary.[11]

Stern[12] has reminded counselor educators that a desperate

---

[5]Alvin R. Mahrer (ed.), *The Goals of Psychotherapy* (New York: Appleton-Century-Crofts, 1967).

[6]*Ibid.*, p. 1.

[7]*Ibid.*

[8]*Ibid.*

[9]Lawrence H. Stewart and Charles F. Warnath, *The Counselor and Society: A Cultural Approach* (Boston: Houghton Mifflin Co., 1965), pp. 17, 18.

[10]A. A. Jones, "Proposed Change of Name of the National Vocational Guidance Association," *The Vocational Guidance Magazine*, 8 (1929–1930), 103–105.

[11]Stewart and Warnath, *Counselor and Society*, p. 15.

[12]Herbert J. Stern, "The Immediate Task of School Counselors," *Counselor Education and Supervision*, IV, 2 (Winter 1965), 93–96.

search for counselor role is futile unless done in relationship to purpose, for role must grow out of a foundation of purpose. Counselor role in the past has been based upon a narrow conception of vocational development. Stern advocates that purpose be found in helping pupils accomplish developmental tasks. Such a purpose will aid counselors to define their appropriate function at whichever level they choose to work.

In an article on counselor role, Stone and Shertzer[13] take the position that each individual counselor must define his own unique role (goals) in his particular setting. This he should do by use of reason, setting up an ideal and then being militant (within reason) in working toward it. They strongly criticize counselors who choose to conform to an inefficient and ineffective status quo because of a lack of tolerance for ambiguity and a high degree of deference to authority.

Cribbin, in his doctoral study dated 1951, examined some 200 guidance texts published from 1935 to 1950, attempting to identify common principles or assumptions. Part of his study was concerned with goal statements, which he grouped under two headings, ultimate aims and proximate aims. The statements consisted of 120 goal statements described by various terms such as "basic aim, major end-goal, central task, primary purpose, crux of the matter, desired end, consummation of guidance, primary objective, supreme end, primary aim, central goal, final purpose, chief aim, final aim, chief interest, and ultimate goal."[14] He found the following ultimate aims of guidance expressed in order of their frequency of statement: (1) best development of the individual, (2) growth in self-guidance and individual maturity, (3) maximizing student satisfaction and social productivity, and (4) helping students to live better lives. Such statements are value laden (for example, *best development, satisfaction, social productivity, better lives*) and are relatively meaningless until what is meant is made explicit. Cribbin criticized these aims for their lack of consideration of a theological and objective consideration that he called "God's Rights."[15]

---

[13]Shelley C. Stone and Bruce Shertzer, "The Militant Counselor," *Personnel and Guidance Journal*, XLII, 4 (December 1963), 342–347.

[14]James J. Cribbin, "A Critique of the Philosophy of Modern Guidance," in Gail F. Farwell and Herman J. Peters (eds.), *Guidance Readings for Counselors* (Chicago: Rand McNally and Co., 1960), pp. 78–93.

[15]*Ibid.*, p. 93.

The proximate objectives, however, he saw as "cogent and valid" and listed them as follows:

1. To develop student initiative, responsibility, self-direction and self-guidance.
2. To develop in the student the ability to choose his own goals wisely.
3. To know one's self, to know the school and to be known by the school.
4. To anticipate, avoid and prevent crises from arising in the lives of the students.
5. To help the student adjust satisfactorily to school and to life.
6. To help the student to recognize, understand, meet and solve his problems.
7. To assist the student in making wise choices, plans, and interpretations at critical points in his life.
8. To help the student acquire the insights and techniques necessary to enable him to solve his own future problems.
9. To help administrators to administer more efficiently by making a maximum contribution to the total school program.
10. To assist teachers to teach more effectively.
11. To develop citizens who will participate in and contribute to the democratic way of life.
12. Miscellaneous objectives; included under this category were such ideas as assisting the home, helping the community, building ethical character, and fostering better human relations and international understanding.[16]

One finds in the professional literature from 1955 to the present a keener interest in the explication of goals, along with a trend toward a more active involvement with values in the counseling process. We are concerned here with the importance of goals to the counseling process rather than with an exhaustive listing of goals as stated in the literature. Also, the focus here is upon explicit statements dealing with goals rather than implicit ones.

## A VARIETY OF GOALS: REVIEW OF THE LITERATURE

In discussing the "unresolved issue" concerning the direction of influence of clients by counselors, Blocher[17] points out that efforts to outline differences between counseling and psychotherapy have in the past dealt largely with methodology. He suggested that a more fruitful

[16] *Ibid.*, pp. 92–93.

[17] Donald H. Blocher, "Issues in Counseling: Elusive and Illusional," *Personnel and Guidance Journal*, XLII, 8 (April 1965), 796–800.

approach would be to deal with it in terms of goals. In this approach he has found two clusters of goals: developmental-educative-preventive and remediating-adjustive-therapeutic. The first set assumes a natural developmental process, reasonably ordered, moving in positive directions in which counseling serves to facilitate these normal processes. The second cluster revolves around removal of pathological components, adjustment to environmental demands, and restoration of mental health. Reasons for confusion of terms is apparent, according to Blocher, in that counselors have served both clusters of goals. Whether the goal clusters will be strengthened or further broken down is an issue remaining for the future.

Walker and Peiffer[18] examined commonly proposed aims such as adjustment in self-terms, contentment of the client, psychological autonomy of the client, adjustment in social terms, the values of the counselor as criteria, and general goals and combined objectives, and found all to be fraught with numerous problems and weaknesses. They question the value judgments of the individual counselor as a criterion for counseling success.[19]

Hadley made a significant point in a reaction to the article by Walker and Peiffer. In his own words:

> Walker and Peiffer clearly point out that the value-judgments of the individual counselor are questionable criteria for counseling success. However, it is indefensible to infer from this that the formulation of counseling goals is independent of the value-judgments of counselors. The mere fact that a goal-statement is offered by counselors implies that it expressed their values. It appears that the extent of agreement as to goals is the crucial consideration here. Agreement by whom? On what points? In what proportion? These, in addition to the purposes in generalizing, are value questions to which counselors collectively must assume the responsibility for providing answers—and which must be answered before significant progress can be made in remedying the inadequacies in our counseling-goal formulations which Walker and Peiffer have so astutely brought to our attention.[20]

According to Hummel[21] there are several popular counselor images: the "problem-centered" image, the "selection and placement"

[18]Walker and Peiffer, "Goals of Counseling," pp. 204–209.

[19]*Ibid.*

[20]Robert G. Hadley, Letter to the Editor, *Journal of Counseling Psychology*, V, 2 (Summer 1958), 152.

[21]Dean L. Hummel, "The Other Counselor," *Counselor Education and Supervision*, IV, 4 (Summer 1965), 171–179.

image, the "adjustment" image, and the "vocational-educational" image. He discussed these and suggested several "realities" to be faced: the national spotlighting of counseling and guidance, the school as a major social institution, the manpower challenge, the college bulge, focus on personal development, and the professional framework. He urged a return to a sane orientation for vocational guidance. He listed the following propositions or goals to which the "Other Counselor" is committed: (1) facilitating positive experiences, (2) being genuine, (3) aiding self-discovery, (4) providing for discovery of knowledge, (5) creating a freedom of choice atmosphere, and (6) allowing for openness. Each of these terms, however, is value laden and demands further clarification.

Mathewson[22] devoted 188 pages of his book *Guidance Policy and Practice* to a discussion of philosophical and cultural foundations for guidance. He advocated a developmental approach based upon a focus on the individual within and interacting with a situational field. The primary purpose of guidance as Mathewson viewed it was "to improve the capability of the individual to understand self and environment and to deal with self-situational relations for greater personal satisfaction and social usefulness in the light of social and moral values."[23] The counselor can influence broad cultural values through action in professional groups and as a citizen play a part in political action. But most important, he can reflect in his being those values to which he is committed. He has the responsibility to *"help his counselee to become a valuing person* in his own right, to understand the values he wants to live by, and to choose and act accordingly,"[24] and to *"educatively communicate the kind of fundamental values* that create and sustain a social millieu that enables individuals to become valuing persons in the first place."[25] Mathewson further stated that the counselor "cannot be neutral about basic human rights, moral values, and democratic processes."[26] The criteria for evaluating values come from a combination of social requirements, spiritual sanctions, biological demands, individual freedom, and cultural themes. In a complex culture that resembles the Greek tragedies, "the counselor, in a humble

[22]R. H. Mathewson, *Guidance Policy and Practice*, 3d ed. (New York: Harper and Row, 1962).
[23]*Ibid.*, p. 134.
[24]*Ibid.*, p. 161. Italics his.
[25]*Ibid.*
[26]*Ibid.*

helping relationship with striving individuals, may be as close to the bedrock of value orientation as it is possible to get."[27] Mathewson viewed the future of guidance as likely to be shaped by the struggle between conservative and liberal educational philosophies. One can observe these conservative or liberal tendencies within the following goal statements.

Ginzberg took a somewhat conservative view of goals by taking issue with what he viewed as two faulty assumptions in guidance. First, he viewed as faulty the assumption that the counselor must deal with the "whole" person, and second, that the counselor has responsibility in helping the student to better understand himself. He suggested, rather, that the "real need" of young people is "to learn more about the educational and occupational world so that they can make better choices."[28] He warned that counselors should not be psychotherapists.

Bray also seems to follow this narrower view. In an article[29] on vocational guidance he implied the fulfillment and use of potential as worthy goals. He restricted guidance to vocational and educational problems and suggested that personal problems should be considered only secondarily. He stressed the right of the individual to his own choices.

According to Bixler[30] counseling is completely ineffective and is gradually losing status value. He advocated rather than counseling an emphasis upon guidance and "directing youth to goals" (not to be construed as a methodology). He does not make explicit the goals he has in mind other than by referring to the goals of education, a reference so broad as to be meaningless.

One would also be remiss not to mention a group of therapists classified as Action therapists.[31] The approaches of this group are based primarily upon learning theory and its members include Wolpe, Salter, Stampfl, the followers of Skinner, and others. All of these approaches share in common a goal either of symptom removal or of

[27] *Ibid.*, p. 163.

[28] Eli Ginzberg, "Guidance: Limited or Unlimited," *Personnel and Guidance Journal*, XXXVIII, 9 (May 1960), 707–712.

[29] Douglas W. Bray, "Vocational Guidance in National Manpower Policy," *Personnel and Guidance Journal*, XXXIV, 3 (November 1955), 194–199.

[30] Ray H. Bixler, "The Changing World of the Counselor II: Training for the Unknown," *Counselor Education and Supervision*, II, 4 (Summer 1963), 168–175.

[31] Perry London, *The Modes and Morals of Psychotherapy* (New York: Holt, Rinehart, and Winston, 1964). See specific references in Chapter 5.

specific behavior change. These approaches fall into two groups in terms of focus: (1) those based primarily upon classical conditioning with an emphasis upon changing old behavior and (2) those based upon operant conditioning with a focus on shaping new behavior. The goals are narrowly focused upon specifics of behavior change, thus often giving the illusion that the therapist avoids value involvement. That value involvement here is at a minimum is true, for the therapist performs much the same function as the physician, merely correcting present dysfunctions. But the therapist with this focus is limiting himself to a very narrow range of problems and sooner or later is likely to be pulled toward treatment of problems involving systems of beliefs, meanings, and values. London has suggested that

> the only alternative to this self-restriction is to deliberately expand the definition of "symptom" to incorporate a wider and wider range of human troubles. This is apparently what many Action therapists have done. But the further this expansion goes, the more tenuous their effort becomes to define symptoms as malfunctions, and the more presumptuous becomes the definition, implied or explicit, of what good functioning is. In effect, this effort produces precisely the same progression of events through which Insight therapists passed. ... The only difference is that problems of general happiness, security, and so forth are now identified as problems of functioning rather than of meaning, and the definition of adequate "functioning" now becomes the property of the therapist.[32]

Techniques are basically amoral. It is the ends served that throw one into the realm of the moral.

Peters advocates a developmental approach to guidance rather than the common distributive-adjustive function, stating that this is the only sound approach for the latter half of the twentieth century. But one must again ask, "Development to what end?" Peters is not highly explicit as to goal, but defines the nature of such guidance as "to assist the immature but growing pupil in a better understanding of himself, to think through with him the meanings of personal choices, to encourage him to optimal academic productivity, to give dignity to his individuality."[33] This statement also needs further definition to avoid the ambiguity of such broad terms.

In 1956 Williamson stressed the cultivation of self-confidence as a legitimate goal and the production of "self-regulating individuals,

[32]*Ibid.*, p. 122.

[33]Herman J. Peters, "The Nature of the Guidance Function," *Counselor Education and Supervision*, III, 3 (Spring 1964), 122–128.

motivated by a sentiment of respect and loyalty to themselves and to others."[34] He viewed the task of the counselor as one of aiding the individual to establish a balance between inner and outer authorities. He also listed the following counseling goals: helping the system to "educate" to follow a course that is "decent, honest, moral, and humane"[35] and helping the client in learning how to make judgments— to choose. It is apparent that Williamson views the counselor as being very much involved in the service of certain "external" (objective) values.

Other writers[36] refer to goals in terms of immediate or impending cultural problems. Berdie speaks of the relationship of two counselor goals, the development of mental health and the development of manpower. To develop mentally healthy individuals is to further the second goal, the development of a productive work force. He views the counselor as playing a major role in the identification and development of talent. There is a hint of deeper value involvement here as he urges counselors to help students and parents to evaluate their attitudes and motivations.

Shoben[37] fights a deterministic view of man, encouraged by materialistic science, which allows individuals to escape responsibility. He reemphasizes man as a moral being and the therapist not as a scientist but as a practicing moralist. Values are presupposed in the mental health movement—how man *should* live, how values and needs can be reconciled, how to judge rightness and goodness of conduct. Decisions in this philosophical realm come from appraisal of human experience and a growth in understanding. Therapy, thus, seems to be an evaluation of one's life goals and the logical consequences of these.

It has been recognized by Wrenn that we must reexamine our current concepts of vocation and vocational counseling. In our so-

[34]E. G. Williamson, "Counseling in Developing Self-Confidence," *Personnel and Guidance Journal*, XXXIV, 7 (March 1956), 404.

[35]*Ibid.*, p. 401.

[36]Ralph F. Berdie, "The Counselor and His Manpower Responsibilities," *Personnel and Guidance Journal*, XXXVIII, 6 (February 1960), 458–463. Rudikoff and Kirk also emphasize motivation of the counselee as an important goal of counseling and one in which the counselor should take an active part. Again, one could ask, motivation toward what end? Lynn C. Rudikoff and Barbara A. Kirk, "Goals of Counseling: Mobilizing the Counselee," *Journal of Counseling Psychology*, VIII (Fall 1961), 243–249.

[37]Edward J. Shoben, Jr., "Personal Responsibility, Determinism, and the Burden of Understanding," *Personnel and Guidance Journal*, XXXIX, 5 (January 1961), 342–348.

ciety, the nature of much of what we call employed work has changed. Its power to bring satisfaction has greatly diminished. It has become necessary to seek a feeling of significance, not in the traditional employed work as has been common but in unemployed activity. Wrenn suggests that the employed and the unemployed aspects of one's life be blended into a whole that will then lead to the *"ultimate of a committed or responsible whole in which one works both for self-fulfillment and for the fulfillment of others.* This is the concept of vocation, of a commitment, a sense of purpose, one's total life in which employed and non-employed work become parts of the whole."[38] This means that the counselor can no longer afford to limit himself to the narrowly vocational in the traditional guidance sense. Rather, he must now help the student define goals and not merely inventory capacities. He must think in terms of life goals and not occupational goals only.

Dreyfus, taking an existentialist position, expresses the goal of counseling as the "elucidation of this client's uniqueness" and "to allow the patient the opportunity to recognize, and then utilize his human potentialities; that is, to be aware of the action-possibilities available to him, and to utilize that which is essentially human within himself."[39]

Blocher advocates human effectiveness as a goal. Recognizing that this term is value laden, he suggests viewing human effectiveness as the product of behaviors best described "in terms of constructs like commitment, competence, consistency, creativity, and control."[40] He then advocates organizing a discipline around the study of those causes (etiology) that underlie effective living.

In a symposium on existentialism in counseling, Arbuckle advocated enhancement of individual freedom as a goal for counseling. In his words: "This is the purpose of counseling—to help the individual to loosen himself from his deterministic shackles, and to come to realize and to see what he has always had—choice and freedom."[41]

In the same symposium Vaughan[42] broadened the goal ex-

[38]C. Gilbert Wrenn, "Human Values and Work in American Life," Henry Borow (ed.), *Man in a World at Work* (Boston: Houghton Mifflin Co., 1964), p. 38.

[39]Edward A. Dreyfus, "The Counselor and Existentialism," *Personnel and Guidance Journal,* XLIII, 2 (October 1964), 114–117.

[40]Blocher, "Wanted: A Science of Human Effectiveness," *Personnel and Guidance Journal,* XLIV, 7 (March 1966), 729–733.

[41]Arbuckle, "Existentialism in Counseling: The Humanist View," *Personnel and Guidance Journal,* XLIII, 6 (February 1965), 558–567.

[42]Richard P. Vaughan, "Existentialism in Counseling: The Religious View,"

pressed by Arbuckle above by listing three aims: (1) fostering freedom within the counselee, (2) improving his encounter with others, and (3) discovering meaning for his existence. He argued that increase in freedom opens one to a fuller experience of value, including religion.

Patterson emphasizes that the counselor definitely has goals and that these are shaped by his values and in turn determine his methodology of counseling as well as his concepts of mental health. Following a discussion of various attempts at goal-setting, he advocated "responsible independence" as a goal for counseling.

> Responsible independence is perhaps an external definition of mental health. From an internal point of view self-actualization perhaps is an expression of the same concept. But a more general and universal or inclusive term is self-esteem. Self-esteem seems to be the essential quality of mental health, and its absence the distinguishing characteristic of mental disturbance.[43]
>
> Counseling and psychotherapy thus would attempt to facilitate the development of individual independence in a client who takes responsibility for himself, his behavior, his choices and decisions, and his values and goals. This would be consistent with the democratic concept of the freedom of the individual, and also with the concept of the responsibility which accompanies freedom. Such a goal is clearly an expression of the values of a democratic society.[44]

Patterson has stated that the counselor must be left free to choose his own counseling goals and should not be required to compromise them. Such goals are long-range in nature and may be in conflict with immediate client goals. The counselor bases his goals upon the assumption "that the client really needs and wants to develop a state or feeling of self-esteem, responsible independence, etc.; so that in reality the goals of the client, though he may be unaware of them, are the same as those of the counselor."[45] The client is still free in that he may choose not to work under the conditions set up on the basis of the counselor's goals.

For Carkhuff and Berenson the goal of counseling centers in helping individuals live as "whole" persons. "The life of the whole person is made up of actions fully integrating his emotional, intellec-

---

*Personnel and Guidance Journal*, XLIII, 6 (February 1965), 553–557.

[43]C. H. Patterson, *Counseling and Psychotherapy: Theory and Practice* (New York: Harper and Brothers, 1959), p. 62.

[44]*Ibid.*

[45]*Ibid.*, p. 64.

tual, and physical resources in such a way that these actions lead to greater and greater self-definition."[46] The following they list as general statements reflecting the implications of becoming whole:

1. The only consistency for the whole person is internal. . . .
2. Creativity and honesty are a way of life for the whole person. . . .
3. Although the way the whole person lives his life is seen by others to be too dangerous, too intense, and too profound, he is in tune with the fact that his real risk involves living life without risk.
4. The whole person realizes that life is empty without acting.
5. The whole person realizes that whatever he does is worth doing fully and well.
6. The whole and creative person functions at a high energy level.
7. The whole person comes to the realization that few men are large enough or whole enough to nourish and love the creative person.
8. The whole person is fully aware that any significant human relationship is in the process of deepening or deteriorating.
9. The whole person realizes that most men say "yes" out of fear of the implications of saying "no," and that most men say "no" out of fear of the implications of saying "yes."
10. The whole person is fully aware that in order to live life in such a way that it is a continuous learning and relearning process, he must periodically burn bridges behind him.
11. The whole person realizes that he is, and must be, his own pathfinder, and travel a road never traveled before.
12. The whole person does not fear living intensely.
13. The whole person is prepared to face the implications of functioning a step ahead or above most of those with whom he comes into contact.
14. The whole person is aware that for most people life is a cheap game.
15. The whole person is fully aware that many of society's rewards are designed to render the creative impotent.
16. The whole person realizes that to emerge within the acceptable levels tolerated by society means institutionalization.
17. The whole person realizes that he must escape traps to render him impotent.
18. The whole person is aware of the awesome responsibility which comes with freedom.[47]

In 1960 Curran[48] described the counseling process as a search for values. The client's self-search leads to ultimate questions regard-

[46]Robert R. Carkhuff and Bernard G. Berenson, *Beyond Counseling and Therapy* (New York: Holt, Rinehart, and Winston, 1967), p. 197.

[47]*Ibid.*, pp. 198–201.

[48]Charles A. Curran, "Some Ethical and Scientific Values in the Counseling Psychotherapeutic Process," *Personnel and Guidance Journal*, XXXIX, 1 (September 1960), 15–20.

ing the meaning of life. The counselor's goal, according to Curran, should be to assist the client in his search and allow him to make his own goal choices. According to his point of view, an increased reasonableness brings increased freedom from defense, which in turn makes possible a more adequate judgment of life goals. Writing from a somewhat perennialist point of view, he spoke of a need to discover the old values that are still valid for our day. These, however, according to Curran, cannot be imposed but must be discovered afresh by each generation.

In a warning of changes to come due to automation, Hart and Lifton[49] also suggest that the counselor will need to become more involved in helping young people develop new value systems. Parents who are in a state of flux and value disruption are not likely to be adequate role models. Once again, the need is more easily described than the solution.

Samler[50] argued that values are at the heart of the counseling relationship and that we must accept without quibbling change in values as a necessary goal in counseling. He recognized that the problems involved are complex but urged that we bring our value commitments to awareness where they can be examined for what they are. It is his feeling that we need a validated and usable system of values and that the scientific study of man can supply the basic data for such derivations, a position similar to Edel's in this last respect. Theories now in existence concerning the healthy personality (Fromm's productive orientation, Sullivan's mature personality, Goldstein and Maslow's self-actualization, etc.) could serve as hypothetical models which could then be tested. Although there are admittedly many hazards here, he states that "our faith must be put on the scientific derivation of desirable behavior, orientation to life, and their underlying values."[51]

> It can be agreed that in some measure *personality appraisal, evaluation of misperception, examination of self-acceptance, resulting change of behavior, acceptance of responsibility,* and *assumption of independence* are common to all counseling tasks. Differential goals are also, of course, to be noted, e.g., *reduction in guilt, accep-*

---

[49]Dale J. Hart and Walter M. Lifton, "Of Things to Come—Automation and Counseling," *Personnel and Guidance Journal*, XXXVII, 4 (December 1958), 282–286.

[50]Joseph Samler, "Change in Values: A Goal in Counseling," *Journal of Counseling Psychology*, VII, 1 (Spring 1960), 32–39.

[51]*Ibid.*, p. 38.

*tance of appropriate feelings of dependence,* and *the experience of feeling.*[52]

Albert Ellis[53] bases his goal for therapy upon an existentialist oriented philosophy of life based upon self-interest. He holds that individuals who live ineffectively do so because of an irrational belief system. The task of the therapist is one of "de-indoctrination" and then of teaching the new and more effective value system to the patient. This approach will be covered in more detail in Chapter 5.

Rudolf Dreikurs[54] emphasizes the Adlerian concept of "social interest" as a goal for therapy. The therapist aids the patient to develop a more effective value system based upon cooperation as opposed to competitiveness and the striving for superiority. In this approach a new social value system based upon equality is promoted. This approach will also be considered in greater detail in Chapter 5.

We turn now to a review of the literature in regard to the selection of goals in counseling.

## THE SELECTION OF COUNSELING GOALS

Berdie[55] raises the question of who should select the goals for counseling and answers by stating that the counselor must determine his own goals. He feels that the counselor's purposes would vary with each client. Also of influence would be the counselor's values, beliefs, attitudes, and place of employment. He feels that the counselee determines his own purposes in counseling.

Horst[56] places much responsibility for the selection and imposition of goals upon the counselor. Although he views the chief objective of counseling as helping the client to "find the course of study or the job which is best for him," he seems to view the counselor as the one to decide what is "best" and "realistic." It is the function of the counselor, according to Horst, to get the client "to accept more realis-

---

[52] *Ibid.,* p. 34.

[53] Albert Ellis, *Reason and Emotion in Psychotherapy* (New York: Lyle Stuart, 1962), and "Goal of Psychotherapy," in Alvin R. Mahrer (ed.), *The Goals of Psychotherapy* (New York: Appleton-Century-Crofts, 1967), pp. 206–220.

[54] Rudolf Dreikurs, "Goals in Therapy," *Psychodynamics, Psychotherapy, and Counseling* (Chicago: Alfred Adler Institute, 1967), pp. 103–112; "Psychotherapy as Correction of Faulty Social Values," *Ibid.,* pp. 113–123; and "Goals of Psychotherapy," in Alvin R. Mahrer (ed.), *The Goals of Psychotherapy,* pp. 221–237.

[55] Berdie, "Counseling Principles and Presumptions," *Journal of Counseling Psychology,* VI, 3 (Fall 1959), 175–182.

[56] Paul Horst, "Educational and Vocational Counseling from the Actuarial Point of View," *Personnel and Guidance Journal,* XXXV, 3 (November 1956), 164–170.

tic goals." He implies that it should be the task of the counselor to decide upon the "appropriate" answer and by some technique then lead the client to it. This would seem to make the client a sort of static entity that, by study, the counselor can know and understand and then mold to the "appropriate" goal. He also assumed a strictly empirical approach, assuming that the "best" is now in existence and can be known by empirical investigation.

In 1958 Williamson criticized the "neutralists" in counseling and urged that the counselor must be in the influence business. He advocated an "open and explicit value orientation in counseling" and urged that the client set his own goals against the external realities of society and make necessary adjustments. The counselor serves the goal of rational problem-solving ability and openly assists the client to examine all questions of values. He questioned the capability of clients to choose "good" goals when left completely on their own in the name of individual development of potential. He raised some pertinent questions:

> Are there any goals of students' development properly predetermined; or do they arise, *sui generis* in the counseling process itself; and, are goals set solely by the counselee himself?
>
> To what purposes and outcomes do we lend our services as counselors? Are they the outcomes of a type that we can justify and accept? Are they socially useful for the "common good," and are they "good" for the individual?
>
> Have we come to view optimum development as justified without regard to standards and forms that bend it toward a "good" goal rather than toward a "bad" end? Do we counselors believe that in counseling "anything goes" or that any kind of development behavior is as good as any other? Do we believe that the fullest growth of one individual inevitably enhances the fullest growth of all other individuals? Are there no relevant and valid standards of growth in individuality? Must any individual choose between the bipolar opposites of absolute autonomy of an individual and object and supine conformity of the individual to someone's (or society's) imposed standards of development—are there no other options to choose in developing one's life?[57]

Such questions, as is generally the case, are left unanswered, but remain to be faced by counselors.

Williamson in 1959 again stressed that counseling techniques could serve either good or bad ends and that the counselor's value orientation is thus vitally important.[58] Man's vocation is an endless

---

[57] E. G. Williamson, "Value Orientation in Counseling," *Personnel and Guidance Journal*, XXXVI, 8 (April 1958), 523.

quest for meaning, and the basic content of counseling, then, must be values—organizing a way of life based upon sound values, beliefs, and life objectives. The counselor's goal should be to influence the direction and forms of development of the counselee. This implies a prior value commitment on the part of the counselor. He suggested five commonly accepted value orientations that it seemed could be viewed as goals for counseling. First, a counselee's choice of school and career should be congruent with his aptitudes and interests, and the task of the counselor is to influence away from choice of career that is incongruent. This implies that the counselor is capable of such wisdom. Second, the choice of a career that offers full expression of a student's interests is valued. Third, activities that have stability are valued. Fourth, we value a "full, rounded life." Williamson also expressed concern over the present self-centeredness of youth as revealed in Jacob's study of the values of American youth and raised questions as to the responsibility of counselors to actively seek to change such an orientation even though the students be satisfied in their self-centeredness.

In another article Williamson continues the same theme of the quest for the "good life" and affirms this as a very important part of counseling. He summarizes the dilemma of modern youth, to be or to strive to become, in these words:

(1) which purposes or life objective to choose in a thoughtful manner; (2) to be or not to be in quest of immediate satisfaction; and (3) to strive to become or not to become one's highest and best potentiality.[59]

The goal of the counselor would be

daily to reconstruct our relationships so that the individual is encouraged as *the* life style of living to strive to become his full potentiality, according to standards of excellence, which he himself has chosen, thoughtfully, in awareness of alternatives.[60]

For Williamson the external standards of excellence are extremely important and the individual cannot be expected to automatically discover these if left on his own.

[58]Williamson, "The Meaning of Communication in Counseling," *Personnel and Guidance Journal*, XXXVIII, 1 (September 1959), 6–14.

[59]Williamson, "Youths' Dilemma: To Be or To Become," *Personnel and Guidance Journal*, XLVI, 2 (October 1967), 176.

[60]*Ibid.*, p. 177.

In an interesting article Krumboltz[61] compared client-centered and behavioristic counseling approaches in regard to values. He stated that both approaches agreed upon behavioral change as the purpose of counseling and both assumed responsibility in further defining the goals of counseling. However, they disagreed in that the client-centered counselor tends to define the same abstract goals for all clients, whereas the behavioral counselor assists the client to define specific goals to be worked toward and which would be different for each client.

Patterson, commenting upon Krumboltz's article, agreed that the broad goals of the two approaches were similar and that specific goals differ. He then questioned that the behavioral counselor would really accept *all* the goals of the client and pointed out that an acceptance of immediate goals may prevent the counselor from recognizing the long-term goals. On the other hand, an acceptance of long-term goals such as self-actualization includes the achievement in some sense of immediate goals. The counselor who does not claim to serve "high sounding and elaborate" goals is not free of such goals and will impose goals whether he is aware of it or not. Thus, it is vitally important for the counselor to be aware of the ultimate goals that he is accepting, since these will be of influence. The basic question is one of goals—the *desirable* in behavior change. Patterson summed it up thus:

> What we need to do is to consider various goals, and the implications of specific techniques for ultimate goals or results, and determine if we can agree upon the ends which we desire and can accept. Then perhaps we can examine techniques in terms of their means to these ends. . . .
> The problem is essentially an ethical or philosophical one, and cannot be reduced to pragmatism or empiricism. One must determine not merely "what works," but what works toward what ends. Neither the individual client nor the individual counselor should choose such goals. All of us, with philosophers and the rest of society, must decide what are the values or goals of counseling, or of life.[62]

Krumboltz, in an article outlining some of the rationale of behavioral counseling, stated the purpose of such counseling as "to help

---

[61]John D. Krumboltz, "Parable of the Good Counselor," *Personnel and Guidance Journal*, XLIII, 2 (October 1964), 118–124.
[62]Patterson, "Comment," *Personnel and Guidance Journal*, XLIII, 2 (October 1964), 124–126.

each client resolve those problems for which he requests help. . . . Within limits, it is each client's wishes that dictate the criteria of success for that client."[63] He stated that the client should determine the end and the counselor the means. He further defined counseling thus: "Counseling consists of whatever ethical activities a counselor undertakes in an effort to help the client engage in those types of behavior which will lead to a resolution of the client's problems."[64] Such statements imply a major responsibility on the part of the client in defining the specific goals for counseling. However, Krumboltz further suggested that there are limitations a counselor might invoke in his acceptance of client goals. The client's problem must fall within the counselor's interests, his competencies, and his ethical limits. In elaborating upon these limits he broadens his definition considerably. If the counselor disagrees with the client's ends, he may seek to help the client to change them to an "appropriate" end—one that can be worked on. Here Krumboltz seems to be doing a reverse and placing the responsibility back on the counselor. One could ask if such goals are of any use, for the counselor could justify any practice in manipulating the client on the basis of his own ethical judgments.

Vance[65] takes an approach similar to that of Krumboltz. She states that it is the function of the counselor to help the client clarify the problem and establish the behavioral goals. Counselor values will influence the process, and so the counselor must be aware of his own values and ethics so that he is aware of what are the desirable or undesirable aspects of behavior to reinforce.

Some writers have observed pitfalls into which the unwary counselor may fall. Here again, it is a matter of which values the counselor in his actual practice serves and whether these values restrict or enhance individual development according to how this is defined in one's ultimate goal.

In 1956 Seeley,[66] using choice as a criterion for goodness or badness, suggested that the whole pyramid of guidance preoccupations should be up-ended in that whatever limits choice limits good.

[63]Krumboltz, "Behavioral Counseling: Rationale and Research," *Personnel and Guidance Journal*, XLIV, 4 (December 1965), 384.

[64]*Ibid.*

[65]Barbara Vance, "The Counselor—An Agent of *What* Change?" *Personnel and Guidance Journal*, XLV, 10 (June 1967), 1012–1016.

[66]John R. Seeley, "Guidance: A Plea for Abandonment," *Personnel and Guidance Journal*, XXXIV, 9 (May 1956), 528–535.

The counselor and the client in counseling are bound together by the pursuit of truth, and the client should be free to become autonomous by means of self-discovery. Adjustment to Seeley was a negative value.

In 1962 Seeley gave warning in discussing the change in America from a scarcity economy to one of abundance and some of the implications he felt it had for counselors. He warned against setting up means and ends for a world that no longer exists—one that is based upon scarcity values. This means also that means of motivation are also changed and counselors "no longer have—or, shortly, no longer will have—hungry little characters whose hungers are your capital assets; the very handles whereby you might expect to handle and hold them."[67] As we mentioned in Chapter 1, Seeley also describes the world in which youth grow up today as one with "a plentitude of means together with a dearth of ends."[68] Recognizing the absurdity of a purposeless world, youth have withdrawn to their own private society, one that repudiates with antagonism the seduction of adult society. This requires counselors who are truly "for" youth and their own discovery of meaning. In Seeley's words:

> I trust that everywhere guidance people and such do think of themselves as a counter-bureaucracy, a counter-administration, the Lenins in behalf of the young amid the Czarist regime of the old, the agents, attorneys and agitators of and for youth, enjoining it only to find itself in its very proper battle, warning it against its all too present temptation to find comfort in compromise, in terms that promise it what is most destructive: a peace without honor, and a plenty without sense.[69]

A warning has been sounded by Shoben[70] against allowing the computer to influence our views of people in the process of formulating ideas of the end-product of therapy. Those who think of man as a machine (the mechanotropes) neglect the human aspects of the relationship they establish. Outcomes of therapy will depend upon the inherent values. In Shoben's words:

> Genuine therapeutic outcomes can be highly diverse, depending in part on the way in which the therapist makes it possible for

[67]Seeley, "Guidance and the Youth Culture," *Personnel and Guidance Journal*, XLI, 4 (December 1962), 302–310.

[68]*Ibid.*, p. 306.

[69]*Ibid.*, p. 310.

[70]Shoben, "The Therapeutic Object: Men or Machines?" *Journal of Counseling Psychology*, X, 3 (Fall 1963), 264–268.

his patient to learn both an explicit system of values and to be critical of it in adapting it for his own uses. ... At any rate, perhaps the crucial learning that occurs in psychotherapy is the acquisition of a functional, critically held, and personally relevant system of human values.[71]

In an article focused primarily upon the goals of the counselor, Feder[72] stresses the importance of individual freedom in a world of machines and overorganization. He calls attention to the dangers inherent in either of two extremes. One he calls "Conantism," with a heavy emphasis upon society, and the other, extreme permissiveness that overemphasizes the individual. It is the task (goal) of the counselor, according to Feder, to aid the individual to discover ways of meeting his needs within a "milieu of social responsibility," as the strength of society will depend upon the quality of individual person-to-person relationships. He refers to the evaluation of our customs and values, the abandonment of the meaningless, and the reconstruction of fundamental values centered in the growth of a productive and responsible self as a worthy challenge. He suggests Huxley's central value core (in *Brave New World Revisited)* of individual freedom, charity and compassion, and intelligence as a model upon which our profession could well build.

Schwebel warns that counselors are also victims of social forces. "Those whose ideology maintains conditions as they are must necessarily become encapsulated, and by the process of selective inattention deny the existence of significant reality impinging upon them."[73]

Brigante,[74] in reference to the ideas of Erich Fromm, warned against the danger of the counselor's viewing people from a "marketing orientation." In this the counselor becomes a salesman, selling his product to employers. When this occurs, there is a danger of serving questionable goals—other-directedness, external goal-internal goal conflicts, and personal involvement of counselors in value conflicts. The counselor, Brigante feels, aids by helping the client to avoid viewing himself as a commodity and by helping him to work out his own value system.

---

[71] *Ibid.,* p. 268.

[72] Daniel D. Feder, "Perspectives and Challenges," *Personnel and Guidance Journal,* XL, 1 (September 1961), 6–10.

[73] Milton Schwebel, "Ideology and Counselor Encapsulation," *Journal of Counseling Psychology,* XI, 4 (Winter 1964), 366–369.

[74] Thomas R. Brigante, "Fromm's Marketing Orientation and the Values of the Counselor," *Journal of Counseling Psychology,* V, 2 (Summer 1958), 83–87.

It is important also to recognize that research is shaped by our goals and values. Froehlich[75] emphasizes the importance of the relation between objectives and research. Research can have meaning only in terms of the objective it serves, and thus research should serve ultimate objectives. Thus, goals, and hence value, serve to shape the direction of research. Rogers has emphasized that

> science cannot come into being without a personal choice of the values we wish to achieve. And these values we choose to implement will forever lie outside of the science which implements them; the goals we select, the purposes we wish to follow, must always be outside of the science which achieves them.[76]

Rogers, in another provocative article,[77] further points out that science is merely a tool used in the service of such prescientific choices of goals made subjectively by individuals. The choice of goals, then, is of vital significance, for they will direct the scientific effort. If static goals such as happiness, contentment, productivity, and the like are chosen, science can be used to discover the means of controlling behavior toward these ends. Such means destroy freedom, and recent experimental evidence reveals that this can happen subtly below the level of the individual's consciousness. These goals, however, are not the sole available choice. Rogers values what he called "process goals." He holds that science can be used to serve these goals by revealing means necessary to produce predictable outcomes. These outcomes, in client-centered therapy, are listed by Rogers as qualities of a person, the client, who has become "more self-directing, less rigid, more open to the evidence of his senses, better organized and integrated, more similar to the ideal which he has chosen for himself."[78] In all forms of therapy, the therapist is engaged in the prediction and influencing of behavior. The direction of this influence is shaped by the therapist's goals in which the client has little choice. If the therapist sets uncertain conditions, such outcomes as listed above become predictable. Such goals grow from values listed by Rogers as valuing

> man as a process of becoming; as a process of achieving worth and dignity through the development of his potentialities; the individual

[75]Clifford Froehlich, "Bedrock for Vocational Guidance," *Journal of Counseling Psychology*, II, 3 (1955), 170–175.

[76]Carl Rogers, *On Becoming a Person* (Boston: Houghton Mifflin Co., 1961), pp. 400–401.

[77]Rogers, "The Place of the Person in the New World of the Behavioral Sciences," *Personnel and Guidance Journal*, XXXIX, 6 (February 1961), 442–451.

[78]*Ibid.*

being as a self-actualizing process, moving on to more challenging and enriching experiences; the process by which the individual creatively adapts to an ever new and changing world; the process by which knowledge transcends itself, as for example, the theory of relativity transcends Newtonian physics itself to be transcended in some future day by a new perception.[79]

Science can serve these values by helping counselors to learn how to unleash them in individuals through helping men to become their own choosers and to value creativity. Such people will be better able to adapt in a changing world.

Nordberg[80] replied to Roger's article. Writing from a Thomistic point of view, he criticized Rogers's paper for what he considered its faulty epistemology. One point he made is of interest to us here. He criticized Rogers for leaving out objective value—that is, need for discovering and pursuing the absolute good. Rogers stated that values derive from two sources: subjective choice and empirical science. Rogers said nothing about why these are the only two sources. Nordberg commented:

A rational value-choice may be "personal" in that one has to choose it for himself, "subjective" in that it involves judgment. "Personal subjective" for Rogers, though, seems to entail a denial that anything objective is involved. This part of his reasoning accepts the premise of positivism—that empirical verification is the only criterion of truth. It is to the doctor's credit that in his more profound moments, he does not believe this.[81]

Nordberg argued that, unless the scientist is in some measure a philosopher and able to see absolute or objective criteria for guiding his choices, his "personal subjective" choice may lead him toward destructive goals, as happened to certain Nazis.

Patterson[82] taking a point of view similar to Rogers's, says that all counseling technique is manipulation of human behavior but that technique of itself is neither good nor bad. It is the goals served by technique that bring forth the value questions, and control falls on a continuum. At one extreme the counselor chooses the final goal of counseling (i.e., happiness) for the client and manipulates the client toward this end. The client in this view is much like an automaton. At

[79] *Ibid.*

[80] Robert B. Nordberg, "Persons and Praxis—A Reply to Rogers," Letters and Comments, *Personnel and Guidance Journal,* XL, 1 (September 1961), 58–59.

[81] *Ibid.,* p. 59.

[82] Patterson, "Control, Conditioning, and Counseling," *Personnel and Guidance Journal,* XLI, 8 (April 1963), 680–686.

the other extreme, manipulation ("operant conditioning") is used toward the goal of "self-determination and self-actualization" of the client. This "frees" him to choose his own goals and to live independently. Patterson recognizes the "genuine, spontaneous concern, interest and understanding of the counselor" as the most powerful reinforcer of optimal personality development.

We now turn to a consideration of the categorization of goals, of which there have been several attempts.

## CATEGORIES OF GOALS: AN AID TO UNDERSTANDING

Byrne,[83] in one of the most complete discussions of goals to be found in the counseling literature, broke goals down into three categories. The first, which he termed immediate goals, consisted of "the moment-by-moment intentions of the counselor during counseling." Intermediate goals, the second category, "relate to reasons why students seek the services of a counselor." The final category, ultimate goals, is derived from the counselor's views of universal man and the nature of life. Byrne viewed ultimate goals as necessary as a base for lesser (immediate and intermediate) goals. Ultimate goals are anchored in the supreme value of man as a being of worth and in his purposive nature. These lend a ring of destiny rather than a timid resignation to mechanistic manipulation. Such terms as "the cultivation of idiosyncracy" by Benjamin, "self-actualization" by Goldstein and Maslow, and "becoming" by Allport reflect such ultimate goals. For Byrne, the key word was apparently purposiveness. One can then think of counseling goals in terms of this suggested hierarchy, with the higher or ultimate goals giving meaning to the lesser goals. Immediate goals are merely instrumental in the service of the higher goals, and intermediate goals are focused primarily upon the remediation of present problems or conflicts. To serve only these lower goals would be to settle for a status quo concept of personality functioning. The task of the counselor in his involvement with individuals and their quest for identity must go beyond mere *remediation* to the *promotion* of growth and development. Such a quest, which involves purpose, also necessarily involves the search for meaning and the development of a philosophy of life. The existentialists have contributed greatly to the formulation of an ultimate goal by focusing on the "givens" of human

[83]Richard H. Byrne, *The School Counselor* (Boston: Houghton Mifflin Co., 1963), pp. 3–25.

nature, which are essential considerations in the human quest. Byrne distilled from existentialism the following points that bear on counseling goals:

1. Being (or becoming) is the state of man in terms of his potential—of what he can become.
2. Being (or becoming) is constantly open to threat.
3. Essential for being (or becoming) is self-awareness, an experiencing of self, and the confrontation of threats to being.
4. A particular man has to be responsible for his own being.[84]

Byrne stated his ultimate counseling goals in the following manner:

> The counselor's goal, firmly based on the human worth of the individual regardless of education, intelligence, color, or background, is to use his technical skills (a) to help each counselee attain and maintain an awareness of self so that he can be responsible for himself, (b) to help each counselee confront threats to his being, and thus to open further the way for the counselee to increase his concern for others' well-being, (c) to help each counselee bring into full operation his unique potential in compatibility with his own life style and within the ethical limits of society.[85]

To serve immediate or intermediate goals without reference to an ultimate goal is to run the risk of allowing one's self to be manipulated by cultural values operating implicitly, which may have questionable outcomes. To serve an explicit ultimate goal is to have a criterion by which the means involved in the service of immediate and intermediate goals may be checked and validated. It is at the level of implicit lesser goals that conflict seems to be the greatest between opposing points of view. In recent years there has been evident a movement toward general acceptance of ultimate goals similar to those stated by Byrne. There is general agreement that the counselor is *for* mankind and *against* all forms of maladjustment. Such value laden terms as *appropriate, best development, socially productive lives, wise choices,* continue to abound in the literature and continue to cover and hide what would be the author's interpretation in terms of his own value orientation. It is thus a difficult task to make such hidden values explicit.

The recognition of ultimate goals by practicing counselors in day-to-day situations is difficult because immediate and intermediate goals are more self-evident. For example, a counselor in the process of counseling will frequently have in mind more immediately practical

---

[84]*Ibid.,* p. 19.
[85]*Ibid.,* pp. 19–20.

goals such as aiding the client to "choose an occupation, prepare for it, enter it, and be successful in it." Such a goal statement could be made equally in varying value systems or ideologies. Such a practical goal derives its meaning from an ultimate goal. In a totalitarian system this goal statement would be validated in terms of service to the state, whereas in a democratically orientated system, validation would be made in terms of the individual. Thus, lesser goals are dependent upon higher goals from which they derive meaning.

> The maximum of freedom requires that there shall be at least moments of life in which a man freely chooses that ultimate goal which prescribes the chain of subordinate choices with which the greater part of his life is necessarily concerned.[86]

Zaccaria,[87] by synthesizing the three developmental theories of Havighurst (developmental tasks), Erikson (psychosocial crises), and Super (vocational developmental tasks), made an attempt to apply the concept of developmental tasks to goals in guidance. He lists a hierarchy of tasks matched to a hierarchy of goals as follows:

| *Range of Goal* | *Developmental Task* |
| --- | --- |
| 1. Ultimate goal | 1. Self-actualization. |
| 2. Long-range goals | 2. General developmental tasks. |
| 3. Intermediate-range goals | 3. Basic developmental tasks. |
| 4. Short-term goals | 4. Subdevelopmental tasks. |

He warns of using developmental tasks in a nomothetic way as is commonly done and rather urges an idiographic application, allowing for individual uniqueness.

As we noted in Chapter 3, choices of goals are based upon certain value assumptions. If the world is viewed in a static manner, goals are likely to be more static. On the other hand, if the world is viewed in a dynamic manner, goals are likely to be more of the process variety. *One, of course, must again remember that any categorization is an abstraction and must not be viewed in a strict, inflexible sense.* Rather, such categories flow into one another with a tendency in one or another direction. Focus upon a developmental model is likely to be tied, as Mahrer found, "to what is 'natural' biologically and genetically. Thus, its philosophical values are tied to concepts of maturity,

---

[86]R. B. Perry, *The Humanity of Man* (New York: George Braziller, Inc., 1956), p. 33.

[87]Joseph S. Zaccaria, "Developmental Tasks: Implications for the Goals of Guidance," *Personnel and Guidance Journal*, XLIV, 4 (December 1965), 372–375.

health, and normal functioning."[88] These need not be, but often are, interpreted as *states* of being rather than as dynamic concepts. Living and dynamic beings cannot be adequately described by nouns; they rather require verbs. Thus, in the existential or self-actualizing model one is more likely to find emphasis upon such concepts as experiencing, becoming, and valuing. The following shows some possible differences in emphasis between process goals and static goals in several areas.

| *Process Goals* | *Static Goals* |
|---|---|
| proaction | reaction |
| being, becoming | finding |
| loving | being loved |
| meaningful striving | pleasure and contentment |
| full use of one's powers | blind idleness |
| perpetual learning and adventure | thumb-twiddling |
| creativity and openness | retirement in future |
| living in present | waiting for the future |
| "true" happiness | "storybook" happiness |

Another method of grouping is to arrange goals according to their specific focus. Mahrer,[89] after analyzing the proposed goals of a number of therapists, felt they could be grouped into several categories. One such category is the reduction of psychopathology, the focus usually being on remediation either in the form of reduced symptomatology or a reduction of defensiveness. A second category focuses upon the reduction of psychological suffering, usually aimed at reducing anxiety and hostility. More recently there has been added within this category an increased emphasis upon reduction of meaninglessness, rootlessness, alienation, aloneness, and feelings of insignificance. A third category is that of fulfillment. Here the aim is to increase the pleasure of living through fulfillment of needs and desires, both physical and psychological. A fourth category focuses upon enhancement of the experiencing process.

> The goal is to feel alive each moment, to experience the concrete process of living and feeling, to have a vital sense of being. There is an openness to experience and to change, a constantly changing commitment to the flow of experience.[90]

The fifth group of goals focuses upon enhancing self-relationships

[88]Mahrer, *Goals of Psychotherapy*, p. 300.
[89]*Ibid.*, p. 259.
[90]*Ibid.*, p. 260.

through increasing self-acceptance and inner-directedness. Enhanced external relationships is the focus of still another group of goals and includes the increase of closeness and intimacy in interpersonal relationships, increased competence in functioning in interaction with one's world, increase in ability to adjust to the demands and limitations of one's external world, and increase in one's social commitment, which includes one's responsibility for the welfare of others. In addition to these six goal categories listed by Mahrer, one might also add the discovery and ordering of values into a consistent philosophy of life as a seventh.

One can note the similarity in the emphases of these groups of goals to C. S. Lewis's description of the three focal points of effective human functioning mentioned in Chapter 1: (1) the individual's internal organization, (2) the individual's relationship to other individuals, and (3) an ordered sense of purpose or meaning in life. These three come into play at one time or another in all types of counseling or psychotherapy, but each school tends to emphasize more strongly one set of goals over another. Some focus primarily upon the internal functioning of the individual, whereas others focus more upon social aspects. The area most likely to be neglected, however, is that dealing with meaning and purpose, for it is here that within the counseling process the more complex and apparent value problems arise.

After summarizing the proposed goals of sixteen therapists, Mahrer[91] classified them into three clusters or families in terms of goal and function: (1) biopsychological developmental psychotherapies, (2) psychological actualization psychotherapies, and (3) reconstructive psychotherapies. All of the families seem to serve the general goals as listed by Mahrer but in addition have, in terms of their ultimate values, tendencies in one direction or another as to social philosophy.

In the first family (including, for example, the Action therapists and Trait-Factor approaches) the emphasis is upon removing blocks to the natural biologically based process of development and growth. *"The goal of psychotherapy is to attain mature, healthy, normal functioning described in terms of the general goals of psychotherapy proposed earlier."*[92] Here there is an underlying assumption of the "goodness" of normality.

[91] *Ibid.*, p. 261.
[92] *Ibid.*, p. 263.

In the second family of actualization therapies (including existentialist and client-centered approaches), the aim is the actualization of potential inherent in the person, this being facilitated by the removal of blocks to experiencing fully one's existence. The "good" life is here equated with optimal functioning in terms of general goals as mentioned previously and a pressing forward into the future.

In the third family, the reconstructive psychotherapies (including Adlerian and Rational and Emotive approaches), the focus is upon a "conceptual system of constructs, basic premises, fundamental ideas, and basic life assumptions."[93] Psychological functioning is here held to be dependent upon this rational system, and the major goal of therapy is to reconstruct and alter that system to the end of producing more effective functioning. The reconstruction in this approach is based upon a definite value system (depending upon the particular school of thought) that is offered as a distinct social-philosophical system approximating optimal functioning.

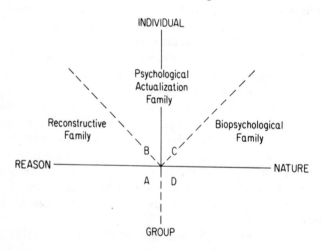

Diagram 8. Assumptions of a social order: families of
psychotherapy.

We can now see a relationship of the three families to social-philosophical assumptions by placing them in our diagram of Chapter 3.

---

[93] *Ibid.,* p. 267.

In the biopsychological developmental family, emphasis is upon the individual's learning to cope with his own nature and the nature of the world. Growing from technical reason it is not surprising that in this school of thought values have been largely ignored. In the psychological actualization family we find an overlap of both quadrants. The emphasis here has been upon the fulfillment of the individual's potential growing from his natural endowments in terms of potentiality but accompanied by a cautious but dynamic movement into the future. The individual creates what he becomes by his choices in regard to the actualization of his natural potentialities. In this family the approach to values has generally been a cautious one, with a fear of the imposition of values upon the individual. In the reconstructive family one finds a clearer structuring of a normative social order and a movement toward it by assisting individuals to at least consider the greater effectiveness they could experience through the adoption of this new value system. The approach to values is not cautious, and the teaching of values is considered to be an important function of either counseling or psychotherapy.

A discussion of goals is difficult to undertake in isolation from the counseling process itself in that philosophy and practice, goals and techniques, do overlap. This discussion of goals will, therefore, continue in Chapter 5, though often, perhaps, implicitly. Let us turn now, in concluding this chapter, to the question of whether or not there are any commonly agreed-upon values underlying the goals of counseling. We must be reminded here that goals, even ultimate ones, are not the same as values. Rather, values form the basis, the criteria, by which goals are chosen.

## COMMONLY AGREED-UPON VALUES

We have raised the question: "Are there any commonly agreed-upon values among counselors?" Since any school of counseling or psychotherapy grows out of a particular culture in response to specific needs, it would seem logical that the basic values of that culture would be strongly reflected in its ethical position. In our society it is not surprising, then, to discover general agreement among counselors upon key values involving the individual and his worth. Buhler[94] referred to what she saw as a relationship between schools of psychotherapy and

---

[94] Charlotte Buhler, *Values in Psychotherapy* (New York: The Free Press of Glencoe, 1962), p. 190.

political philosophy, although she was reluctant to claim a causal relationship. One could anticipate some conflicts among counselors when the values of society begin to conflict, for example, when democratic values clash with the materialistic values of a sensate culture.

Albert, writing about American values, described a set that have been central and explicit. "These have developed since 1776," and have been "reported by observers from Tocqueville to such contemporary writers as Myrdal, Lerner, and Kluckhohn." These have their origin in the Declaration of Independence and the Constitution:

> Equality; liberty; justice; democracy, understood as the sovereignty of the people; the right of private property; and individual responsibility, freedom and initiative, circumscribed only by avoiding harm to others and by concern for the general welfare.[95]

One finds wide agreement in the counseling literature upon these values at this abstract level. Agreement becomes foggier as these values descend to the level of action.

There is general agreement as to the rationality of the individual, with an optimistic belief in the capability of the individual to choose for himself in a responsible way.

> Moral and philosophical themes in guidance have not been grounded in nihilism, hedonism, fatalism, or skepticism. What seems to underly the faith of guidance philosophers is strong belief in logical reasoning, foresight, prudence and the capacity of people to plan and conduct their affairs within foreseeable limits. . . . At bottom, guidance depends upon a belief in supremacy of reason and problem solving in the direction of life activity.[96]

A source of generally agreed-upon values can be found in any consensual statements of the profession, provided that these are a true consensus. One such source is to be found in the aims expressed through professional publications. Samler, as editor of the *Personnel and Guidance Journal* in 1955, stated the aims of the publication as

> basically to reinforce and implement the beliefs (1) that the personnel and guidance counselor is a worker in the scientific tradition; that he must attempt to find out not only what works but also why it works, and (2) that personnel and guidance work rests upon a basic and deeply-rooted respect for the individual human being, his ability

---

[95]Ethel M. Albert, "Conflict and Change in American Values: A Cultural Approach," *Ethics*, LXXIV, 2 (October 1963), 19–33.

[96]Mathewson, *Guidance Policy* p. 73.

under proper settings to mobilize his resources, and the great variety of acceptable differences among individuals.[97]

He then added that this statement "attempts only to make explicit what now is pretty obvious and is reflected in every issue of the Journal."[98]

Another source is a statement issued by the American Personnel and Guidance Association regarding developments that seemed to threaten the right of individual freedom by using counselors as instrumentalities to "force" students into positions that would solve the nation's manpower shortages. This statement was printed in the March 1958 *Personnel and Guidance Journal* "as a permanent record of the principles which should determine future national action by the American Personnel and Guidance Association."

> This is a statement defending the right of every individual to freedom of choice. Its purpose is to safeguard against the forcing of high-ability people into specific "needed" occupations. Emphasis is rather placed upon developing to the full every individual's potentialities and thus assuring excellence in all areas. The statement holds that national manpower shortages can be alleviated without destroying freedom of choice. This can be done through education by assisting individuals to know their potentialities, interests, and values; to develop them through education; to know the complex and rapidly changing career picture; to become motivated to develop their potential as well as to relate it to the opportunities existent in society.

The American Personnel and Guidance Association upholds the following principles:

1. Freedom to choose one's life work.
2. For freedom to flourish:
    a. students must learn (progressively) about themselves.
    b. students must learn about change and career opportunities.
    c. students should be motivated to explore the best outlets for their talents.
    d. students must be instilled with a sense of responsibility and become good stewards of talents.
3. Professional counselors must be available at all levels.
4. Waste of human resources can be reduced by guidance.
5. Counselors have obligation to both the student and society in assisting growth of potential and utilization of skills for needs of society.

[97]Samler, Editorial, *Personnel and Guidance Journal,* XXXIV, 1 (September 1955), 41.
[98]*Ibid.*

6. Adequate staff is necessary so that professional counseling can take place. Without counseling, other aids are not fully effective.[99]

Another important source of value consensus is to be found in the code of ethics of the profession. An ethical system or code of ethics is a guideline for action based upon commonly held values. To be meaningful, a code of ethics should reflect not only the agreed-upon values of the profession represented but also values generally accepted by the society the profession serves. An adopted code of ethics is then a gauge of the most basic values agreed upon by the profession.

The history of the development of a professional code of ethics among guidance workers is another example of the lack of explicit concern over value issues. Early texts for the most part have not concerned themselves with ethical or philosophical matters, and any concern with ethics has focused mainly upon the issue of confidentiality. Wrenn made the following statement in an article published in 1952: "It is a sad commentary on the maturity of our profession that the published literature on ethics in counseling can be discussed quite briefly." [100]

Before a group can state an ethical code, it must first seek out commonly agreed-upon underlying values and responsibilities. Following a series of such attempts at definition of common values, the American Personnel and Guidance Association published in October, 1961, its adopted code of ethics. In the preamble it is stated, "This service of the educational, scientific, and professional organization is committed to profound faith in the worth, dignity, and great potentiality of the individual human being,"[101] and under Section B., Counseling, "A counseling relationship denotes that the person seeking help retain full freedom of choice and decision and that the helping person has no authority or responsibility to approve or disapprove of the choices or decisions of the counselee or client."[102]

An examination of the code reveals what might be called the consensual values of the profession.[103]

---

[99]American Personnel and Guidance Association, "A Statement of Policy Concerning the Nation's Human Resources Problems," *Personnel and Guidance Journal,* XXXVI, 7 (March 1958), 454–455.

[100]Wrenn, "The Ethics of Counseling," *Educational and Psychological Measurement,* XII, 2 (Summer 1952), 161–177.

[101]American Personnel and Guidance Association, "Ethical Standards," *Personnel and Guidance Journal,* XL, 2 (October 1961), 206–209.

[102]*Ibid.,* p. 207.

[103]*Ibid.,* pp. 206, 207.

1. "Profound faith in the worth, dignity, and great potentiality of the individual human being."

2. Respect for the right of the individual to full freedom of choice and decision.

3. Service to society based upon the above two commitments.

Street, in a report of the study by the National Education Association's Educational Policies Commission on "Manpower and Education" concluded by "emphasizing the great hazard to democratic values unless those guidance principles are operative which respect the right of a student to a meaningful and honest picture and the freedom to choose for himself."[104]

Such, then, is the guiding purpose of the profession; but even within these commonly held tenets there exist the seeds of conflict—the compromise between society and the individual, between man and men. "The problem of values arises only when men try to fit together their need to be social animals with their need to be free men. There is no problem, and there are no values, until men want to do both."[105]

This makes ethical matters problematic in counseling as long as one approaches them in a dualistic manner. There exist conflicting loyalties on the part of the counselor to the client, society, the employing institution, the profession, and to himself. The subjectivism of the individual clashes with the objectivism of societal standards. Such conflicts can be resolved only by recourse to a framework of values. Although an ethical code may serve as a guideline, the final judgment rests upon the individual counselor, his values, and his perception of the axiological dilemma. To make such decisions requires great moral courage and integrity on the part of the counselor.[106]

This discussion anticipates the need for an examination of the concept of freedom, which appears to be central to the purposes of counseling and guidance within a democratic society. This value (freedom) along with another that is closely related to it, the dignity of the individual, seem to form the consensual values of the profession, and we shall turn to a discussion of these in Chapter 7. We now turn to a consideration of values in the counseling process.

[104]Paul Street, "Guidance: The Century's Educational Necessity," *Personnel and Guidance Journal,* XXXV, 7 (March 1957), 462.

[105]Jacob Bronowski, *Science and Human Values* (New York: Harper and Row, 1956), p. 70.

[106]Wrenn, "Ethics of Counseling," pp. 161–177.

# chapter 5

# Values in the Counseling Process

One cannot live without encountering the problem of values. Certainly, one cannot go through psychotherapy without becoming involved, implicitly or explicitly, in the problem. Nor can one engage in psychotherapy as a therapist without bringing certain convictions about values into one's work. These convictions may or may not be specifically communicated to the patient, but they underlie the therapist's activity; they help determine the goal he sets for himself and his patient; and they are consciously or unconsciously reflected in his questions, statements, or other reactions.[1]

## COUNSELOR: NEUTRAL OR VALUE ORIENTED?

There is some difficulty in separating writings that have dealt primarily with values in the counseling process from those that deal with goals, for the two areas necessarily overlap.

As previously cited, Green, in what is one of the first articles raising questions concerning values in the therapeutic process, referred to the history of modern psychotherapy as "an unsuccessful struggle to evaluate the role of social values."[2] He stated his thesis in two points: one, that therapists *must* deal with values, and two, that therapists would be better off if they were explicitly aware of what they were doing. He defined social values as "simply standards of morality and conceptions of other's welfare, supported by the groups of which the given person is a part,"[3] and said that their authority derives neither from logic nor science but rather from a transcendental "ought." Obligations are invoked by men by conformity to group standards to allow individuals to achieve their goals. He viewed all

---

[1]Charlotte Buhler, *Values in Psychotherapy* (New York: The Free Press of Glencoe, 1962), p. 1.

[2]Arnold W. Green, "Social Values and Psychotherapy," *Journal of Personality,* XIV, 3 (March 1946), 199–228.

[3]*Ibid.*, p. 199.

behavior resulting in the need for psychotherapy as social and involving "a conflict between self-and-others and between self-values and other(s)-values. In part, all neuroses refer to a moral struggle."[4] He discussed the social values served by the therapeutic systems of Freudian psychoanalysis, adjustment therapies, social reform theories, and client-centered therapy. He concluded by listing two common shortcomings of therapists: first, a failure to keep distinct three value areas—the counselor's, the client's, and the client's social group; and second, a sociological naivete.

Buhler, in her study of values in psychotherapy, stated that

knowingly or unknowingly, *the therapist conveys to the patient some of his thinking about values.* This seems to be the case even in the most nondirective, or seemingly purely interpretive, approaches. It seems that the therapist conveys to the patient something beyond his understanding of the patient's motivation struggles. He reveals, knowingly or unknowingly, on rare or more frequent occasions his own personal *reaction,* his *point of view,* or even his *position* in matters of consequence. And of course he cannot help revealing, beyond the technically acquired model, attitudes of "poise, patience, fairness, consistency, rationality, kindliness, in short—his *real* love for the patient," some of his own personality characteristics.[5]

Buhler pointed to the vital question of seeking possibilities between the two extremes of *"leaving the patient to find his values and beliefs himself "* or of *"actively inducing beliefs in him."*[6]

Since Green's article in 1946, a number of writers have referred to the importance of the counselor's own value orientation in counseling. There has been a movement away from viewing the counselor as a neutral and uncommitted (at least in the counseling interview) professional whose function is primarily that of a mirror—merely reflecting back to the client his own impressions of himself. One can question if the following quote by Counts is not also applicable to many counselors who attempt to remain neutral.

There is the fallacy that the great object of education is to produce the college professor, that is, the individual who adopts an agnostic attitude towards every important social issue, who can balance the pros against the cons with the skill of a juggler, who sees all sides of every question and never commits himself to any, who delays action until all the facts are in, who knows that all the facts

[4] *Ibid.,* p. 200.
[5] Buhler, *Values in Psychotherapy,* p. 3.
[6] *Ibid.,* p. 6.

will never come in, who consequently holds his judgment in a state of indefinite suspension, and who before the approach of middle age sees his powers of action atrophy and his social sympathies decay.[7]

Walters describes a more involved value-oriented posture for the counselor.

> The therapist usually conceives of himself and is often represented as the detached dispassionate scientist. A more realistic view would see him as an involved participant with an interest in the outcome, following a sectarian psychotherapeutic doctrine or combination of doctrines, the selection and practice of which are tinctured by his own basic philosophy of life.[8]

Arbuckle[9] traces the development of counseling from medicine, via Freud, explaining how it has been viewed primarily as a science. He notes the discrepancy between viewing humans in a scientific way, seeing them as objects, and relating to them in a deeply involved relationship that moves one into the realm of philosophy and of values, feelings, and ideas. Science can determine only what *is*, but the counselor needs to ask *why* as well as *how*, and so the philosophical aspect takes on much importance. Arbuckle suggests that the "trained" counselor (technique oriented) asks *how* but the "educated" counselor asks *why*. He strongly affirms that we need more "educated" counselors.

Shoben, quoting Davis, emphasizes that the role of those concerned with the prevention and therapy of psychopathology is "not that of a scientist but that of a practising moralist in a scientific, mobile world."[10]

Boy and Pine give a chapter in their new book to the counselor's sensitivity to the valuing process and refer to counseling as the "processing of values."[11]

The school counselor who is not sensitive to the existence of

---

[7]George S. Counts, "Dare the School Build a New Social Order?" in Ronald Gross (ed.), *The Teacher and the Taught* (New York: Dell Publishing Co., 1963), p. 185.

[8]Orville S. Walters, "Metaphysics, Religion and Psychotherapy," *Journal of Counseling Psychology*, V, 4 (Winter 1958), 249.

[9]Dugald J. Arbuckle, "Counseling: Philosophy or Science," *Personnel and Guidance Journal*, XXXIX, 1 (September 1960), 11–14.

[10]Edward J. Shoben, Jr., "Personal Responsibility, Determinism, and the Burden of Understanding," *Personnel and Guidance Journal*, XXXIX, 5 (January 1961), 342–348, quoting K. Davis, "Mental Hygiene and the Class Structure," *Psychiatry*, 1 (1938), p. 65.

[11]Angelo V. Boy and Gerald J. Pine, *The Counselor in the Schools: A Reconceptualization* (Boston: Houghton Mifflin Co., 1968), p. 34.

values within himself and the degree to which they affect his functioning is much like an automobile that rejects the importance of an engine.[12]

After discussing man's search for values and then listing some of the important humanistic values of the counselor, they summarize the process thus:

> Counseling, then, is a relationship in which the counselor provides the client with a communicating atmosphere that gives the client the opportunity to become involved in the discovering, processing, and synthesizing of values.
>
> If the school counselor is to bring a substantive quality into his relationships with students, he must become sensitive to values— their existence, their relevancy, and how they affect his being. He must also become aware of the interplay between his values and those of his clients and, in turn, the struggle within the client as he attempts to discover his personal values and their relationship to values exterior to himself.[13]

Taylor[14] refers to some important philosophical issues regarding the counselor's own value position. She recognizes a commonality in views of reality that approaches universality and advocates that the counselor become involved in the social and moral aspects of counseling.

> Since . . . all guidance is postulated on freedom of choice, every theory of counseling implies an ethical position. It is ethical because it springs from responsibility for choice on one hand and specific metaphysical hypotheses concerning what is preferable on the other. For those who see nondirective counseling as absolute freedom (and there are many who do not), the ultimate goal may be suggested; "Know Thyself" since there are no absolute values toward which the counselor may guide.
>
> Is each man's world so unique that counselor and counselee travel only transient parallel paths, preventing communication of valid views of the non-self world? Indeed not. Individual's worlds of non-self bear so much similarity that in daily life we may and do act as if they were one world. A criterion of the need for therapy is whether the client is "out of touch with reality." This reality then consists of fairly universally agreed upon aspects. Because the client's picture is *not* that of others we know he needs help. Perhaps the lines of counselee-world and counselor-world may not meet, but they progressively approach each other. Therefore in the guidance

---

[12] *Ibid.*, p. 18.

[13] *Ibid.*, p. 35.

[14] Charlotte P. Taylor, "Social and Moral Aspects of Counseling," Letters from Readers, *Personnel and Guidance Journal*, XXXV, 3 (November 1956), 181.

conference not only the self-world relationships should be investigated, but the nature of the world itself as interpreted by both individuals.

If we can draw no fine lines in ethics, we may at least see a pattern of human conduct which is psychologically and ethically "good." Furthermore, it is a familiar one, found in various expressions in the philosophies of most cultures. . . .

Rather than abandoning the social and moral aspects of counseling, we should strive to enlarge them, commensurate with the best and finest knowledge we have in the fields of psychology and ethics.[15]

A master's thesis by Lowe serves to focus more attention upon the role of the counselor's own values in the counseling process. His thesis was that there exist irreconcilable differences as to the end counseling should serve. In an article derived from his thesis he states:

The point of this article is that the involvement of the psychologist's own values in the applied field creates an ethical dilemma. The dilemma exists because the psychologist as a scientist cannot know to which of mankind's brave new worlds he is to be beholden. . . .

. . . The dilemma of the practicing psychologist is compounded by the existence of a multiplicity of competing sets of values, for one value orientation tends to exclude all others.[16]

Following a brief review of the literature and an analysis of the four value orientations of naturalism, culturalism, humanism, and theism, he concludes that for the counselor "there is no single professional standard to which his values can conform."[17] Should he subscribe to one set of absolutes he would cease to be scientific and would become the proponent of a social movement. If, however, he were to base his values upon the values of a plurality, he would have decided in favor of culturalism. If the therapist is aware of his value orientation, it will at times clash with that of the client. If he is not aware of his orientation, he will hold his values as self-evident and attempt to impose them upon the client. The counselor finds himself truly in a dilemma. Lowe suggests four possible alternatives to the dilemma: (1) ignore the problem, (2) contrive a blend or synthesis of value orientations, (3) assume absolute truth, and (4) show objective and impartial concern for the

---

[15] *Ibid.*

[16] C. Marshall Lowe, "Value Orientations—An Ethical Dilemma," *The American Psychologist,* XIV (1959), 687.

[17] Lowe, *Value Orientations in Counseling: An Ethical Dilemma,* M.A. thesis, Ohio State University, p. 125.

client's value orientation and assist the client to make a choice from the possible alternatives. He ends his thesis with the following statement.

> The conclusion we come to then is that differences in value-orientations cannot be resolved, each orientation having adherents whose beliefs should be respected. We suggest that each counselor have a greater understanding of the values of both himself and others. We suggest also that the counselor be honest enough intellectually to admit the philosophic bias under which he operates.[18]

There is growing agreement that the counselor cannot avoid bringing his values with him to any human relationship. Browning and Peters[19] stress that the counselor cannot avoid the consideration of ultimate values in counseling. Neither can he avoid operating according to some philosophical point of view, be it "some form of Idealism, Realism (Christian or otherwise), Pragmatism, Naturalism, or Existentialism (again religious or otherwise)."[20]

Grater[21] calls attention to the fact that the counselor's values regarding what is *productive* client behavior during a counseling interview may subtly and without the counselor's awareness control the sort of behavior that takes place. If, then, the client is a highly dependent sort of person, the counselor may actually reinforce such dependency under the illusion that the client is showing *productive* behavior, pleasing the counselor. This kind of client will usually come to counseling with something "important" to discuss, for in this way he can "please" the counselor in an attempt to negate his feelings of inferiority and worthlessness.

There is also the possibility that the client may pattern himself after the counselor in order to win approval or for some other reason. Walker and Peiffer,[22] quoting Wolberg, state that

> no matter how passive the therapist may believe himself to be, and no matter how objective he remains in an attempt to permit the patient to develop his own sense of values, there is an inevitable incorporation within the patient of a new super-ego patterned after

---

[18]*Ibid.*, p. 131.

[19]Robert L. Browning and Herman J. Peters, "On the Philosophical Neutrality of Counselors," in Peters and others (eds.), *Counseling: Selected Readings* (Columbus: Charles E. Merrill, 1962), pp. 363–371.

[20]*Ibid.*, p. 370.

[21]Harry A. Grater, "When Counseling Success Is Failure," *Personnel and Guidance Journal*, XXXVII, 3 (November 1958), 323–325.

[22]Donald E. Walker and Herbert C. Peiffer, Jr., "The Goals of Counseling," *Journal of Counseling Psychology*, IV, 3 (Fall 1957), 204–209, quoting Wolberg.

the character of the therapist as he is conceived by the patient. There is also almost inevitably an acceptance by the patient of many of the values of the therapist as they are communicated in interpretations or direct suggestions or as they are deduced by the patient by his association with the therapist. Sometimes these values are not in the best interests of the patient.[23]

## COUNSELOR INFLUENCE: DEGREE AND DIRECTION

There have been several empirical investigations that support the view that counselor values do influence the client. Rosenthal,[24] in a much quoted study, hypothesizes: (1) that values, and particularly moral values, do change in psychotherapy, (2) that the patient learns to accept the moral values of the therapist and that this is accompanied by alleviation of psychological distress, and (3) that values of the type measured by the Allport-Vernon Scale of Values would not be systematically influenced because they would not ordinarily be at issue. Utilizing twelve patients at a psychiatric clinic as a sample, he administered tests at the beginning and at the end of therapy. His results revealed that improved patients had revised their values in the direction of the therapist's, the unimproved patient's values became less like the values of the therapist, and that, as predicted, no significant changes occurred on the Allport-Vernon Scale. One could raise some questions here concerning the validity of the study due to the small N and also as to whether there would be a transfer of results from a clinic to another different setting. This study is often quoted in the literature in support of counselor influence upon values.

In a study related to that above, Schrier[25] presented evidence of a relationship between improvement and the extent of identification by the client to the therapist's need system.

Another study of a similar type was done by Farson and involved the process of introjection in the psychotherapeutic relationship. He described his study thus:

> Using Q methods of personality analysis the self-descriptions of eighteen clients and their six therapists were compared before and after client-centered therapy to investigate the possibility that the

[23] *Ibid.*, p. 207.

[24] David Rosenthal, "Changes in Some Moral Values Following Psychotherapy," *Journal of Consulting Psychology*, XIX, 6 (1955), 431–436.

[25] H. Schrier, "The Significance of Identification in Therapy," *American Journal of Orthopsychiatry*, XXIII (1953), 585–604.

personality of the therapist is introjected by his client. Six colleague judges were asked to rank the therapists as to their psychological adjustment, therapeutic competence and the likelihood that their clients would come to resemble them. The findings suggest that if introjection occurs, it is most likely to occur in the case of less competent and less adjusted therapists.[26]

The limitations of this study were also many, including a small N and the fact that data collection was separated by several years.

Landfield and Nawas[27] also investigated the effect of therapists' values upon improvement. They used thirty-six college students and six psychotherapists. Their findings confirmed their hypotheses that a minimal degree of communication between client and therapist in the client's own language dimension is essential for improvement in psychotherapy and that improvement is accompanied by a shift in the present-self of the client toward the ideal of the therapist as described within the framework of the client's language dimension. The results thus agree with Rosenthal's, but (the writers add) with reservations. There seemed to be an influence by therapist's ideals, but *"at the same time* some of them are shaking themselves free from dependence on the therapist's language framework."[28] More research is needed before one can state with great validity that clients do move toward an acceptance of counselor values.

While there now seems to be general agreement that the counselor does influence the client and cannot avoid it, the questions of how values are actually communicated and how values should be handled within the counseling relationship remain open.

Blocher is one who saw this issue of whether or not the counselor influences the client as being primarily resolved and as

> really no longer an issue. Writers as different in orientation as Williamson (1958) and Patterson (1958) agree that counselors do, should, and cannot avoid influencing clients. The relevant questions which survive around this part of the issue concern only directions and degrees of influence.[29]

---

[26]Richard E. Farson, "Introjection in the Psychotherapeutic Relationship," *Journal of Counseling Psychology,* VIII, 4 (Winter 1961), 337–343.

[27]A. W. Landfield and M. M. Nawas, "Psychotherapeutic Improvement as a Function of Communication and Adoption of Therapist's Values," *Journal of Counseling Psychology,* XI, 4 (Winter 1964), 336–341.

[28]*Ibid.,* p. 340.

[29]Donald H. Blocher, "Issues in Counseling: Elusive and Illusional," *Personnel and Guidance Journal,* XLIII, 8 (April 1965), 796–800.

There still exists a continuum as to degree and direction of influence, falling between the two poles of a cautious approach on one hand, where the counselor attempts to keep his personal value judgments out of the counseling process in order to insure that the client has freedom to find his own values, and an active attempt to induce certain values in the client on the other.

Historically there seem to be three periods representative of changing approaches in the counseling and guidance movement, and these parallel to a certain extent those mentioned by Buhler and previously referred to. First of all, there seems to have been a period of active techniques, extending from the beginning of the movement through the thirties. Known as directive counseling, this approach primarily emphasized vocational aspects. The counselor was viewed as the authority, with certain responsibility to guide the client correctly. The second period, starting with Rogers's protest against the more "directive" techniques, advocated that the counselor should be neutral and nonjudgmental, leaving the client to make his own choices without undue influence on the part of the counselor. The third period seems to be growing out of the recognition that counselors cannot avoid being an influence and seems to be moving us into a period of more active involvement once again. However, the type of involvement is important, and the kind of values served takes on increased importance.

Patterson[30] has reemphasized that a philosophy of counseling is an organized system of values and that these values will influence the counselor's goals as well as his techniques. Important here are the values held regarding the nature of man. If the counselor believes that man is inherently evil and that his tendency is toward evil, however defined, he is going to be more active in helping the client control his evil impulses and serve the "right" values. However, if he views man as inherently good, with a basic positive tendency, his emphasis will be upon allowing his client to express his positive nature and to help him rid himself of the hindrances to such expression. The impartation of values in this case would not be necessary since they are "built in." One may also take a middle approach and see man as neither evil nor good, but neutral. His basic tendency of growth may move in either direction. Here again, the counselor would view the learning of posi-

---

[30]C. H. Patterson, *Counseling and Psychotherapy* (New York: Harper and Brothers, 1959), p. 56.

tive values as an important part of the counseling process.

Walker,[31] in an article analyzing the philosophical basis of Rogers's theory, pointed to some important value issues regarding one's view of the nature of man and how this affects one's counseling behavior. Suggesting that Rogers was primarily a follower of Rousseau (Man is basically good but has been corrupted by society), he contrasted his theory with what he called Freud's Augustinian view. The following Rogerian considerations make sense if one believes that man is inherently good: (1) if man is good, nothing need be added and nondirection (if not neutrality) makes sense; (2) goals and aims are built in to the individual and so the problem of goals rightly becomes peripheral and goals are important only as signposts of the developmental process; (3) most value questions can be ignored, since the client will arrive at the proper values if the obstacles are removed; and (4) problems of society and the individual must arise at a supraindividual level, for it is society that corrupts and not man. The Freudian-Augustinian view, in contrast, views man not as essentially good but as evil, or at least as neutral with potential for evil. If one holds this view of man, the following premises would make sense: (1) a neutral role on the part of the counselor cannot be justified, for if the counselee has any tendency to move in other than positive directions, he must not be permitted to follow his own impulses; (2) goals become vitally important, for if goals are not built into the individual to be released in the counseling process they must derive from counseling in some more fundamental sense; and (3) it therefore cannot be taken for granted that value problems are self-resolving within the counseling process.

Rogers, reacting to the above article, objected mildly to the use of categories (in that they destroy uniqueness) but was pleased with the philosophical focus of the article.

> I feel pleased that such a discussion in print calls attention to the value orientation, to the philosophical substratum, of every form of psychotherapy. One cannot engage in psychotherapy without giving operational evidence of an underlying value orientation and view of human nature. It is definitely preferable, in my estimation, that such underlying views be open and explicit, rather than covert and implicit.[32]

[31]Donald E. Walker, "Carl Rogers and the Nature of Man," *Journal of Counseling Psychology*, III, 2 (Summer 1956), 89–91.

[32]Carl R. Rogers, "A Note on 'The Nature of Man,'" *Journal of Counseling Psychology*, IV, 3 (Fall 1957), 199.

He then sought to clarify his own position.

> I do not discover man to be well characterized in his basic nature by such terms as fundamentally hostile, antisocial, destructive, evil. I do not discover man to be, in his basic nature, completely without a nature, a *tabula rasa* on which *anything* may be written, nor malleable putty which can be shaped into *any* form. I do not discover man to be essentially a perfect being, sadly warped and corrupted by society. In my experience I have discovered men to have characteristics which seem inherent in his species, and the terms which have at different times seemed to me descriptive of these characteristics are such terms as positive, forward-moving, constructive, realistic, trustworthy.[33]

Kemp[34] involved himself in the same discussion on the nature of man by responding to Rogers's reply. He placed emphasis upon the spiritual aspect of man's nature, urging that this is necessary to a view that embraces the "whole" person. This, in Mowrer's terminology, is the "something more" of man's existence. Kemp criticized Rogers for identifying freedom with reason. "Neither Rogers or Freud recognized that man is free to violate both the necessities of nature and the logical systems of reason."[35] Man's freedom can be used either constructively or destructively. He pointed to a growing consensus that the counselor's beliefs make up a basic and integral part of the counseling relationship and that these include the natural, the rational, *and* the spiritual aspects of man's nature.

It is only natural that counseling philosophy would reflect the democratic ideology of our culture, and so there does seem to be agreement upon certain key principles of this ideology by both those who would be more active in expressing values in counseling and those who would be more passive. The following is an expression of such agreed-upon principles:

1. The belief that human life, happiness, and well-being are to be valued above all else.
2. The assertion that man is master of his own destiny, with the right to control it in his own interests in his own way.
3. The determination that the dignity and worth of each person shall be respected at all times and under all conditions.
4. The assumption of the right of individual freedom; the recognition of

[33] *Ibid.*, p. 200.
[34] C. Gratton Kemp, "Another Note on Counseling and the Nature of Man," Comments and Letters, *Journal of Counseling Psychology*, VIII, 2 (Summer 1961), 186–188.
[35] *Ibid.*, p. 187.

the right of each person to think his own thoughts and speak his own mind.[36]

In addition to the particular view of the nature of man held, the main differences in approach to values in the counseling relationship seem to stem also from the particular interpretation of the subjectivity or objectivity of value. If values are entirely subjective in nature, it would seem that there would be little need for any sort of external confrontation of values in counseling. However, if values are at least somewhat objective, it would seem logical that becoming aware that such values exist would be an important learning, for one would not be able to choose that of which he was not aware.

We shall now turn to a discussion of various approaches to values in counseling. The following categories are not to be interpreted rigidly but rather as groupings used to aid in understanding the various approaches taken. No one can completely delete the objective or subjective side of value. However, certain theorists have a tendency to emphasize one aspect more than the other. They are grouped according to this tendency.

### Active Approaches

Williamson, in a series of articles, tended to emphasize the objectivist approach to values as well as a neutral view of man—that is, he viewed man as neither good or bad but capable of developing in either direction. He expressed a fear of extreme individualism central to certain counseling philosophies as well as an extreme togetherness that would stifle individuality. He advocated a dual commitment to both the individual and society. His concern with objective values seems clear in his view of the counselor as a representative of authority (although one that is loving), to bring about conformity to law and order.[37] He viewed "forced counseling" as not necessarily bad. Again, his emphasis on client's being confronted by external values is evident. In the loving relationship, the counselee (misbehaving) must come to understand his relationship to authority and thus come to accept new values. Williamson made it clear repeatedly that the counselor is not neutral, that he is on the side of morality and law and order. He also recognized the subjective side of value experience and saw a need for a balance between inner and outer authorities. The counselor is repre-

---

[36] Patterson, *Counseling and Psychotherapy*, p. 57, quoting Hand's postulates.
[37] E. G. Williamson, "The Fusion of Discipline and Counseling in the Educative Process," *Personnel and Guidance Journal*, XXXIV, 2 (October 1955), 74–79.

sentative of the right kind of freedom, freedom with responsibility. Williamson strongly emphasized that the counselor is "obligated" to help the client discover and commit himself to a value system. In so doing, the counselor does not impose his values upon the client but aids by "teaching" the client various value options from which he then makes his own choice. The counselor should "educate" the client to follow a course that is "decent, honest, moral, and humane." The counselor "teaches" values by teaching a rational approach to problem-solving by weighing the probable outcomes of choices and by teaching responsibility as well as the privilege of choice. The client also will learn values indirectly through the counseling process. The counselor's every action would be indicative of some value, either implicit or explicit. The counselor must be aware of his value commitments, must constantly examine them and their effect upon the counseling process, and should not be afraid to make them explicit when appropriate. The counselor is always an influence upon the client in the choice of a value orientation, but the client always makes his own choice. Williamson emphasized the "search" as the most important experience in dealing with values. He viewed all education as being a quest for value orientations.

> I hold the view that, with regard to character formation, education should function to *introduce* each student to "role-models" from which he *may* select the ones which he considers to be appropriate to his aspirations and on whose pattern he builds his own life —introduces, not indoctrinates, imposes, or requires slavish acceptance.[38]

> On some occasions, the relationship may be characterized as direct teaching through explicit explanations, suggestions of possible hypotheses, assistance in searching for relevant facts (aptitudes, interests, motives, etc.) that illuminate the counselee's problems, and so on. On other occasions, the teaching method may be one of friendly, encouraging listening. And, not infrequently, the counselee takes the posture of a teacher of himself.[39]

In another article Williamson dealt with the value options available to clients in regard to values chosen or adopted by an individual as a basis for his life style. He views the counseling process as a key

---

[38]Williamson, "The Counselor as Technique," *Personnel and Guidance Journal*, XLI, 2 (October 1962), 108–111.

[39]Williamson, "Value Orientation in Counseling," *Personnel and Guidance Journal*, XXXVI, 8 (April 1958), 522.

locus for the teaching of values. The counselee should become aware of the values he lives and should be made aware of possible value alternatives. The counselor is active in the process:

> Essentially, incorporating the problem of value choice into counseling practices requires that we become thoughtful philosophers and logicians and that we learn more complex techniques of conversing with students about complex concepts and questions involved in the pursuit of the good life.[40]

He lists eight systems of value hierarchies and advocates that counselors become "more sophisticated and mature" in understanding the ramifications of philosophy. The counselor needs to explicate his own value hierarchy so that the student can perceive him as a possible role model.

Berdie expressed agreement with Williamson's position. He stated that

> it is strange that psychologists who are kin to those who contend that all of our problem-solving abilities, perceptions, and bodily reactions are influenced by our attitudes and beliefs, are the same ones who contend the values and attitudes of the counselor should or can play a minimum role in counseling.[41]

He added that the counselor should attempt to select employment in an institution that would be acceptant of his own values and needs.

It is apparent from the following statement that Sorenson's thinking also is similar to that of Williamson's:

> Perhaps everyone will agree that it is the function of the school to help the individual increase the number of alternatives available to him. This concept, that the school generally, and counselors in particular, should help the individual to increase the number of choices available to him now and in the future, seems to me to constitute one of the major ethical assumptions underlying the profession of school counseling.[42]

Samler also takes a strong position for active involvement with values on the part of the counselor. He states that "intervention" by the counselor in the client's values is an actuality and should be accepted as a necessary part of the process. (In a footnote he suggests

[40]Williamson, "Value Options and the Counseling Relationship," *Personnel and Guidance Journal*, XLIV, 6 (February 1966), 620.

[41]Ralph Berdie, "Counseling Principles and Presumptions," *Journal of Counseling Psychology*, VI, 3 (Fall 1959), 179.

[42]Garth Sorenson, "Pterodactyls, Passenger Pigeons, and Personnel Workers," *Personnel and Guidance Journal*, XLIII, 5 (January 1965), 432.

that "intervention" is a stronger word than he intended but that it is a close approximation.) He further states that such intervention is beyond dispute and is accomplished by means of a basic relationship technique. One learns values by experiencing and not by exhortation. (One could question whether this is always the case. Whereas it is true in counseling that such exhortation causes defensive reactions in the client, it seems possible that exhortation at times could also be *experienced* as meaningful.) Intervention must be based upon a scientifically validated value model, and the counselor must be careful to bring his values to awareness.

> We must examine our present value commitments and carry them sharply into awareness, on the light of our growing knowledge of human behavior we must ourselves map the country and travel a road of our own choosing. We should be able to accept without quibbling the objective in counseling of modification of client behavior and therefore of attitudes and values. With the purpose unequivocally clear our task remains that of determining how it can best be accomplished whatever our present commitments.[43]

Collins is another who expresses an active approach to values in counseling. He refers to the counselor as a "value catalyst"—that is, one who encourages the examination of values by students. In order to qualify for such a role, the counselor must have a tough and logical mind, have a catholic education including psychology, sociology, and philosophy. "What is being said here is that a counselor working with students in value-choice must be an intellectual, not a moralist; a man qualified by education, sensitivity, and insight to presume to be a dispenser of wisdom."[44]

Fullmer and Bernard also suggest an active approach on the part of the counselor when they state that "the age of permissivism is giving way to a rebirth of realism in psychology and education,"[45] and "counselors must know how to give direction to, and specify purposes for, individuals."[46] Because it is impossible for counselors to conceal their values and because they are in reality in a position of influence upon the youngsters, the counselor should use this influence toward a proper end. Throughout the book they reiterate their theme of

---

[43]Joseph Samler, "Change in Values: A Goal in Counseling," *Journal of Counseling Psychology*, VII, 1 (Spring 1960), 36.

[44]Charles C. Collins, "Junior College Counseling: A Critical View," *Personnel and Guidance Journal*, XLIII, 6 (February 1965), 549.

[45]Daniel W. Fullmer and Harold W. Bernard, *Counseling: Content and Process* (Chicago: Science Research Associates, Inc., 1964), p. 14.

[46]*Ibid.*, p. 15.

*interrupt* (the life stream)-*intervene-influence.* They advocate that the counselor assist youngsters to develop a more mature system of values. "The focus of the counseling process is to help the counselee develop a mature way of valuing, based on his own internal, intrinsic worth."[47]

The group of therapists known as the Action therapists[48] (mentioned in Chapter 4 and including Wolpe, Salter, Stampfl, the followers of Skinner, and others) also falls within the more direct group. Based upon conditioning theory, either classical or operant, the therapist assumes the responsibility for what takes place as well as for the end result and focuses upon manipulating the environment (including the verbalizations of the therapist, which are considered not for their meaning but just as another set of stimuli) in such a way as to produce desirable behavior change in the client. Because the great emphasis of these approaches has been on rigorous experimental science, it is not too surprising that there has been little attention given to questions of value. To the "hardheaded" scientist, facts are facts and values are the loose ambiguities of a mystical humanism. But this does not excuse the Action therapist from facing the issue. London lays it on the line when he says:

> The lack of overt concern with social philosophy or some hypothetical moral order does not free the Action therapist from any involvement in these issues. Indeed, the fact that he is so courageous (or stupid) as to himself assume responsibility for his work, must make him more alert to the implications it has for the social order and his own, as well as his patient's role in it.[49]

---

[47] *Ibid.*, p. 138.

[48] See J. Wolpe, *Psychotherapy by Reciprocal Inhibition* (Stanford: Stanf University Press, 1958); J. Wolpe and A. A. Lazarus, *Behavior Therapy Techniqu* (New York: Pergamon Press, 1966); A. Salter, *Conditioned Reflex Therapy* (New Y Creative Age Press, 1949); Perry London, *The Modes and Morals of Psychothel y* (New York: Holt, Rinehart, and Winston, 1967), particularly "An Epitaph for Ins t; Action Therapy," pp. 70–125 and "Commentary on Chapter 5," pp. 234–256; F. Skinner, *Science and Human Behavior* (New York: The Macmillan Co., 195 I. Goldiamond, "Stuttering and Fluency as Manipulatable Operant Response Classe in L. Krasner and L. P. Ullman (eds.), *Case Studies in Behavior Modification* (New rk: Holt, Rinehart, and Winston, 1965); I. Goldiamond, "Self-control Procedures ir er-sonal Behavior Problems," in R. Ulrich, T. Stachnik, and J. Mabry (eds.), *Con l of Human Behavior* (Glenview: Scott, Foresman and Co., 1966); and W. Isa , J. Thomas, and I. Goldiamond, "Application of Operant Conditioning to Reinstate rbal Behavior in Psychotics," *Journal of Speech and Hearing Disorders,* XXV (1960), -12.

[49] Perry London, *The Modes and Morals of Psychotherapy* (New York: Holt, Rinehart, and Winston, 1964), pp. 124, 125.

And again:

> No matter how much he specifies his goals, or limits his attack
> to the alleviation of clear-cut symptoms, the fact remains that some
> symptoms of dysfunction are sources of psychological distress pre-
> cisely because they are rooted in what may equally well be seen as
> systems of meaning; and whenever this happens, an effective therapy
> is likely either to change behavior to satisfy a meaning system or
> change the system to justify a behavior. Even the fact that meaning
> can be described as a semantic imposition on reality, and that lan-
> guage, indeed thought itself, can be construed as a collection of
> conditioned responses so gross that they always involve some move-
> ment of the skeletal musculature has, finally, no bearing on the
> case.[50]

Glasser[51] is another who advocates a direct approach. Basing his
theory upon the concept that all misbehavior is irresponsibility rather
than mental illness, he, then, advocates the teaching of responsibility
as the main emphasis in psychotherapy. According to Glasser, to
become responsible is to learn to fulfill the two basic psychological
needs with which psychotherapists are concerned: *"the need to love
and be loved and the need to feel that we are worthwhile to ourselves
and to others."* Ignoring the past and focusing upon the present and
future, the process of therapy consists of three stages:

> First, there is the involvement; the therapist must become so
> involved with the patient that the patient can begin to face reality
> and see how his behavior is unrealistic. Second, the therapist must
> reject the behavior which is unrealistic but still accept the patient
> and maintain his involvement with him. Last, and necessary in vary-
> ing degrees depending upon the patient, the therapist must teach the
> patient better ways to fulfill his needs within the confines of reality.[52]

On what basis does the therapist judge behavior to be realistic
or unrealistic? In answering this question, the particular therapist's
value system must come into play. In reality therapy such a judgment
would be based upon Glasser's definition of responsibility—"the ability to fulfill one's needs, and to do so *in a way that does not deprive
others of the ability to fulfill their needs."*[53] Irresponsibility then
follows from the reverse of this definition. The categorical imperative
for reality therapy seems to be the following:

[50]*Ibid.*, p. 123, 124.
[51]William Glasser, *Reality Therapy: A New Approach to Psychiatry* (New York:
Harper and Row, 1965).
[52]*Ibid.*, p. 21.
[53]*Ibid.*, p. 13.

> We believe that almost all behavior which leads to fulfilling our needs within the bounds of reality is right, or good, or moral behavior, according to the following definition: *When a man acts in such a way that he gives and receives love, and feels worthwhile to himself and others, his behavior is right or moral.*[54]

In the process of therapy, the therapist's values become directly involved as an important part of the process. The therapist plays the role of value catalyst as well as model of responsibility.

> The therapist must be a very responsible person—tough, interested, human, and sensitive. He must be able to fulfill his own needs and must be willing to discuss some of his own struggles so that the patient can see that acting responsibily is possible though sometimes difficult. Neither aloof, superior, nor sacrosanct, he must never imply that what he does, what he stands for, or what he values is unimportant. He must have the strength to become involved, to have his values tested by the patient, and to withstand intense criticism by the person he is trying to help.[55]

There is, however, the recognition that it is the patient who must face up to his own values, and this is done as the therapist helps him to confront himself and his own ideas of responsibility. "The patient rather than the therapist must decide whether or not his behavior is irresponsible and whether he should change it."[56] "The skill of therapy is to put the responsibility upon the patient and, after involvement is established, to ask him why he remains in therapy if he is not dissatisfied with his behavior."[57]

Glasser further advocated that feelings of worth are closely tied to one's ability to maintain satisfactory standards of behavior. This, then, means that when one works with problems concerning an individual's feelings of worth he has entered the realm of morality. Values, then, become an important part of the therapy process. Interests, hopes, fears, opinions, and values (defined by Glasser as the individual's own personal ideas of right or wrong) become central to the process:

> We must open up his life, talk about new horizons, expand his range of interests, make him aware of life beyond his difficulties. . . .

[54] *Ibid.*, p. 57.
[55] *Ibid.*, p. 22.
[56] *Ibid.*, p. 28.
[57] *Ibid.*, p. 29.

*When values, standards, and responsibility are in the background, all discussion is relevant to therapy.*[58]

Glasser thus confronts the problem of morality in psychotherapy very directly and boldly:

> Admittedly, the introduction of morality into psychotherapy may draw criticism from many sources. Some people argue that a great strength of conventional psychiatry is that it does not involve itself with this age-old question. It would be easier for us if we could avoid the issue also, but we cannot. People come to therapy suffering because they behave in ways that do not fulfill their needs, and then ask if their behavior is wrong. Our job is to face this question, confront them with their total behavior, and *get them to judge* the quality of what they are doing. We have found that unless they judge their own behavior, they will not change. We do not claim that we have discovered the key to universal right or that we are experts in ethics. We do believe, however, that to the best of our ability as responsible human beings, we must help our patients arrive at some decision concerning the moral quality of their behavior.[59]

An important question here would be whether or not the therapist has the right to influence the individual along his own or society's conception of what is right or wrong. In critique of Glasser's point of view, Rollo May had this to say:

> Since . . . the distinction is not made between the moral standards of the patient and those of the therapist, the stage is set for the values of the therapist to be enforced upon the patient at worst, and at best the mores of society to be handed over to the patient under the caption of "adjustment" and "mental health." I understand Dr. Glasser's therapy was worked out originally in his function as psychiatrist in an institution for delinquent girls. This makes sense: the psychopathic personality is the one clinical type which is agreed to be without "conscience" to begin with, and cannot be reached without developing in the patient some social sense. But to extend this type of therapy to every kind of patient is hopelessly to confuse the whole problem of neurosis and mental illness, and to make the therapist society's agent for the destruction of the patient's autonomy, freedom, inner responsibility, and passion.[60]

But is it not possible that the individual still can remain free to choose, even when confronted by the therapist's idea of what is "good"? Could it be that the individual has already decided against his

[58] *Ibid.*, p. 31.
[59] *Ibid.*, p. 56.
[60] Rollo May, *Psychology and the Human Dilemma* (Princeton: D. Van Nostrand, 1967), p. 181.

present value system when he enters therapy?

Albert Ellis[61] is another who fits within the direct approach. Self-defeating behavior, according to Ellis, results from an irrational and inconsistent belief system, which produces anxiety (self-blame) and hostility (blame of others). The individual perpetuates irrational beliefs within himself by means of self-indoctrination, which includes a pessimistic evaluation of himself. Ellis's A-B-C theory expresses that the anger or hostility experienced at point C where the individual becomes upset is not due to the external stimulus which is point A, but is rather a result of the "nonsense" the individual tells himself (point B) about what happened at point A. The task of the therapist is to "deindoctrinate" or "depropagandize" the individual, which involves a direct attack upon the individual's irrational belief system. As Ellis puts it:

> I consistently persuade and argue the patient out of his firmly held irrational and inconsistent beliefs. And I unhesitatingly *attack* his neurosis-creating ideas and attitudes after first demonstrating how and why they exist.[62]

Another part of the process consists in teaching the individual a new existentialist oriented philosophy of life, and Ellis apparently assumes that this is what individuals *ought* to believe.

> I vigorously attack the notion that his intrinsic value to himself depends on the usual socially-promulgated criteria of success, achievement, popularity, service to others, devotion to God, and others.[63]

He recognizes the danger of the therapist's being authoritarian in a pernicious way[64] but feels that the danger is minimized by the therapist's being aware of the possibility. But the therapist has the right to let his values be fully known in the therapeutic session.

> First of all, being a human being, he [the therapist] must have values; and it is pointless to pretend that he doesn't. Secondly, being well trained and presumably little disturbed himself, there is a good chance that he will tend to have saner, more workable values than his patients, and that he will be able to present these in a reasonably objective, unpunitive, understanding manner. Thirdly, since he will

---

[61]Albert Ellis, *Reason and Emotion in Psychotherapy* (New York: Lyle Stuart, 1962), and "Goals of Psychotherapy," in Alvin Mahrer (ed.), *The Goals of Psychotherapy* (New York: Appleton-Century-Crofts, 1967).

[62]Ellis, in Mahrer, *Goals of Psychotherapy*, p. 213.

[63]*Ibid.*, p. 214.

[64]Ellis, *Reason and Emotion*, p. 367.

consciously tend to communicate his values to his patients, it is better that he do so overtly rather than covertly, with full consciousness of what he is doing. Fourthly, the more open he is about presenting his own values, the more spontaneous and unartificial, the more courageous and committed to his own views, he is likely to be.[65]

The therapist, then, openly proclaims his value system, and for Ellis the key focus is "self-interest" as opposed to "social-interest."[66] It is believed by Ellis that social interest will follow from this rather than precede it.

There are several who represent an Adlerian point of view,[67] another direct approach, and for our purposes we will focus upon the approach of Dreikurs. For Dreikurs, the changing of the value system is essential as a part of psychotherapy. He analyzes the faulty goals of the individual, helps him become aware of them, and then, in the reorientation phase of therapy, makes him aware of more effective goals which Dreikurs bases upon his interpretation of Adler's concept of the "logic of social living."[68] This logic represents basic laws for cooperation based upon a concept of human equality. Every individual has a basic need to belong, and if he cannot belong in useful ways he will try to achieve belonging through being "useless." "The goal of psychotherapy is more than emotional adjustment; it is actually social adjustment."[69] However:

> Adjustment ... means not mere conformity to existing standards, but the movement toward an improved social organization

[65] *Ibid.*

[66] *Ibid.*, p. 322.

[67] Rudolf Dreikurs, "Goals of Psychotherapy," in Mahrer (ed.), *Goals of Psychotherapy*; Don Dinkmeyer, "Contributions of Teleoanalytic Theory and Techniques to School Counseling," *Personnel and Guidance Journal*, XLVI, 9 (May 1968), 898–902; Don Dinkmeyer, "Developmental Counseling in the Elementary School," *Personnel and Guidance Journal*, XLV, 3 (November 1966), 262–266; Rudolf Dreikurs, "The Adlerian Approach to Psychodynamics," in Morris Stein (ed.), *Contemporary Psychotherapies* (New York: The Free Press, 1961), pp. 60–79, and "The Adlerian Approach to Therapy," in *Contemporary Psychotherapies*, pp. 80–93; Rudolf Dreikers, *Psychodynamics, Psychotherapy, and Counseling* (Chicago: Alfred Adler Institute, 1967), especially "Goals in Therapy," pp. 103–112, and "Psychotherapy as Correction of Faulty Social Values," pp. 113–123; Marven O. Nelson, "Individual Psychology as a Basis for the Counseling of Low Achieving Students," *Personnel and Guidance Journal*, XLVI, 3 (November 1967), pp. 283–287.

[68] Alfred Adler, *Social Interest: A Challenge to Mankind* (New York: Putnam, 1939).

[69] Mahrer, *Goals in Psychotherapy*, p. 104.

which will better fulfill the requirements of the "ironclad logic of social living."[70]

The goal then is to aid the individual to accept values based upon cooperation in place of values inimicable to cooperation.

Four such attitudes with their counterparts are: "1) social interest—hostility; 2) confidence in others—distrust and suspicion; 3) self-confidence—inferiority feelings; 4) courage—fear."[71] Common mistaken social values are the desire for self-elevation, perfectionism, fear of mistakes, personal success, and overemphasis upon reason and objectivity. Such mistaken values war against the movement toward usefulness in the individual.

Other subsidiary goals are the formation of a satisfactory therapeutic relationship with the patient, helping the patient to restore faith in himself, and the encouragement of realization of inner freedom.

> Inner freedom and social interest are not contradictory, but supplementary. Only a free person can truly be a social person, not the victim of social and other pressures, but a free agent as a social being.[72]

The achievement of a sense of belonging is the key motivational factor for the individual, and the achievement of social interest, including social usefulness, is the key goal.

### Less Active Approaches

Perhaps the most dramatic evidence of the move in counseling from a position of neutrality to a more active recognition of value influence is to be found in the recent writings of Rogers. Rogers has moved to a recognition of value influence in the counseling process. "One cannot engage in psychotherapy without giving operational evidence of an underlying value orientation and view of human nature. It is definitely preferable, in my opinion, that such underlying views be open and explicit, rather than covert and implicit."[73] The approach, however, is still cautious.

> I think that I would be in total agreement with the notion that we do have a value impact on the people with whom we deal. The important question is: "What values do we hold and what is that

---

[70]Dreikurs, *Psychodynamics, Psychotherapy, and Counseling*, p. 114.
[71]*Ibid.*, p. 115.
[72]Mahrer, *Goals in Psychotherapy*, p. 111.
[73]Rogers, "A Note on 'The Nature of Man,' " p. 199.

impact?" It seems to me as I have tried to puzzle over this issue—and I am sure my own thinking has changed and will continue to change on it—that the imposition of lesser values is philosophically most dubious. I don't know by what right I, as a counselor, have any earthly business imposing my plans, choices, or values on the person with whom I work. Yet there is one value which, if held by the counselor, can become predominant in the situation without running into that philosophical difficulty; that is, if the counselor truly values the self-directed development of this individual and that's a value I wouldn't hesitate to hold in a relationship with a client. It's a value which, from my point of view, I would see no harm in being present in the relationship. On the other hand, if it becomes something quite different, that I value being scholarly and he doesn't, for example, then I think one can be strongly criticized, at least from the philosophical point of view, for imposing those values on the individual.[74]

Patterson indicates this change in Rogers's thinking also when he states:

The proposal that the counselor not only should be aware of and has a right to his own moral attitudes and values, but should sometimes express them in the counseling relationship, is consistent with recent developments in client-centered thinking. Stressing that the therapist should be himself in this relationship with the client, Rogers in an unpublished paper suggests that the therapist should express his own feelings as he experiences them.[75]

Arbuckle indicates agreement with Rogers when he holds that the basic central core of the counselor's value system must rest in the "integrity and the dignity and the rights of the individual man over all else."[76] In Arbuckle's view, values are very much a part of the person and should not be viewed as something separate and external. This is the existential view that "puts man above the culture, existence above essence, individual morality above legal morality."[77] He questions the assumption that the teacher who is in possession of a value not possessed by the client or student should teach this value to the student. He further questioned whether it is possible for the counselor

---

[74]Rogers, in Willis E. Dugan (ed.), *Counseling Points of View* (Minneapolis: University of Minnesota Press, 1959), p. 31.

[75]Patterson, *Counseling and Psychotherapy*, p. 73.

[76]Dugald S. Arbuckle, *Counseling: Philosophy, Theory and Practice* (Boston: Allyn and Bacon, 1965), p. 265.

[77]*Ibid.*, p. 266.

to accept the client and at the same time to view him as having inadequate values. Arbuckle's position is highly subjectivist, implying that all values must come from somewhere within man rather than from preexisting truths and values. The supreme value to Arbuckle seems to be freedom.

> The existentialist would feel that the individual may live in a physical world which is, in a sense, determined, but the human individual, the existential self, the spirit of man, is not bound by any set of determined chains. Man basically *is* free, and any man can come to learn and to grow and to become the free person he is. This is the purpose of counseling—to help the individual to loosen himself from his deterministic shackles, and to come to realize and to see what he has always had—choice and freedom.[78]

The counselor who holds to this value, according to Arbuckle, will view the world in which we live as relative rather than absolute.

One can question the tenability of a strict subjectivist position on the basis of how the individual comes to know his values. To say that values are learned means that they originally come from the culture. It is true also to say that man creates his own values, but he does not create them from nothing. He, in a sense, discovers them, but also creates them, for the meaning he attaches to them will be unique to him. Values, like good music, prove themselves within culture. The poor or useless become sifted out and the better or useful are carried on. Each generation does not have to create tools and ideas anew. Neither do values have to be reinvented; this is true of normative as well as instrumental values. Men create meanings for themselves from what already may be present by interacting with the value possibilities and choosing those that have the most meaning to them in terms of their perception of truth and according to their constructive intent. They then also become responsible for their choice. This is evidently what Curran was referring to when he stated that to discover the old values that are still valid for our day will

> free us from the more recent, possibly Kantian, ethical concept that all personal values must be imposed from without which has come not to mean either by parents, society or even more threatening and dangerous, by the state. It would restore again the possibility of starting out . . . on a thrilling personal pursuit of oneself in a fierce

[78]Arbuckle, "Existentialism in Counseling: The Humanist View," *Personnel and Guidance Journal*, XLIII, 6 (February 1965), 562.

and independent search for reasonable self-values and yet allow that one would ultimately come by this process, not to violent rebellion and anarchy, but to ancient and secure traditional values.[79]

Although Arbuckle did not like the idea of external values, he seemed to be saying much the same thing when he said that the values chosen by an individual "might be like those of yesterday, or they might be like those of tomorrow, but man lives his life and creates his values. He never goes back to what once was, although he may become like what once was."[80] For Arbuckle it is the individual and his choice that is the important point.

To be one-sided in favor of subjectivism is to fail to see that there is an objective side to the value experience. This may bear with it the danger of becoming lost in meaninglessness, especially if it becomes coupled to conformity, to following a crowd, in order merely to find security from belonging. As Lowe put it:

> The dilemma of culturalism is that it allows itself to be caught in a vicious circle—our society can be like a dog following its tail. If there is nothing external that it can follow, it is doomed to meander meaninglessly in circles. The hope for the world is in following after the most sublime, and not after the most painfully obvious.[81]

Rogers has been criticized for not recognizing the external aspects of value in his theorizing. He has claimed a positive force that comes from *within* man and drives him toward self-actualization. Lowe is one of these critics.

> Humanistic psychology can first of all be criticized for absolutizing American activism when it is only a cultural phenomenon. Rogers may tell us quite open-mindedly that he has discovered a drive towards self-assertiveness in all his clients, but he does not tell us how many of these clients were unrelated in any way to the middle class, which judges personal worth by the amount of achievement. What Rogers boasts of so proudly as self-actualization may be but the pathology of a culture whose members are frightened at being cut off from past traditions and rush pellmell into the future, as if they were animals in stampede. Today the absolute nature of self-

---

[79]Charles A. Curran, "Some Ethical and Scientific Values in the Counseling Therapeutic Process," *Personnel and Guidance Journal*, XXXIX, 1 (September 1960), 15–20.

[80]Arbuckle, *Counseling: Philosophy, Theory and Practice*, p. 272.

[81]Lowe, "Value Orientations," pp. 687–693.

actualization seems threatened on the one hand by the corporation, which, in the organization man, grinds out its own cultural type, and on the other hand by increasing contact with other cultures, which are in many ways superior to our own even if they produce little change over many centuries.[82]

Each man is very much a part of his culture and one cannot escape this fact. Although what Lowe says may be true, it is likely that self-acceptance plays an important part in Rogers's successes in psychotherapy. If this be the case, it is necessary to ask what it is in the way of values that a person accepts within himself and whether these come solely from within.

Green,[83] another critic of Rogers on this point, speaks also in regard to the derivation of these values. He views movement in client-centered therapy not as growth but as retrogression. Rather than moving forward, the client moves backward to a deeper acceptance of the norms he had learned earlier and in this process becomes emancipated, in that the code of morals now becomes his own rather than the detached "musts" of his parents. The client accepts the code as his own choice and no longer needs to rebel further because of value conflicts. Client-centered therapy as representative of a democratic-individualistic-liberalistic tradition subtly leans toward the reinforcement of specific social roles and goals of this ideology.

> If the individual has a modicum of insight into himself and his problems he will be likely to make a choice of goals wisely, Rogers asserts. This is tautological, for what is the criterion for "wisdom" if it is not a choice of goals that are socially and morally approved both by the therapist and the persons and groups with whom the client is currently interacting.[84]

From studying some of Rogers's typescripts of his counseling sessions, Green went on to indicate that in spite of the fact that "Rogers claims that the therapist must possess no moralistic or judgmental attitude whatsoever, it is interesting that in every *single* case he describes as successful the client always attaches himself to goals, or accepts roles, that would meet the hearty approval of any Methodist minister."[85]

> What client-centered therapy does is allow free expression of moral conflicts in an atmosphere that is permissive of hostile verbali-

---

[82] *Ibid.*, p. 690.
[83] Green, "Social Values and Psychotherapy," p. 212.
[84] *Ibid.*
[85] *Ibid.*

zations against those imposing moral norms, and at the same time, through the imposition of "limits," made sufficiently tense to frustrate the self-aggrandizement tendencies. *The client who has sufficiently incorporated early moral norms of conduct, learning that he does not have to continue fighting against them in this permissive yet limited relationship, after talking out his aggressiveness and hostility, allows socially acceptable roles and goals, incorporated prior to the development of the specific self-aggrandizement trend, to become reincorporated at a deeper level of the self.* Very simply, what client-centered therapy does is set the stage for a heightening of the battle between early conscience and later "selfish" strivings.[86]

One can also equally criticize the extreme objectivist position. The objectivist counselor would, on the basis that values are all external, seek to impose them upon the client in a teaching or indoctrinating manner. One cannot deny the importance of choosing one's own values, of creating meaning from one's unique experience, but neither can one deny that our experience takes place in relationship to a culture that is external and that it imposes itself upon us—that is, confronts us with value options.

Barry and Wolf also took what might be called a cautious approach to dealing with values in counseling. It was their contention that value judgments should not be expressed by the counselor in counseling. Since such judgments can be expressed either verbally or nonverbally, the counselor must be aware of what he is communicating. They listed basic principles for their approach to counseling, which they called "Dynamic Developmental Counseling."

1. "No subject is taboo in the counseling session."[87]

2. The individual is given "a chance to discuss what is important to him—his values, motives, feelings, aims, realities—in an absence of value judgments."[88]

3. Understanding is basic and must be "so complete that the counselor can know and feel the values, motives, aims, and emotions of the counselee."[89]

4. The counselee must always "be allowed to travel at his own pace."[90]

5. "The counselee must be allowed to cope with his own problems

[86] *Ibid.*, p. 214.
[87] Ruth Barry and Beverly Wolf, *Motives, Values, and Realities* (New York: Bureau of Publications, Teachers College, Columbia University, 1965), p. 198.
[88] *Ibid.*, p. 199.
[89] *Ibid.*, p. 201.
[90] *Ibid.*, p. 202.

by means of the new learnings that result from the self-understanding and confidence he gains."[91]

The counselee must be free to discuss what he wants to discuss without being judged, for value judgments on the part of the counselor would terminate the counseling because of a negation of understanding. Barry and Wolf stated that

> most school counselors feel that they must go on record as pointing out errors in a youngster's values when and if they occur (from the counselor's point of view) and must stand up and be counted on the side of school values. Perhaps they should, but *never* in the counseling interview.[92]

It was their feeling that the controversy and difficulty over values in the counseling process stems from a failure to distinguish between the teaching and counseling functions. There is a vast difference between these two—the teacher's contribution to learning being much more direct and involving lecturing, informing, and advising. These, to Barry and Wolf, were antithetical to counseling, since the counselor "teaches" in another way and "teaches" other values. He " 'teaches' acceptance, understanding, and faith in the individual by living them in the counseling room."[93]

Smith[94] placed great emphasis upon the counselor's understanding of values, for by understanding what values are as well as their interplay, he can best prevent the introjection of his own value system. The counselor seems best able to understand value interplay when he is sensitive and empathic in the counseling relationship. If the counselor fails to understand the client's perceptions he is most likely to accept client judgments that parallel his own. He suggests that we need better methods for aiding counselors to understand their value systems.

Vaughan[95] stressed existential values similar to Arbuckle's but included more of an objective value orientation. He listed three aims of the existential approach to counseling: fostering freedom within the counselee, improving his encounter with others, and discovering

---

[91]*Ibid.*, p. 203.

[92]*Ibid.*, p. 199.

[93]*Ibid.*, p. 200.

[94]David W. Smith, "Value Systems and the Therapeutic Interview," in Peters and others (eds.), *Counseling: Selected Readings* (Columbus: Charles E. Merrill, 1962), pp. 372–378.

[95]Richard Vaughan, "Existentialism in Counseling: The Religious View," *Personnel and Guidance Journal*, XLIII, 6 (February 1965), 553–557.

meaning for his existence. (One could note in passing that these three goals are similar to the example given by C. S. Lewis.)[96] Vaughan stated that previous counseling theories such as psychoanalysis have presupposed meaning in life (hedonism) and others such as Rogers's have avoided the problem by assuming that the process itself is enough to provide meaning. He viewed freedom as a means of opening the individual to a fuller value experience, including religion. He thus would hold that there are values external to man's experiencing. The counselor must pose the existential questions of death, purpose of life, meaning of suffering, and others. The counselee, however, must always discover his own answers.

We have discussed approaches to values that have tended either more strongly to the objectivist side or to the subjectivist side. We now come to a consideration of some approaches that emphasize a balancing of the subjective and the objective; we refer to them as synthesis approaches.

### Synthesis Approaches

May, from an existentialist position, has taken a broader value orientation, including a balancing of the subjective and objective aspects of value experience. His focus upon the subjective aspect of man's value experience can be readily seen in his discussion of some of Nietzsche's thought.

> One of his most crucial existential emphases is his insistence that the values of *human* life never come about automatically. The human being *can lose his own being by his own choices*, as a tree or stone cannot. Affirming one's own being creates the values of life.[97]

The subjective aspect, however, is not considered in isolation from the objective, that is, of the being who is there to his immediate world.

> The person and his world are a unitary, structural whole; the hyphenation of the phrase being-in-the-world expresses precisely that. The two poles, self and world, are always dialectically related. Self implies world and world self; there is neither without the other, and each is understandable only in terms of the other. It makes no

---

[96]C. S. Lewis, *Mere Christianity* (New York: The Macmillan Co., 1952), pp. 70-71.

[97]Rollo May, Ernest Angel, and Henri F. Ellenberger (eds.), *Existence* (New York: Basic Books, 1958), p. 31.

sense, for example, to speak of man in his world (though we often do) as primarily a spatial relation. The phrase "match *in* a box" does imply a spatial relation, but to speak of a man *in* his home or in his office or in a hotel at the seashore implies something radically different.[98]

And again, "World is the structure of meaningful relationships in which a person exists and in the design of which he participates."[99]

One finds a close similarity between this type of thought and that in Zen Buddhism. Berger[100] related this thought to counseling psychology in an article discussing Zen Buddhism drawn from the writings of Watts and Suzuki. Such thought abhors the interference of Aristotelian dualism with a fuller awareness of experience. Zen views both self and nonself as part of total experience representing a mutual relationship between subject and object. Subject "creates" object and object "creates" subject. Any attachment to form limits and obstructs pure experience. One must be cautioned, however, in carrying similarities beyond this, for they spring from differing philosophical traditions.

May also emphasized that one of the distinguishing characteristics of man is that he "can experience self as subject and object at the same time."[101] He can be aware of having a world and being related to it or with it. Between self and world one's relationship is experienced as meaning.[102] To lose consciousness of either the self or the world is to lose consciousness of the other. This relationship also implies responsibility, for one cannot be a self unless he responds.[103] From this, May drew his definition of freedom growing from this relationship between self and world. "Freedom is the individual's capacity *to know that he is the determined one*, to pause between stimulus and response and thus to throw his weight, however slight it

[98] *Ibid.*, p. 59.

[99] *Ibid.*

[100] Emanuel M. Berger, "Zen Buddhism, General Psychology, and Counseling Psychology," *Journal of Counseling Psychology*, IX, 2 (Summer 1962), 122–127.

[101] May, "Freedom and Responsibility Re-examined," in Esther Lloyd-Jones and Esther M. Westervelt (eds.), *Behavioral Science and Guidance: Proposals and Perspectives* (New York: Bureau of Publications, Teachers College, Columbia University, 1963), pp. 95-110.

[102] See Eugene Gendlin, *Experiencing and the Creation of Meaning* (New York: The Free Press of Glencoe, 1962).

[103] See an interesting discussion of responsibility and its meaning in May, *et al.*, *Existence*, p. 74.

may be, on the side of one particular response among several possible ones."[104]

Because man exists in relation to a world, freedom must always include social responsibility, for freedom is limited by this world. It is a dialectic process—not man *over* the world but man *in* and affected by his world. Values, then, assume relationship between self and world, for "there is no such thing as truth or reality for a living human being except as he participates in it, is conscious of it, has some relationship to it."[105] This relatedness to the world also includes the counselor and is a part of the counseling relationship. May emphasized that the whole topic of the "technical-objective" and the "understanding-subjective" attitudes to counseling has been based on a false dichotomy. A restatement needs to be made upon the basis of the concept of the existence of the client as a *being-in-the-world* and the counselor as a participant in that world.[106]

May viewed values as an important part of counseling and one that cannot be avoided whenever one deals with human beings. However, he viewed these underlying ethical aspects of counseling more in terms of presuppositions concerning what is happening. The counselor must recognize these to avoid imposition, but this does not necessarily mean that an explicit discussion of ethics will come up in the counseling process.

> Values are presupposed in every step the counselee makes in his own integration, but not in the sense that the counselor's values or even society's values are handed over or subtly implied as the only possible ones or the preferred ones. The counselor can best help the counselee arrive at his own values by admitting (though it need not necessarily be verbalized) that he, the counselor, has his own values and has no stake in hiding the fact, but that there is no reason at all that these will be the most meaningful or fitting values for the counselee himself.

> Values should be by definition creative, not static, always emerging and growing, not accepted full-blown. The important thing is to help the other person in his own *act of valuing.*[107]

[104] May, "Freedom and Responsibility," in Lloyd- Jones and Westervelt, p. 103.
[105] May, "The Emergence of Existential Psychology," in May (ed.), *Existential Psychology* (New York: Random House, 1961), p. 17.
[106] *Ibid.*, p. 29.
[107] May, "Freedom and Responsibility," in Jones and Westervelt, pp. 95–110.

The approach, then, to May was a somewhat cautious one of being the Socratic "midwife."

> As Kierkegaard remarked about Socrates, "How rare the magnanimity" of a helper who can be sufficiently concerned with the other person's self-realization and sufficiently free of his own need to dominate that he is willing to be merely an "occasion" for the other's achievement of his own values.[108]

There are a number of other writers who took somewhat of a middle position. Here the emphasis was upon the counselee's choosing his own values, but in relation to a world outside himself. Here there seemed to be more recognition that the counselor has a right to his own values, that he need not hide them, and that being open about them does not imply necessarily that these are best for the counselee.

Mathewson took this approach, as is apparent in the following statement:

> It would seem that certain injunctions might be placed upon the counselor as a professional practitioner. First, his first concern will be to *help his counselee to become a valuing person* in his own right, to understand the values he wants to live by, and to choose and act accordingly. And second, the counselor will reflect and *educatively communicate the kind of fundamental values* that create and sustain a social milieu that enables individuals to become valuing persons in the first place. This means that the counselor cannot be neutral about basic human rights, moral values, and democratic processes.[109]

Mathewson recognized individual values as well as societal values, with a connecting relationship between the two exemplified by his "self-situational" approach upon which he grounds his ideas. Mathewson held that the criteria by which the values of valuing persons can be judged grow from a combination of social requirements, spiritual sanctions, biological demands, individual freedom, and cultural themes. This is a position not unlike that of Edel and his concept of the valuational base. In times of great instability, there is a greater focus upon the individual as the source of value. Again:

---

[108] May, "Historical and Philosophical Presuppositions for Understanding Therapy," in O. Hobart Mowrer (ed.), *Psychotherapy: Theory and Research* (New York: The Ronald Press, 1953), p. 43.

[109] Robert H. Mathewson, *Guidance Policy and Practice* (New York: Harper and Row, 1962), p. 161.

> In times that resemble Greek tragedies, we come back to the center of all human activity, the individual himself, and rely upon there being a sufficient number of relatively autonomous individuals to form nuclei from which health for the whole organism may ultimately spread. ... In such a situation, the counselor, in a humble, helping relationship with striving individuals, may be as close to the bedrock of value orientation as it is possible to get.[110]

Mathewson was not specific as to the approach the counselor would take in dealing with values, but one could infer from most of what is said that the counselor, although he should never impose values, plays an important part in calling attention to value options. For example:

> If there is any social channel through which the individual may learn to serve values beyond himself or may learn to transcend narrower class values for broader cultural outlooks, it is in and through educational opportunity. Thus the counselor may be justified in arousing motivations in individuals that will orient them upon developmental possibilities beyond caste and class, looking toward broader realms of social service.[111]

London[112] is another who assumes a middle approach. He criticizes Insight therapy for leaving the question of morals entirely to the client (a complete subjectivist emphasis), morals that may, at times, and at the extreme, be directly opposed to the counselor's own moral scheme. He further criticized the Action therapists for taking the opposite stance (a thoroughly objectivist one) of basing the moral scheme strictly upon the views of the therapist, even though it may conflict at times with the client's views. He avoids these two extremes by following the model established by Mowrer, which includes a combination of insight and action, based neither upon the client nor the therapist alone as an effective judge of proper goals but rather upon a dual effort to posit "a good life possible only in society." It appears that, cast in this role, the therapist becomes a representative of society, but, in a sense, even more than this. The view of community is an idealistic one of community at its optimum good, and commitment is urged in this direction. The individual is to commit himself to an "ideal" but is to live in the "real" society.[113]

---

[110] *Ibid.*, pp. 162, 163.
[111] *Ibid.*, pp. 49, 50.
[112] London, *Modes and Morals.*
[113] *Ibid.*, p. 143.

London sees the Action therapists as focusing strictly upon symptoms and internal functioning of the individual for which the individual needs a doctor. The Insight therapists focus upon problems of meaning for which individuals need a priest. In between these two problem areas (at a middle level of values) there is overlap where individuals need some of both—they need to learn in what way life could be more meaningful as well as how to live or act toward the resulting goals. Thus, this forms a system comprising both the subjective and objective value considerations.

Barclay,[114] in an examination of five articles and a book criticizing the testing movement, emphasizes that the counselor's values will show in the counseling interview but that it is not the task of the counselor to impose values upon the client. Rather, it is to help the client examine his values and acquire problem-solving ability. In order to assist the client to discover his own values, it is important that the counselor be "open," a characteristic that may be misconstrued by critics as indicative of ambivalence and tolerance for a "drifting value system." This posture, however, is necessary to the client's discovery of his own values. He also stresses the importance of the counselor's understanding philosophy, which has important implications for counselor education programs. Barclay does not see the counselor's "openness" as being a rigid sort of thing that is completely value neutral, for

> a well-trained counselor knows he cannot allow his commitment to the individual to sanction anti-social and illegal behavior. The counselor in the school is dedicated to the proposition that facility in individual problem solving is both beneficial to society and conducive to the highest personal fulfillment in that society.[115]

The way to development of responsibility is paved "through the living example of teachers and counselors who believe in the dignity of the individual and his right to set his own values."[116]

Shoben advocates a return to a recognition of human responsibility as a goal in counseling and in the service of this goal urges an active, Socratic-like role for the counselor in dealing with values. In this role, the counselor is not a scientist but rather a practicing moralist. That is, any consideration of mental health must consider how a man should live, how his needs and values can be reconciled, and how

---

[114]James R. Barclay, "The Attack on Testing and Counseling: An Examination and Reappraisal," *Personnel and Guidance Journal*, XLIII, 1 (September 1964), 6–16.
[115]*Ibid.*, pp. 9, 10.
[116]*Ibid.*, p. 10.

he can properly judge "goodness" or "rightness." The key to the development of human responsibility according to Shoben is understanding. The counselor serves this important function by the encouragement of understanding. This assumes the necessity of certain types of knowledge, and Shoben emphasizes the "humanistic traditions represented in history, literature, and philosophy,"[117] for it is this tradition that aids the definition of the "good life" and guides men's choices. He then recommends an active role for the counselor in the value quest. Rather than playing a nonevaluative role, he suggests that the counselor be more active to the point of evaluating (making value judgments) as well as advice-giving. This, however, is not to be done by strong command but rather by merely offering alternatives as possibilities to be considered. He reemphasizes the point made by Rogers that the counselor who is a "real person" has his own firm value orientation and, being secure, has no need to impose this upon others. From a Socratic orientation, the main goal is the "examined life." Shoben also views the counselor as an important role model, one that he refers to as the "good parent," meaning one who is very actively involved with values but who always cares deeply for the individual. On this point he stresses that "love is not enough" in and of itself. The counseling relationship is merely the means that allows the "working through" to happen. Love is not the end but the base from which other objectives emerge, the main goal of counseling being a "developmental experience."

> From a sought-out respect and regard for the client, the counselor is able to confront him with the more unsavory segments of his character and motivation, to explore with him the fitness of his conduct to his always developing sense of values, and to insist on his examining more closely his implicit purposes, the probable consequences of his methods of persuing them, and the alternatives that are available for his consideration. It is in this kind of confrontation, exploration, and examination that the process of "working through" consists, and it is improbable that it will be accomplished unless it rests on a base of genuine concern.[118]

Krumboltz suggests the need for more than mere understanding and reflection of feeling on the part of the counselor when dealing with certain types of client problems.

[117]Shoben, "Personal Responsibility, Determinism, and the Burden of Understanding," p. 346.
[118]Shoben, "The Counseling Experience as Personal Development," *Personnel and Guidance Journal*, XLIV, 3 (November 1965), 228–229.

Some clients wish only that someone will listen to their problems and try to understand them. Such clients already have all the necessary facts and skills at their command, and need only a genuinely interested listener to help them put the pieces together.

But other clients are not so fortunate. . . . Many are trying to reach serious decisions in their lives in the absence of relevant information or with gross misinformation. Not only do they not know the answers to some vital questions; they do not even know what questions to ask. With such clients, a counselor's understanding is not sufficient. The counselor has to seek out the information he needs in order to arrive at a wise decision.[119]

Neither does this involve a breach of freedom, for as Krumboltz puts it:

Clients want to be influenced by counselors. Their freedom is not increased by the failure of counselors to influence them. Quite the contrary. Their freedom is restricted if the counselor is not willing to use whatever procedures give his clients a better opportunity of achieving their goals.[120]

In another article Krumboltz stresses that it is the client who must choose the goals and the counselor the means.[121] Such goals, however, must be acceptable to the counselor's value orientation. He defines counseling as consisting of "whatever ethical activities a counselor undertakes in an effort to help the client engage in those types of behavior which will lead to a resolution of the client's problems."[122] This may mean that the counselor become involved in an active analysis of values. He lists the following as illustrative of counseling goals in which he may become engaged by involving the client in these procedures:

Generating a list of all possible courses of action.

Gathering relevant information about each feasible alternative course of action.

Estimating the probability of success in each alternative on the basis of the experience of others and projections of current trends.

Considering the personal values which may be enhanced or diminished under each course of action.

---

[119]John D. Krumboltz, "Parable of the Good Counselor," *Personnel and Guidance Journal*, XLIII, 2 (October 1964), 122.

[120]*Ibid.*, p. 123.

[121]Krumboltz, "Behavioral Goals for Counseling," *Journal of Counseling Psychology*, XIII, 2 (Summer 1966), 153–159. He also makes this point in "Behavioral Counseling: Rationale and Research," *Personnel and Guidance Journal*, XLIV, 4 (December 1965), 383–387.

[122]Krumboltz, "Behavioral Counseling."

Deliberating and weighing the facts, probable outcomes and values for each alternative.

Eliminating from consideration the least favorable courses of action. Formulating a tentative plan of action subject to new developments and opportunities.

Generalizing the decision making process to future problems.[123]

At times it may be the task of the counselor to assist the client in the formulation of goals.

Nash[124] examines seven concepts implicit in a philosophy of school counseling: prediction, testing, conformity, efficiency, authority, values, and finitude. He bases his analysis upon the assumption that the problem of human freedom lies at the heart of a philosophy of counseling. In regard to values, he holds that the counselor has the right to explicit value judgments, but for the purpose of self-revelation rather than indoctrination. The counselor must always maintain a respect for the client's right to develop his own value system. It is his contention that judgments made by the counselor in this way do not contradict the concept of positive regard.

Patterson[125] discusses a new trend toward the intentional influence of client values by the counselor, a trend at least partially supported by research evidence. This approach is in direct contrast to the position commonly held by most therapists that the counselor should be careful not to impose his values upon the client. He recognizes that the counselor will and cannot avoid influencing his client, but gives the following reasons why he felt it is probably not justifiable to attempt direct manipulation:

1. While there are no doubt some generally, or even almost universally accepted principles or ethical rules, these do not constitute a philosophy of life.
2. It is too much to expect all counselors to have a fully developed adequate philosophy of life ready to be impressed on the client.
3. The counseling relationship is not the appropriate place for instruction in ethics and a philosophy of life.
4. An individual does not develop a system or code of ethics, or a philosophy of life from one source, or in a short interval of time.
5. It would appear to be best for each individual to develop his own unique philosophy, and not to be deprived of the experience of doing so.

---

[123]Krumboltz, "Behavioral Goals."
[124]Paul Nash, "Some Notes Toward a Philosophy of School Counseling," *Personnel and Guidance Journal*, XLIII, 3 (November 1964), 243–248.
[125]Patterson, *Counseling and Psychotherapy*, chapter 4.

6. We must still accept the right of the client to refuse to accept any system of ethics, or any philosophy of life.[126]

Patterson is careful to say that this does not mean that the counselor will not discuss ethics, values, or philosophy. It is only to say that he will not be concerned about the influence he has upon the client in these directions. He is a constructive influence by "being himself."

It is also possible that the counselor will express his own values, but when so doing he must be careful to identify them as his own without making an outright attempt to impose them upon the client. The counselor may also from time to time supply information concerning values.

> There may also be times when the counselor, whether by request of the client or not, feels it necessary or desirable to inform the client of the attitudes, standards, or values of society, or the ordinary or generally accepted rules of ethics and morality. In a more or less rational problem-solving type of counseling, for example, where there is a lack of information on the part of the client, the counselor may attempt to supply this lack.[127]

Patterson suggests that the approach discussed by him in openly dealing with values has several advantages in counseling.

> By recognizing that the counselor's moral attitudes and values do enter into counseling it prevents the counselor from erroneously believing that he is neutral. Freed from this belief, and the feeling that it is necessary or desirable to be neutral, the counselor is better able to recognize and accept his own values. He then can be aware of them in the counseling relationship; and, when he feels that the counseling relationship would be improved or furthered by his expressing his own attitudes and feelings, he can do so. That is, he can freely be himself, without guilt about doing so, or without feeling that he should not have any feelings. Finally, this approach contributes to the openness of the counseling relationship, without violating its client-centeredness. In fact, the relationship is probably more client-centered.[128]

The counselor does not teach values as such, but he does implement values by an expression of his philosophy of counseling, which is in reality his philosophy of life.

Murphy asks, "Shall personnel and guidance work ... attempt to impart a philosophy of life?" While recognizing that "no one knows enough to construct an adequate philosophy of life," he states that

---

[126] *Ibid.*, pp. 70–71.
[127] *Ibid.*, p. 71.
[128] *Ibid.*

"nevertheless if he who offers guidance is a whole person, with real roots in human culture, he cannot help conveying directly or indirectly to every client what he himself sees and feels, and the perspective in which his own life is lived."[129] He gives three answers to his original question. First, the counselor cannot help transmitting what he is, and, therefore, his personality is far more important than his techniques. Secondly, "It is not true that the wise man's sharing of a philosophy of life is an arrogant imposition upon a defenseless client." Arrogance is rather the attempt to manipulate by certain skills in order to guide "wisely." Third, one system of values is *not* as good as another, or counselors would not have chosen to be counselors. "Those who can guide boys and girls, men and women, into a life full of zest in pursuing personal interests and at the same time serving the larger needs of a cooperative commonwealth are imposing nothing arbitrary; they are giving their clients a sounder as well as a richer life."[130] However, he warned against attempting to guide without a stable philosophy of one's own.

Buhler assumes an active approach to values in counseling. At a Los Angeles study group on values she declared herself "in favor of informative as well as value statements at certain specific occasions. Her rationale is that we live in a time of tremendously fluctuating values with a tremendous, ever-increasing impact of rapid scientific advances on man's interpretation of life's meaning and purpose."[131] The therapist can on occasion "briefly survey for the patient the trends of our time. He can structure for the patient the changes in value orientation and *Weltanschauung* that are taking place and can advise him regarding different possible solutions among which he might choose."[132] The when and the "how" however, need to be established by further research. She formulated general principles that most therapists have in common:

1. Present-day psychotherapists strive to help the patient to a better understanding of himself in order to help him to *face and accept* reality as it is and to *master his own life* better than he did before;
2. Most modern psychotherapists want the patient to *work through his problems by himself* as much as possible, with the therapist being mostly an intermediary in the process of self-understanding, rather than

[129]Gardner Murphy, "The Cultural Context of Guidance," *Personnel and Guidance Journal*, XXIV, 1 (September 1955), 4–9.
[130]*Ibid.*, pp. 8, 9.
[131]Buhler, *Values in Psychotherapy*, p. 25.
[132]*Ibid.*

a teacher or a knowing authority;

3. The present-day therapists base their work mostly on their *personal relationship* with the patient and on the interpretations that they give to the patient's motives, development, affects, and behavior;

4. The therapist's training, experience, and personality that determine this procedure may vary greatly. But regardless of their theoretical bias and their therapeutic approach, they will have to help the patients to cope with their lives, with the goal of *functioning better than before*, of *mastering their lives*, and of conceiving of *life as worthwhile*.[133]

Little has been done to help the counselor in his task of dealing with values in the counseling relationship. Buhler describes the counselor's plight as he faces this complicated task:

1. He is left to his own devices in determining whether the values, value problems, and value conflicts of his patient are healthy or neurotic.

2. He must use his own judgment not only regarding the patient's insight potential but also regarding the factor which we called the patient's value potential and which determines the patient's eventual ability to apply the insight he acquired in action.

3. Furthermore, he must clarify the position he himself wants to take with respect to his patient's value system and value considerations.

4. Apart from this he must have come to terms with the values implied in the theory to which he subscribes and which may not in all respects correspond with his own feelings about things.[134]

The individual counselor is thus left to himself to decide how he will deal with values in counseling. His answer will reflect his own unique philosophy. To reiterate a point made earlier, a point made also by some of the writers in our review of literature, the counselor cannot afford to remain ignorant of his own values and philosophical assumptions.

[133] *Ibid.*, pp. 27, 28.
[134] *Ibid.*

*chapter* 6

# The Counselor and Religious Issues

The question of religious values and their importance has recently been recognized as a crucial problem within education. The need for recognition of moral and spiritual values as an important part of the public school curriculum is emphasized by the Educational Policies Commission of the National Education Association.[1] Also, in the book *Perceiving, Behaving, Becoming* it is stated that

> adequate persons are, among other factors, the product of strong values. The implication seems to be clear, then, that educators must be interested in and concerned with values. Unfortunately, this is not the case in many schools and classrooms today. The emphasis is too often on the narrowly scientific and the impersonally objective. . . . Children often get the idea in school that how they feel and what they think is not very important compared to scientific and objective facts. Without fully realizing it, we have sometimes taught children that personal meanings have no place in the classroom. . . . Education must be concerned with values, beliefs, convictions, and doubts of students.[2]

There is little dispute over the need for teaching values in the public school but rather over how they should be handled. The Commission listed values upon which American people in general agree, but it was in the realm of religion and the part played by it in the transmission of values that much controversy existed. Each denominational group would like to have its particular "way" taught in the public school. The problems this would create are readily recognized when one tries to adapt a common school to a pluralistic society.

---

[1]Educational Policies Commission, *Moral and Spiritual Values in the Public Schools* (Washington, D. C.: National Education Association, 1951).

[2]Association for Supervision and Curriculum Development 1962 Yearbook Committee, Arthur W. Combs, chairman, *Perceiving, Behaving, Becoming*, (Washington, D. C.: National Education Association, 1962).

Whatever position a school takes, it cannot avoid being an influence. "The entire life of the school, every classroom, every teacher, every activity, makes its contribution, *plus or minus*, to the understanding and appreciation of moral values."[3] Education is itself a moral enterprise, for "the aims of education presuppose some ideals of human nature . . . and such ideals are supported by value judgments."[4] Education "has been the means by which the adult generation transmits to the oncoming generation the internal equipment it deems necessary for the good life."[5] According to Malinowski, "the whole system of education is determined by value."[6]

The important question pertains to the school's role in the promotion of values and what this role should be. It is relatively easy to transmit and even to modify knowledge about "things" in the classroom, but knowledge of one's self and of values must come only by unique individual experience.

> Since man, unlike lower animals, has no genetically determined inborn mechanisms for governing inter-personal relations, he has to learn in each generation how to manage with other men; and since he has been on earth only half a million years or so, he is, naturally, still in elementary school so far as learning how to get along with his fellows is concerned.[7]

The individual gains self-knowledge and knowledge of how to get along with others only through interaction with others and, in so doing, learns the how, what, and why of his behavior in its effect and influence upon others.

The question that is important to us pertains to the role of the counselor regarding problems concerning religion. Some therapists, with Freud, would deny the validity of religion but would recognize for at least some people the strength and consistency of a religious philosophy. Walters referred to a letter written by Freud to his friend Oskar Pfister, a Swiss Protestant clergyman who practiced psychoanalysis:

[3]Educational Policies Commission, *Moral and Spiritual Values.*

[4]Herbert Feigel, *Aims of Education for Our Age of Science: Reflectings of a Logical Empiricist,* Fifty-fourth Yearbook of the National Association for the Study of Education (1955), p. 324.

[5]Huston Smith, "Values—Academic and Human," in Marjorie Carpenter (ed.), *The Larger Learning* (Dubuque: William C. Brown, 1960).

[6]Malinowski, quoted by Theodore Brameld, *Cultural Foundations of Education* (New York: Harper and Brothers, 1957), p. 198.

[7]Jules Henry, *Culture Against Man* (New York: Random House, 1963), p. 11.

In the letter Freud complained about the kind of patients who came for analysis, describing them as "often very poor material." "You, on the other hand," he wrote, "have young people with recent conflicts who are attached to you personally, and who are in a suitable state for sublimation. ... You are in the fortunate position of leading them on to God and reconstructing the conditions of earlier times, fortunate at least in the one respect that religious piety stifles neurosis.[8]

However, Freud generally viewed religion as the "universal neurosis."[9] To him, religion was basically nothing but a wish fulfillment. Others, such as Ellis, have viewed religion as a hindrance to mental health and thus something to be attacked in the therapeutic interview.

Others, and their numbers seem to be growing, view religion as being, at least for some people, a healthy force in their lives. Allport, in reacting to Freud's view of religion as the "universal neurosis," made the following exception:

One cannot ... take the religious sentiment, when it exists in a personality, at its face value. A more balanced view of the matter would seem to be this: *sometimes* one cannot take this sentiment at its face value, and sometimes one can. Only a careful study of the individual will tell. In a person in whom the religious factor serves an obviously egocentric purpose—talismanic, bigoted, self-justificatory—we can infer that it is a neurotic, or at least immature, formation in the personality. Its infantile and escapist character is not recognized by the subject. On the other hand, in a person who has gradually evolved a guiding philosophy of life where the religious sentiment exerts a generally normative force upon behavior and confers intelligibility to life as a whole, we infer that this particular ego-formation is a dominant motive and that it must be accepted at its face value.[10]

Walker and Peiffer[11] pointed up a danger in judging points of view solely on the basis of their origins, for this is to evaluate illogically on the mere basis of description. As in Freud's ideas of religion, it is to say that all religion is false because it originates in a wish fulfillment.

[8]Orville S. Walters, "Metaphysics, Religion, and Psychotherapy," *Journal of Counseling Psychology*, V, 4 (Winter 1958), 247.

[9]See Sigmund Freud, *The Future of an Illusion* and *Totem and Taboo*.

[10]Gordon Allport, *Personality and Social Encounter* (Boston: Beacon Press, 1960), p. 104.

[11]Donald E. Walker and Herbert C. Peiffer, "Description, Not Evaluation: A Logical Confusion in Counseling," *Journal of Counseling Psychology*, IV, 2 (Summer 1957), 111, 112.

Allport[12] declared that psychologists (and one might add counselors) have no right to ignore religion when it is a part of so many people's lives. If one is to work with the whole person, his religious beliefs are from time to time going to enter into the process of counseling.

Wrenn[13] viewed psychology and religion as complementary, the former focusing upon the nature of self in life and the latter upon the meaning or significance of life. These functions, however, overlap, and when the religious problems come up in a counseling session, numerous questions are raised. The counselor cannot afford to pretend that religious problems are not a reality, and it is difficult to know how to handle such problems. The counselor can at least recognize and study the significance of religion in personality development, be prepared in advance to deal with these problems as he would with any other, and clarify his own religious feelings and values in order to be more aware of their effect in counseling. In a complex culture it is a must to have a carefully considered value system, for judgments of "rightness" will reflect this system.

Mowrer strongly advocates that psychologists look to religion as an important part of man's life. He feels that psychologists have missed the whole point of religion, the point being that religion has had psychological survival value. He sees a need for psychologists to recognize the "something more" of living rather than to settle for mere bodily survival (with the mind serving the body in this function) as the chief end of man. The "something more" is recognized in a growing trend toward a greater focus upon the mind in its complexity, having its own conditions for survival.[14] These conditions may not only be different from bodily comforts but may even be in conflict with them. Thus, there is and must be a new focus upon value questions.[15]

Walters is another who emphasizes the dangers of ignoring metaphysical aspects of a person's conflicts and the serious limitation this can be to therapy. In dealing with human beings one soon finds himself beyond the limits of science and in the realm of philosophy.

[12]Walters, "Metaphysics, Religion, and Psychotherapy."

[13]C. Gilbert Wrenn, "Psychology, Religion, and Values for the Counselor," *Personnel and Guidance Journal,* XXXVI, 5 (January 1958), 331–334.

[14]See O. Hobart Mowrer, "Some Philosophical Problems in Psychological Counseling," *Journal of Counseling Psychology,* IV, 2 (Summer 1957), 103–111.

[15]See also Mowrer, "Christianity and/or Psychoanalysis?" Unpublished paper presented at the American Personnel and Guidance Association Convention, Boston, Massachusetts, 1963.

Walters speaks of the necessity for the therapist to actively encounter the patient's value system, but at the same time differentiated between the role of the therapist and the role of the priest. "The goal of both professions is to help the patient achieve full self-affirmation. They may collaborate fruitfully, but neither should try to replace the other."[16] He emphasizes the fact that there is no mature science of man but only "doctrines of man." Therapists thus choose not between a scientific as opposed to an unscientific view but from various philosophies. It would be just as difficult for the therapist who is negative and hostile to religion to accept and understand the client's religious meanings and values as it would be for the religiously oriented counselor to accept the atheistic humanist's point of view.

In a symposium on "Religious Factors and Values in Counseling," [17] several writers commented on pertinent factors. Curran drew several parallels between counseling and religion. Counseling and religion have common factors in the sort of relationship formed, namely, a commitment of one's self to another, what in religion would be referred to as love and perhaps in counseling as a deep or total trust or acceptance. (Unconditional positive regard, to use Rogers' term.) This is also similar to relationship to God in religion where all is bared in a total trust. A second common factor involves depth of communication. Third, there is found in each type of relationship love and acceptance, and fourth, a genuine optimism which in religion is expressed as salvation. He further stated that, though there are commonalities, the two relationships are different, but also supplement one another. Religion represents a "third dimension," which is spiritual but nevertheless (as Augustine stated) represents a need in man.

> This third dimension, for the religious man, goes beyond the somatic world of pain and the psychological world of conflict and fear to a Divine commitment mutually shared between God and man. It is an "I-Thou" relationship with God where, in relationship and dialogue with the Divine, man has confidence and security in an ultimate "being and becoming" in the fullest complete sense of self unfolding and fulfillment at the highest level of his own personality.[18]

[16]Walters, "Metaphysics, Religion, and Psychotherapy," p. 247.

[17]"Religious Factors and Values in Counseling: A Symposium," *Journal of Counseling Psychology*, VI, 4 (Winter 1959), 255–274.

[18]Charles Curran, "The Counseling Relationship and Some Religious Factors," *Journal of Counseling Psychology*, VI, 4 (Winter 1959), 269–270.

Kagan points to the close relationship between psychology and religion and to the difficulty of understanding just where psychology ends and theology begins. He stresses the need to distinguish between normal guilt and neurotic guilt and existential anxiety and pathological anxiety. He also adds support to the value of psychotherapy as an "I-Thou" (love) relationship.

> Recent psychiatric studies lead to the conclusion that where there is hope there is greater success in enduring pain, in healing and prolonging life. Hope vanishes when the need to belong, the need to be loved and the need to believe are unmet. . . .
>
> Because our society is no longer made up of integrated communities with religious orientation, there is a crisis in meeting the need to believe.[19]

Mann, as a part of the same symposium, stressed the importance of religious values and orientation to ego organization. He argued that if religion does anything (whether true or not) it is probable that it accounts for more adequate ego organization. He stated that there is now a movement away from the traditional view that the therapist should not impose values upon the client toward holding a point of view "that religious values, not imposed but proffered or made available, are not so irrelevant to the therapeutic process as had formerly been imagined."[20] He suggested that religious values comprise an important aspect of mental health. He discussed a value framework consisting of three possible levels of ego organization. First, the level of "the values of relatively immediate gratification" is recognized. Second is the level of "the values of social responsibility," and third, "the values of a philosophy of existence."[21] These levels are each different, but yet interact. In level one, the main concern is adjustment of the personality. Mann suggested a possible danger here if the psychotherapist leaves the person at this level with the danger of further breakdown due to a failure to meet the ego's deeper needs for orientation and meaning. Level two involves the person's involvement with other individuals, which also may involve conflicts between level one

[19]Henry E. Kagan, "Psychotherapy as a Religious Value," *Journal of Counseling Psychology*, VI, 4 (Winter 1959), 265.

[20]Kenneth W. Mann, "Religious Factors and Values in Counseling: Their Relationship to Ego Organization," *Journal of Counseling Psychology*, VI, 4 (Winter 1959), 259–262.

[21]*Ibid.*, p. 260. These three areas of ego organization seem to keep recurring in the literature, although expressed in different ways. C. S. Lewis referred to these similar levels in *Mere Christianity*, pp. 70-71.

and level two. "What is suggested therapeutically is the necessity of extending and strengthening the ego organization to include what can be called an 'adaptive potential' in the face of difficult social requirements."[22] The third level involves the development of a philosophy of life. Here one is not concerned only with bodily survival but also with psychological survival. In the therapeutic process the mere getting rid of old inadequate beliefs is not enough without reorganizing some new ones and integrating such religious values with the reorganizing ego. He recognized a danger, however, in that it may be possible for the religiously oriented counselor to get carried away with his own ideas and beliefs.

> The clergyman employed in clinical work will have to stand guard against his own need to trespass upon the apparent theological insufficiencies of the patient. Otherwise, he will reap the bitter fruits of his compulsion: a rebellious patient who will not return for counseling, or a submissive devotee who has temporarily buried his pathology under the superficial signs and symbols of religion.[23]

Segal dealt more with the actualities of religious value communication by the counselor in the counseling process. He stressed the contractual character of the counseling relationship, with the client telling and the counselor listening toward the end of helping the client to act out of choice rather than compulsion. It is possible, he felt, for values to become a hindrance in this process, for "to the extent that either the counselor or the client allows his own values to impede the honest evaluation of the client's problems and his feelings about them, to this extent values interfere with the goals of the helping relationship."[24] To avoid this problem, the counselor must become aware of his own values in order to keep them from interfering. Segal saw no real conflict between various value orientations, as long as the counselor is truly committed to help the client to "freer choice." The counselor's religious values should have no place in counseling if the main concern is to attempt to get the client to accept them, for this would only lead to an increased compulsion on the part of the client. However, resistance to religious values can also stem from compulsion. The counselor can come to understand the dynamics of value conflicts only by focusing upon the emotional dynamics they hold for

---

[22]*Ibid.*, p. 261.

[23]*Ibid.*, p. 262.

[24]Stanley J. Segal, "The Role of the Counselor's Religious Values in Counseling," *Journal of Counseling Psychology*, VI, 4 (Winter 1959), 271.

the client. Segal thus argued for an active involvement on the part of the counselor with the client's values, but only to better understand them and to assure that the client is accepting or rejecting them on the basis of his own choice and not because of compulsion.

Meehl, in the same symposium, focused upon some of the methodological problems of dealing with values in counseling. He suggested that, because current viewpoints are so widely diverse, we cannot be dogmatic about any one approach. He suggested four possible approaches to dealing with values in counseling: first, having the counselor expand to a pedagogic role; second, defining a new profession like psychotherapy, which would be recognized strictly for "value counseling"; third, shifting roles (at the appropriate moment the counselor would structure a change of procedure when in the area of values with the consent of the client); fourth, improving the attitudes and techniques of counselors so that values can be dealt with without subtle imposition upon the client's religious thinking and feeling. Of the four possible approaches, he took a position favoring the last. He held that the counselor could be quite active without forcing imposition and that a "reality-confrontation" within the value thinking of the client may not be as drastic and "directive" as we think. The counselor would thus function in a role similar to the Socratic gadfly, assisting the client to tighten his system of beliefs and to insure that they are logical and noncontradictory. Although Meehl favored an active approach to dealing with values, he did "plead for therapeutic 'openness,' as contrasted with postulational exclusion of value-questions and religious conflicts from the domain of real problems that patients face."[25]

Curran[26] took a perennialist view of axiology and applied it to Rogerian (or client-centered) counseling. In counseling, the client actually goes back to traditional values of Western civilization, he felt, by discovering them afresh. This involves a change of perception through the psychotherapeutic process. Perceptions of the "good" change, and with this change come changes in choice and action. There is a movement from narrow goals to broader ones, with an

    [25]Paul E. Meehl, "Some Technical and Axiological Problems in the Therapeutic Handling of Religious and Valuational Material," *Journal of Counseling Psychology*, VI, 4 (Winter 1959), 258.
    [26]Curran, "Some Ethical and Scientific Values in the Counseling Psychotherapeutic Process," *Personnel and Guidance Journal*, XXXIX, 1 (September 1960), 16.

accompanying increase of meaning. There is also a greater reasonableness and a movement toward the more ultimate value questions dealing with the meaning of life itself. He believed that the traditional values held promise and when rediscovered would free us from the Kantian imposition of values and give a sense of belonging to the culture that produced us.

As one's perceptions change along with the changing value orientation, one's choices and actions also change as one becomes committed to the perceived "good life." Drawing upon research evidence, Curran stated that

> the superimposed image is itself an apparent good and that the self tends to move towards this apparent good until its perceptions are broadened and the reasoning and insightful process of the personality, in this case brought out through counseling, brings out from the background the real good, the total perceptual field.[27]

When this occurs, the previous narrow focus is rejected and the person now acts from a broader base.

Arbuckle[28] was critical of denominational religion primarily because of what he saw as its hypocrisy in the way the religious organization has treated man and also because of its narrow absolutism. He preferred to view religion in a broader sense based upon an existential humanistic approach to man. Although the explicit views of man for counselors and for religionists in many cases are similar, Arbuckle viewed some traits and characteristics associated with organized religion and many of its spokesmen as contradictory to a philosophy of counseling and a detriment to the development of a therapeutic relationship. Some of these were the desire to convert and to change, conflicts with the sin question (original or otherwise), problems concerned with morality and virtue, the tendency toward the control of human behavior rather than acceptance of it, and the matter of faith and belief. Most of these problems seem to stem from a rigid belief in religious and moral absolutes. Some more religiously oriented counselors would disagree with several of Arbuckle's points. First of all, he seems to lump all denominationally oriented counselors under the very broad umbrella of organized religion. Second, he implies that one who holds to absolutes would be unable to accept another person who

---

[27] *Ibid.*
[28] Dugald S. Arbuckle, "Counseling: Philosophy or Science," *Personnel and Guidance Journal*, XXXIX, 1 (September 1960), 11-14.

differed with him. There are, perhaps, some semantic difficulties here with the word absolutes, for it seems that one could be, in Allport's sense, "half-sure and wholehearted," and yet accept the other individual who disagrees. This is perhaps what Arbuckle meant when he asked:

> Is it possible to be accepted by your church as a good and devout and faithful member, and be able to say to yourself, "I think I'm right, but it doesn't really matter too much if it turns out that I am wrong, and you are right, as well you might be." If he can feel this way, then it might be possible for him to be completely acceptant of an individual whose value system, as well as religion, differed sharply from his own. If he cannot feel this way, it would be rather difficult for him to accept another individual when he is saying to himself, "You are, of course, quite wrong."[29]

Nevertheless, there are counselors who would not make agreement as important a matter concerning acceptance. Blocher, for one, took this stand. He stated that "acceptance does *not* mean the absence of moral judgment about a client's behavior. Judgments about behavior are an inescapable part of being a valuing human being. Acceptance does mean a belief in the worth of the client."[30] If this be the case, it would seem to be a matter involving one's personal hierarchy of values. If one's belief in the worth of the individual and in his right to make his own choices, which includes the right to disagree, is higher than his need to *push* his religion, it would seem that it would be possible for the counselor to accept his client. However, if the reverse of this is true, it would seem that acceptance would be an impossibility. If one were to make agreement with the client a rule for accepting him, it seems that, pushed to its logical conclusion, it would be impossible to accept a client, for rarely would the client and counselor agree on all points. Also, if this were the case, the client would not need counseling.

The criticism of absolutes is also questionable, for one might hypothesize that everyone has some absolute. For example, would not a belief in the worth of the individual be an absolute and one that the counselor need not fear?

Crawford argues that commitment can find meaning only in

    [29] *Ibid.*, p. 15.
    [30] Donald H. Blocher, *Developmental Counseling* (New York: The Ronald Press, 1966), p. 145.

terms of a moral absolute. It is his argument that relativism (a firm belief in it) is a moral absolute.

> *If one is committed, then the object of at least the highest commitment must be an absolute.* . . . For the sake of brevity consider only the reply quickly supplied by the psychologists, "How ignorant this writer is! Does he not know that there are no absolute truths, everything is relative!" This declaration is itself an absolute which they say is true. They appeal to what they deny to prove their point. A more fitting way to state it would be, "There are no absolute truths except this one."[31]

He goes on to argue that "the nature of man is such that he needs a commitment" but that it is also true that "it is possible to have no commitment." Man needs a sense of purpose, of meaning, in his life. He argues that if it is a matter of which absolute we choose, then we are faced with either reexamining the issue of religion in the schools or of continuing to engender a moral vacuum by teaching relativism, which is itself a religion. Crawford urges that all religions be brought into the schools and that emphasis be placed upon the moral absolute of everyone's loving his neighbor as himself. His emphasis upon the counselor's openly professing his value commitments is clear. "If the counselor believes in something (i.e. has a commitment), why be ashamed of it?"[32]

Winborn, commenting on Crawford's article, dismisses him as a neoscholastic and attributes the weaknesses of the neoscholastic position to his article. In reference to Archibald MacLeish, Winborn states:

> He argues that if *all* men were free to search for the truth which is true for them, then a better world will be created. In one essay, "To Make Men Free," he has presented this challenge. "We are free to make the future for ourselves. And we are free because it is the man who counts in this country: always and at every moment and in any situation, the man. Not the Truth but the man: not the truth as the state sees the truth or as the mob sees the truth, but the truth as the man sees it, as the man finds it, for himself as man."[33]

This view places the worth of man high on a hierarchy and would assess absolutes as meaningful only in terms of an individual's percep-

---

[31] Claud C. Crawford, "Commitment," *Personnel and Guidance Journal,* XLIV, 9 (May 1966), 907.

[32] *Ibid.,* p. 909.

[33] Bob Winborn, "Comment on Crawford," *Personnel and Guidance Journal,* XLIV, 9 (May 1966), 910.

tion and acceptance of them as meaningful. It is in this quest for meaning that the counselor is instrumental.

> Counselors will continue to be called to assist individuals as they search for individual truths, examine the value options that are inherent in the alternatives that are deliberated. This calls for a commitment to the individual and his search for a meaningful existence rather than a commitment to any one system of values that transcends "the characteristics of individuals, nations, and peoples."[34]

One might add that unless religions are considered within the schools, it is questionable that individuals will become aware of the value options open to them.

Crawford,[35] in another article, discusses once again the need to bring religion back into the schools. He lists the following counselor functions that pertain to the problem of religious liberty: first, the counselor's inescapable responsibility in becoming involved in moral concerns in counseling; second, the counselor's involvement in religious concerns which he defined very broadly as "a philosophy of life to which one is committed." He mentions the religions of materialism, nationalism, naturalism, subjectivism, relativism, as well as theism, which have already played a part in being indoctrinated in the schools. He suggests three proposals concerning religion in the school: (1) religion must remain in the schools, (2) if religious liberty is to be functional in the public school, all religions must be welcome and free to speak, and (3) since counseling is a private confidential relationship, the religious persuasion of the school counselor needs to be known to the students and the community ahead of time. It appears that there would be a number of problems involved in this last aspect, not the least of which would be the possibility of prejudice in the hiring of counselors. It would seem that this approach of making the religious persuasion of the counselor known would have meaning if a counselor were unable to accept those who disagree with him. However, if he can accept them as they are and merely work to help them in the clarification of their own thinking about values, it is questionable that any indoctrination need take place. There is a need to clarify the role of the counselor as opposed to the role of the teacher regarding this problem of religion in the school, and we shall deal with it shortly.

[34] *Ibid.*

[35] Crawford, "The School Counselor and Religious Liberty," *Counselor Education and Supervision*, VI, 3 (Spring 1967), 208–209.

Crawford concludes his article by making the following suggestions for counselor education:

1. That counselor educators write and make public their philosophical (i.e., religious) orientations;
2. That college students in counselor preparation be given time all through their preparation to develop, modify, and state definitively their philosophy, and that its acceptable writing be one condition for graduation and certification;
3. That the public schools insist that one condition for employment of a school counselor be his willingness to make public his written philosophy.[36]

One would need to recognize that a written philosophy may be quite different from the philosophy which one lives. However, in counselor education a written philosophy would be an important first step in making one's beliefs explicit to himself and then in giving him something to measure his actual working philosophy against. It is perhaps true that not enough attention is given to the matter of personal philosophy in counselor education. Considering the nature of public schools, suggestion 3 seems unworkable to this writer.

To be concerned with the "whole person" in public education means that religion cannot be ignored, for it is an important part of the individual's life (speaking in the broad definition of religion used by Crawford, as a philosophy of life to which one is committed). To ignore formal religion in the public school is to advocate its unimportance and to indoctrinate subtly in some other religion such as naturalism or relativism. The question remains as to how this problem should be handled and what the counselor's role should be.

In the previous consideration of the subjective and objective value question, it was argued that both subjective and objective values must be accepted as complementary parts of the value question. If this be the case, it would be logical to argue that the school must give attention not only to the subjective aspects of religious experience (that is, the creation of meaning by the individual) but also to the objective aspect, the making explicit of value options. How can this be done? I would suggest that it can be done through the utilization of counselor and teacher roles as they now exist. The counselor can serve the function of working with the individual at a deeply personal level in the weighing of alternatives, the clarification of feelings, and

[36] *Ibid.*, p. 209.

the creation of meaning based upon a clear explication of one's own constructive intent. Religion can be meaningful to people only when they are left free to choose. Religion cannot be manufactured as a tool to mental health.

> We are faced by a paradox: religion can be therapeutic only when it is not so regarded; when, instead, it is paid allegience as a thing-in-itself. No utilitarian need can ever determine the realm of the sacred, which is concerned with revealed truth and ultimate ends. Religion does not lend itself to prescription.[37]

The teacher serves the function of dealing with facts, with the world "out there" and a confrontation of it. In this position, the teacher is much more free to "teach" values. It cannot be assumed that each individual somehow automatically knows all that he needs to know concerning value alternatives. This is the error of the extreme subjectivists. Frondizi states that

> esthetic and moral education does not consist in calling the young man's attention to certain questions of fact, or consequences produced by certain actions, but also in focusing his very eyes upon the presence of values which his inexperienced observations have not as yet discovered.[38]

The Association for Supervision and Curriculum Development also makes this clear by stating that

> within the broad limits of good taste both students and teachers should be free to explore and test values without restraint or fear of criticism. Teachers must stand for something if for no other reason than to give children something to push against. Values, beliefs and convictions must be admitted to the classroom situation. They must be respected and cherished if students are to develop their own beliefs and values. Ethics, morality, human feeling and emotion need to be part of the curriculum if the school intends that teachers and classrooms will affect student behavior significantly.[39]

This means, though, that the teacher must be honestly involved. "If it is values in education we are talking about, then emotional involvement is one of the critical issues in the relationship between the children and the teacher. It isn't something that is going to be taught by movies."[40] It seems that bringing religion into the classroom,

[37] Arnold W. Green, "Social Values and Psychotherapy," *Journal of Personality*, XIV, 3 (March 1946), 206.

[38] Risieri Frondizi, *What Is Value?* (LaSalle, Ill.: Open Court, 1963), p. 108.

[39] Association for Supervision, *Perceiving, Behaving, Becoming*, p. 201.

[40] Ronald Lippitt, "Value Issues for a Classroom Change-Agent," in Theodore

however, in most cases is simply not being done.

An idea with great possibilities in this matter is what Brameld has called "defensible partiality." He suggests the open presentation and discussion of as many value systems (or religions) as there are proponents of them. There would be a free examination as well as defense of all positions within a climate of acceptance and understanding. The promotion of this would require teachers specially trained in group work in order to maintain the climate of understanding and acceptance. This approach is based upon the idea that

> *what we learn is defensible in so far as the ends we support and the means we utilize are able to stand up against exposure to open, unrestricted criticism and comparison. What we learn is partial in so far as these ends and means still remain definite and positive to their democratic advocates after the defense occurs.*[41]

Such courses would be taught by teams of teachers of preferably different value orientations, as well as by invited priests, ministers, and others from the community who would present their own philosophies. This approach is no doubt fraught with a number of problems, but it does appear workable. Counselors in this type of program would serve the individual by assisting him to work through some of his own thoughts and feelings regarding his confrontation with value issues.

An interesting possibility in the handling of values within counseling is what Buhler refers to as "constructive exploration." In this process the counselor avoids giving direction but assists in making the client aware of his own implicit considerations. Bertocci and Millard, citing Brightman, have offered general principles that might be useful in the counseling relationship in aiding the client to test his considerations. These are not universal moral laws to be imposed upon people. They are, rather, universal principles that individuals "ought" to follow in the quest for a philosophy of life. They are principles of rational action and must be self-imposed. They are guides to rational action and not formulas for the good life. They may be stated as follows:

1. Principle of Consistency: *Each person ought to choose consistently or logically.* In other words, he ought not to choose on the basis of conflicting or contradictory intentions, or choose conflicting and

Brameld and Stanley Elam (eds.), *Values in American Education* (Bloomington: Phi Delta Kappa, 1964), p. 171.

[41]Theodore Brameld, *Education for the Emerging Age* (New York: Harper and Brothers, 1961), p. 157.

contradictory actions, or choose conflicting and contradictory means and ends.[42]

2. Principle of Autonomy: *"All persons ought to recognize themselves as obligated to choose in accordance with ideals that they acknowledge."* This means that morality must be self-governed and recognized as such. Self-rule is the very foundation of morality.[43]

3. Axiological Principle: *"All persons ought to choose values that are consistent with each other, harmonious and coherent, not values that are conflicting, contradictory, or incoherent."*[44]

4. Principle of Consequences: *"Each person ought to consider and on the whole approve of the foreseeable consequences of his actions."*[45]

5. Principle of the Best Possible: *"Each person ought to choose the best possible values in every situation and, hence, if possible, improve every situation."*[46]

6. Principle of Specification: *"Each person, in any given situation, ought to develop the value or values specifically relevant to that situation."*[47]

7. Principle of the Most Inclusive End: *"Each person ought to choose a coherent life in which the widest possible range of value is realized in accordance with a life plan."*[48]

8. Principle of Individuality: *"Each person ought to realize in his own experience the maximum values of which he is capable in harmony with all other moral principles."*[49]

9. Principle of Altruism: *"Each person ought to respect all other persons as ends in themselves and, as far as possible, cooperate with others in the production and enjoyment of shared values."*[50] The counselor who is aware of such principles as these is able to reflect them in the counseling process, thus assisting the client to better evaluate the quality of his choices.

[42]Peter A. Bertocci and Richard M. Millard, *Personality and the Good* (New York: David McKay Co., 1963), p. 432, citing E. S. Brightman, *Moral Laws* (New York: Abingdon Press, 1933), p. 98.

[43]*Ibid.*, p. 450, citing Brightman, p. 106.
[44]*Ibid.*, p. 481, citing Brightman, p. 125.
[45]*Ibid.*, p. 495, citing Brightman, p. 142.
[46]*Ibid.*, p. 509, citing Brightman, p. 156.
[47]*Ibid.*, p. 532, citing Brightman, p. 171.
[48]*Ibid.*, p. 551, citing Brightman, p. 183.
[49]*Ibid.*, p. 574, citing Brightman, p. 204.
[50]*Ibid.*, p. 597, citing Brightman, p. 223.

In summary, we might state that the task of the counselor in dealing with values in a pluralistic society is complex; this is especially so if he lacks a sound foundation upon which he can base his judgments of both goals and methods in the counseling process. But is there any base upon which he can establish a firm footing? In an age rocked with change and uncertainty, is there any common value core that cuts beneath the mere superficial and yet above the more profound depths of belief where much conflict and controversy exist? It is to such questions that we must now turn.

# chapter 7

# Freedom: A Valuational
# Base for Counseling?

## TOWARD VALIDATION

Is there a value base that can be made explicit and validated that can serve as a guide in counseling and against which practice can be evaluated? The logical place to look for such a base would be in the philosophy of value, but in doing so one finds a complex and somewhat disappointing picture. Edel speaks for the philosophers when he says:

> The quest for values in educational theory is a vast subject. In our day it follows no well-worn path. There is no fixed ethical theory, nor set of virtues, nor list of commandments, nor inventory of goals, nor even perhaps fixed constellation of ideals, about which I could say: "Here is what the moral philosopher swears by. Take it ye educators, and apply it to your discipline. My task is done." You all know this as well as I do. If it were not so, the quest for values would pose no problems.[1]

There are no easy or quick answers. The best one can hope for at present is to be able to sort out some of the complexities and bring what he can to the task of making application to educational problems. This is the intent here, by clarifying and elaborating upon what was discovered to be the common core of belief in Chapter 5, namely, the multifaceted concept of freedom.

One of the greatest barriers to any question of values in American life has been relativism. Since as Americans we value pluralism and stress the right of the individual to be different, the search for any one criterion for value judgments becomes problematic. How can one set up a criterion of value that will not restrict the individual or impose

---

[1]Abraham Edel, "Education and the Quest for Values," *The Philosophical Forum*, XX (1962–1963), 17.

unwanted values upon him? The value of freedom deserves serious consideration in serving this purpose.

The essential quality of freedom is that it allows man room to be himself, to be creative, to make choices and be responsible for them. Freedom allows man to choose higher values if he desires. It allows him to follow his own quest for truth, to develop his own philosophy of life. Freedom is a matter of degree. We must talk in terms of *more* or *less* rather than of *presence* or *absence*. Freedom involves man in his individual functioning, in his functioning with others, and in his search for meaning. It has many facets, and man is confronted by choices involving them. Freedom can be at least part of a base from which one can examine and evaluate practice. This seems to be what Gardner was referring to when he said:

> We are beginning to understand how to educate for renewal but we must deepen that understanding. If we indoctrinate the young person in an elaborate set of fixed beliefs, we are ensuring his early obsolescence. The alternative is to develop skills, attitudes, habits of mind and the kinds of knowledge and understanding that will be the instruments of continuous change and growth on the part of the young person. Then we will have fashioned a system that provides for its own continuous renewal.
>
> This suggests a standard in terms of which we may judge the effectiveness of all education.[2]

It is my intent here to propose certain evidence that contributes to validation. Freedom is here viewed as both end and means. As end, it is a goal to be strived for both internally and externally, and, in this sense, it is an ideal that will never be completely realized either at the individual or the societal level. A free society must always demand more from its citizens than they will be able to give or there is danger of lapsing into a lethargic status quo. As means, freedom becomes the raw material of further purposeful choice. As individuals become more free, they can better choose among further more ultimate ends. They can choose to openly examine available value orientations, to examine their own value orientations, to submit them to open examination by others, to choose when and if to change, and to accept the responsibility for their choice.

The statement that only means can be validated but that ultimate ends must be chosen arbitrarily contains a thread of truth. It is an expression of the complexity of the task of establishing valid crite-

[2]John Gardner, *Self-Renewal* (New York: Harper and Row, 1963), p. 21.

ria by which to judge the value of ends, in our case, freedom. One must admit some arbitrariness in this choice, but any choice must have the support of some evidence to win its worth as a "best" alternative. In a day of crisis such as the present, one can ill afford to take the easy road of the merely arbitrary. "Our only hope of escape from intransigent presents lies in an examination not alone of whether we are doing what is right or good, but, more fundamentally, of what it means to make the claim that an action is right or good."[3]

Though the founders of our country offered no explicit valuation of their fundamental beliefs ("We hold these truths to be self-evident") they were motivated by the realization of a need for a new order. This order was in direct opposition to the then existing rigid systems of class and caste. Anchored in strict belief in Natural Law, the individual emerged with freedom to achieve. Such beliefs as set down in the Declaration of Independence and the Constitution were the result of a consensus—a consensus that seems to be a growing tide in history. One can witness today the struggles for freedom and self-realization among the new nations. Peoples previously held in bondage of ignorance are now rising to make new demands for their personal rights. Though there is yet much oppression, one can still witness the cry of the masses for the Liberté, Egalité, Fraternité demanded in the French and American revolutions. In the communist countries, although the surge forward is interpreted as historical necessity, it is also promoted by the dream of future security, freedom, and self-realization. Witness also the breaking of old molds within the Catholic Church and a new look at the principle of freedom. All of these point to a growing consensus of a belief in freedom as necessary to man's sense of dignity and his self-realization.

The core of such consensus can be found by searching for common or universal goals of mankind, and considerable progress has been made in this direction. Edel, a leader in the construction of a valuational base, describes the narrowing of indeterminacy of values and a growing scientific basis for consensus of human "goods."[4] Brameld, in referring to Edel's concept of the valuational base, recognizes as did Edel that the validation of such a base is far from complete and conclusive, but that

[3]Elizabeth F. Flower, "Present-Day Disagreements in Moral Philosophy," in F. C. Gruber (ed.), *Aspects of Value* (Philadelphia: University of Pennsylvania Press, 1959), p. 19.

[4]Edel, *Ethical Judgment* (New York: The Free Press of Glencoe, 1955).

> *given the knowledge we possess of the nature of man and his striving for fulfillment, some values are much more universally consistent with this knowledge than are other values.* More human beings converge upon the goal of peace, certainly, than they do upon that of war. More human beings cherish the goal of human brotherhood than they do that of mutual hatred. More human beings consider desirable an economic order that will produce abundance than they do one of scarcity and poverty. By the same token, more human beings value freedom as the goal of providing concrete opportunities for their development than they do slavery or degradation. All of these values, moreover, are increasingly global in scope.[5]

Science does not create values but only produces raw materials (knowledge) from which humans can discover and prescribe values.[6] And science, as Bronowski has so clearly revealed, demands freedom as its atmosphere or truth-seeking must soon suffocate.

There are perhaps few people who would honestly desire to return, if they could, to live in some past age. Perhaps the primary reason can be found in an unwillingness to give up the comforts that are the fruits of modern technology. As a result of the progress of science, modern man is more free from pains, burdens, and discomforts than were his ancestors. Science has proved to be a blessing to man (as well as a curse when used for improper ends) that has brought unprecedented fulfillment of man's lower needs. Defining science very simply as "knowledge at the upper limit of its development,"[7] we can relate this to freedom. There are many needs of man that have not yet been met. Science is on the threshold of new and important breakthroughs in an attempt to further man's comforts and also his development. Few would argue that this is not "good." But without freedom of inquiry and communication, one aspect of freedom, science cannot flower. "Truth-seeking" is dependent upon the degree of freedom permitted. Thus, we can validate freedom as a necessary ingredient to further scientific progress toward "truth." The society of scientists can serve as a model of the unity that can be achieved on such a basis.

Because of a general fear of indoctrination and other authoritarian methods, many educators have feared to set up any purpose that is utopian, idealistic, or absolutistic in any sense. In an age rocked by

[5]Theodore Brameld, *Cultural Foundations of Education* (New York: Harper and Brothers, 1957), p. 236.

[6]J. Bronowski, *Science and Human Values* (New York: Harper and Row, 1956).

[7]Ralph B. Perry, *The Humanity of Man* (New York: George Braziller, Inc., 1956), p.7.

crisis, we are learning more of the importance of well-chosen goals and commitment to them. The totalitarian systems of government have perhaps been most successful in educating toward their ends because they have not feared firm commitment. Our situation demands that we reexamine some of these old fears in the light of new knowledge. Perhaps defining our ends more clearly and pressing all possible means into their service need not be as restricting and narrowing as we think.

> There is an escape from this dilemma if we look to the grounds on which indoctrination is condemned. Why does the critic find the Nazi method, the communist method, the strict parental or scholastic method objectionable? Because it is narrow, rigid, and authoritarian. But if he is against these things he must be *for* their opposites: namely breadth, flexibility, and freedom.
>
> These opposites and other kindred ideas themselves define an end—an end that can be methodically and consistently pursued if it is to be realized. The weakness of educational self-criticism is its failure to acknowledge and make explicit the positive purpose which underlies its scruples. It protests against authority, rigidity, and narrowness—in the name of *what?* It hesitates to name the name lest it be itself guilty of the same faults and because it fails to proclaim a positive end of its own, it lacks the dynamism which springs from conviction and enthusiasm.[8]

Related to this is the fear of prejudice and bias. Unless one examines each issue carefully, one can fall into the danger of backing into one's convictions. To be guilty of this is to examine what our "enemies" believe and then jump to the assumption that the opposite must be correct. Perry refers to this in regard to the teaching of morals.

> The remark that the moral teacher must take the risk of being considered prejudiced is also revealing. Morality *is* a prejudice—a prejudice in favor of justice and benevolence. The use of this word suggests that it is a petty eccentricity, an arbitrary peculiarity, like preferring blondes to brunettes or French dressing to mayonnaise. But if morality means that "the things that bring all men together are greater than the things which keep them apart," as indeed it does, it underlies all human institutions, including education itself.[9]

A question can be raised, and legitimately at this point, as to whether such a choice of freedom as ultimate goal is not a cultural bias. It is a bias. Although freedom may be allowed to exist in a variety of

[8] Perry, *Realms of Value* (Cambridge: Harvard University Press, 1954), pp. 426–427.

[9] *Ibid.*, pp. 429–430.

social systems, it is believed by this writer that it is only whenever the dignity of man is valued in the deepest sense that freedom is prevalent and valued in the deepest sense of the term. The dignity of man as an ideal is expression of trust and belief in man as a free and autonomous being, as end rather than means. Such a society must provide education that will develop free men, for it is free men who will develop such a society. This bias is not only cultural in a restrictive sense; it goes much beyond, for it looks to the nature of man that approaches universality. It recognizes all men as desiring independence of thought, speech, and action in fulfilling their deepest needs. It may be true that there is a cultural readiness that is required for a nation to be able to function with freedom. A man does not break his fetters overnight and automatically emerge as a responsible and independent being. That this is true reemphasizes the need for a truly liberating education. Freedom is not easily won. It grows as men in their true natures grow. The counselor has the privilege and great challenge of assisting such growth.

The value *freedom* might be considered an ideal. As such and phenomenologically viewed, it "falls somewhere along the range between what is urgent and what is wished for."[10] It is not the supreme "good" but is a pathway to the "good," necessary in a pluralistic society where every individual is responsible to define a supreme "good" for himself. It is for this reason that freedom is here chosen as the core value for an evaluational base over such other alternatives as "truth," however defined, etc. The ideal of freedom gives the individual liberty to follow a quest for his own "good." Freedom allows room also to move in a direction that is detrimental, and for this reason one must consider it within its particular context to determine whether it is of a hindering or a fulfilling type.

Rather than command, dictate, or affirm, freedom as an ideal attracts. It pulls man, for it offers enhanced possibility for fulfillment. It is always out of reach in an absolute sense but at the same time is within reach to a relative degree. It is abstract and, as we have noted, not easily defined, and for this reason ideals in general have suffered criticism. For example:

> Every group, in every age, has had its "ideals" for which it has striven as if men had blown bubbles into the air, and then entranced by their beautiful colors, had leaped to catch them. In the very

[10]Edel, *Method in Ethical Theory* (Indianapolis: Bobbs-Merrill, 1963), p. 324.

processes of analysis and deduction, the most pernicious errors find entrance.[11]

And again:

> *Ideals.* An ideal is entirely unscientific. It is a phantasm which has little or no connection with fact. Ideals are very often formed in the effort to escape from the hard task of dealing with facts, which is the function of science and art. There is no process by which to reach an ideal. There are no tests by which to verify it. It is therefore impossible to frame a proposition about an ideal which can be proved or disproved.[12]

This is the view of the hard-headed scientist. However, it would seem once again that such a view fails to see the urgency of the times in which we live as well as the importance of fixing our pursuit into the future upon ends worth serving. Ends do not come about automatically unless, of course, "any road will do."

> In human life, evaluation of ideals is given special urgency by the fact that a new generation is constantly growing up. Unless one is simply to equip it with older attitudes in spite of changing conditions, or unless one simply imparts a sense of momentous tasks to be done, leaving the content of these tasks as a kind of value vacuum to be filled in by chance, careful attention to the nature of ideals and criteria for their evaluation are indispensible.[13]

Freedom, as an ideal, proposes a positive and fulfilling process of existence. Being a value at the "middle level" (that is, not being concerned with the trivia of mere relative preferences nor with the highest theological and ultimate goals upon which men would differ), it functions in such a way as to organize other values under it. For example, tolerance and positive regard, as well as other humanistic values important to democratic living, are incorporated under it. Of the values underlying a democratic society freedom is to be found at the top of the hierarchy.

To choose freedom as an ideal is a valuing process in itself, and to evaluate our choice we are in need of criteria by which to do so. But to choose criteria for evaluation is to make another value judgment, and so the process could continue ad infinitum. Hence, we must recognize that there is always a value assumption underlying any choice of criteria for evaluation.

[11] *Ibid.*, quoting W. G. Sumner, *Folkways.*
[12] *Ibid.*
[13] *Ibid.*, p. 323.

Edel[14] suggests the following seven points of reference for deciding the merits of strengthening or supplanting an ideal: strength of foundations, intensity, motor power or dynamism, genuineness, attainability, effectiveness, and necessity. These rest upon the value assumption of *"maximum achievement, in rich experience, of the aims of the mass of the people of the globe,"* as a good.[15] It is further assumed that most counselors would subscribe to this. The justification based upon these criteria will necessarily be continued throughout this chapter, but we shall consider them briefly here. Let us now examine freedom as an ideal by using these criteria.

### Strength of Foundations

The foundations of freedom are grounded in the nature of man. As we have noted previously, man experiences himself as making choices and desires to do so. When he is constrained he expresses resentment or hatred in one form or another.[16] As he experiences more freedom (as defined in this chapter) growth becomes more possible and the individual can allow himself to change in order to serve greater human values.

> The good society is, thus, the one which gives the greatest freedom to its people—freedom defined not negatively and defensively, but positively, as the opportunity to realize ever greater human values.[17]

### Intensity

This point of reference refers to the attractiveness of the ideal to the individual in the face of its "far-off" characteristics. Here it must be recognized that individuals can experience increased freedom in the "here and now," no matter what their state. The possibility is always there, no matter how small the degree, and thus has great attractability. One must not fail to recognize, however, that men also try to "escape from freedom" to avoid being responsible. This, though, is a result of being in bondage within a frightening world, and as one

---

[14] *Ibid.*, pp. 336–337.

[15] *Ibid.*, p. 353.

[16] Rollo May, *Man's Search for Himself* (New York: The New American Library, Inc., 1967), especially chapter 5. Also published in hardcover (New York: W. W. Norton & Co., Inc., 1953).

[17] *Ibid.*, pp. 137–138.

gains courage he can move out into ever widening circles of freedom. As such, freedom is both means (to greater freedom) and end (a future ideal toward which one can press). Freedom thus has great attractability as the individual gains in courage and each victory over determinism makes it all the more attractive.

### Motor Power or Dynamism

This refers to the power (or intensity) of the ideal to spur to action. Here again freedom as an ideal has this capacity. One needs but look at the history of the struggle for freedom to recognize it as a motivating force. As to inner freedom, one may have more doubt, for the psychotic, for example, may resist psychological freedom. But this does not mean that the dynamic potential is not there. The therapist, when faced by individuals who resist freedom, must assume that such dynamism lies somewhere below the surface and that, as the individual increases his awareness and becomes more courageous, such a positive force is awakened. This, in actuality, generally proves to be the case.

### Genuineness

The genuineness or authenticity of freedom depends upon two factors. First is how it is held by the individual; for example, is it held authentically? Second, what are the consequences that flow from it? The first would seem to refer to honesty within the individual and whether or not the ideal is held by his own choice or by externally compelling forces. This would have to be judged separately in each unique situation. As to consequences, the test would be one of responsibility or irresponsibility. Is the ideal held in such a way as to enhance human values, or is it held in such a way as to subtly manipulate individuals to meet some other hidden needs? Again, the answer must come from an analysis of the ideal in action.

### Attainability

One must recognize that we do not refer here to freedom as a static goal with some fixed quantitative measure. Rather, we refer to it as a dynamic that can be experienced in varying degrees and so once again reference is made in terms of more or less rather than of presence or absence. In this regard freedom fulfills the demands of this point of reference, for as previously stated, it is always attainable to some degree at any moment but still retains the characteristic of always offering more than one could possibly grasp. It is thus a compelling force but at the same time a satisfying one.

### Effectiveness

Reference here is to the effectiveness of the ideal to produce, within a historical context, the meeting of the needs upon which it is based. The ideal of freedom rests upon the need for self-fulfillment within a world in which one considers others and their right to self-fulfillment. Responsibility is again a key word. It appears that only within a context of minimal responsible freedom can self-fulfillment in this sense occur. As such, freedom according to our definition is effective as an ideal.

### Necessity

Edel states that

> An ideal whose achievement is indispensable to the fulfillment of a mass of accepted values, or, sometimes, to the very possibility of striving for them, will be said to possess *ethical necessity.*[18]

Thus judged, freedom would seem to fit this description, especially within our present-day world of change, alienation, loneliness, and lawlessness. In such a time we must of necessity focus upon flexibility, openness, and creativity—all aspects of freedom as ideal. But now, let us go on to further clarify the various meanings of freedom.

To the man on the street, freedom may seem very simple to understand. It may be something he feels he has or does not have. It may mean to him a specific governmental form or a particular cultural pattern, but however he perceives it, to him it seems simple enough. But it is such naive realism as this that adds to the prevalent confusion as to what freedom really is and how it may be defined. The philosopher must look at the problem very circumspectly, for one man's freedom may be another man's prison. The naive realist defines freedom through the lenses of his own vested interests. Such narrow personal views make the choice of freedom as a cultural and personal goal problematic. Educators, although enthusiastic in their support of freedom as a goal, have not been immune to using the term with ambiguity, and philosophers have debated the problems concerning freedom throughout the centuries without successfully delineating a clear and definitive answer upon which all could agree. Brameld suggests several reasons for this difficulty.

[18]Edel, *Method in Ethical Theory*, p. 347.

One difficulty is that their formulations have usually rested upon metaphysical or otherwise speculative and unverifiable presuppositions that are denied by philosophers holding alternative (and often equally deniable) presuppositions. Another difficulty is that their formulations may unconsciously but no less basically reflect varying cultural patterns—patterns that express freedom differently because the ways men actually live individually and collectively likewise differ.[19]

Perhaps it is because freedom is so close to man's inner nature that it is so difficult to conceptualize. It is not an easy task to define and thus make static what by nature is an ongoing process—something that is experienced, whether personally or culturally. As Griswold puts it:

The last word on freedom will never be spoken. Deeds, rather than words, are its most eloquent testimonial. We shall never complete our definition of freedom because, while we recognize it as the absence of restraint, its truest meaning must always be subjective.[20]

Although we may not be able to state a closed and final definition of freedom, it is imperative that we trace it to its source, that we discover its foundation, for at its root one should be able to discover commonalities. It is an understanding of freedom as a universal (as applicable to all men in all situations) that we seek rather than as a particular (applicable only to particular men in particular situations).

But what is the source? To discover the source of freedom one must look to man and to his basic nature. It is here that we must look for a verification for our goals by whatever knowledge philosophy and the behavioral sciences can provide.

In the choice of freedom as a worthy goal for counseling (as well as for all of education) one finds his weightiest evidence within the basic nature of man himself. Although there are different kinds of freedom (at least in emphasis)—freedom of speech, cultural freedom, academic freedom, freedom from want, etc.—the basis of our discussion here shall be grounded upon what can be called "freedom of choice."

Freedom of choice ... means that a man who consciously comes to a decision between two or more genuine alternatives is free to do so and is not completely determined by his heredity, education,

[19]Brameld, *Cultural Foundations*, p. 224.
[20]A. W. Griswold, *Liberal Education and the Democratic Ideal* (New Haven: Yale University Press, 1959), p. 114.

economic circumstances and past history as an individual. While a
person's choices are always conditioned and limited to a marked
extent by such factors and by the situation that currently faces him,
he possesses a decisive element of freedom in determining whether
to do this or that.[21]

Man does experience himself as choosing, and along with the
choice that he experiences as a free one there is the accompanying
recognition that he could have chosen otherwise. One of the everyday
experiences of choosing can be exemplified in common speech.[22] A
person chooses his words as he communicates and at times searches
for the "proper" words. Or, in writing, one expresses himself freely
within the self-imposed limits of his topic, and the writer feels that he
could have written otherwise. This feeling of having the power to have
taken a different course of action is basic to the whole idea of responsibility. Because an individual feels that he could have done differently,
he also feels responsible *(respondere,* the one who can answer) for the
outcome of his choice.

## FREEDOM VERSUS DETERMINISM

Any theory of values then must suppose that man does indeed make
choices and does act upon those choices. But the various theories
differ as to what is involved in such choice-making. Weiss suggests
four basic meanings of freedom, meanings that must be distinguished
from one another for the sake of clarity.[23]

1. *Freedom from.* This meaning refers generally to freedom from
restraints, and its focus is primarily external. If a person is kept prisoner he is not free to do what he wishes. Some writers refer to this
freedom as freedom of action. This meaning is not controversial, there
being wide recognition that it does exist and there is little question
about it.

2. *Freedom to.* This meaning refers to inner decisions of inten-
tion whether the result is overt or covert. It involves choice on the part
of the actor, thus involving goals and responsibility. This meaning

---

[21]Corliss Lamont, *Freedom of Choice Affirmed* (New York: Horizon Press,
1967), pp. 16, 17.

[22]*Ibid.,* p. 37.

[23]Paul Weiss, "Common Sense and Beyond," in Sidney Hook (ed.), *Determinism
and Freedom* (New York: Collier Books, 1961), p. 233.

is highly controversial, and some philosophers have denied that anything other than freedom of action exists.

3. *Freedom for.* This meaning is similar to "freedom to," but it involves the power of commitment to ends plus the ability to work and carry them out. This is also a controversial meaning for the reasons given in number two above.

4. *Freedom with.* By this is meant the freedom to live in harmony with other equally free men.

The controversy has raged traditionally over the question of whether or not man is really free to make decisions of the type mentioned in numbers two and three, above. The battle lines have been drawn between the determinists and the libertarians.

The determinists, following a naturalistic and positivistic orientation, have argued that human behavior follows laws just as natural phenomena do and that therefore whatever we call choices have their causal explanation. One can think of a continuum between the two poles of freedom and determinism with all men's beliefs falling somewhere between. The determinists, on the one hand, vary in their points of view, but all would insist on some measure of external causality apart from the will and determination of the actor. The libertarians, on the other, insist that decisions are not caused in the same way that natural phenomena are caused, but that man can choose for himself, can assert his will, and thus is exempt minimally from any causality of natural law. On the argument between these two positions hangs the question of obligation and responsibility, for how can a man be responsible for that over which he has no control? Mothershead suggests that "most contemporary determinists would agree that the dilemma of moral responsibility arises because of a misunderstanding of natural law."[24] The task of natural law is primarily descriptive. It is based upon probability that events occurring together in the past will also occur together in the future. "Scientific laws do not compel human behavior; they are rather descriptions of it. If the behavior were different, the laws would be different. No sensible determinist denies that human choices make a difference in the world—that is, that they are themselves causes."[25] One must "distinguish between compulsion and necessitation on the one hand and determination and causation on the other. Human choices like all natural events are determined,

---

[24] John Mothershead, Jr., *Ethics* (New York: Henry Holt and Co., 1955), p. 53.
[25] *Ibid.,* p. 54.

but they are not, in all cases, compelled or coerced."[26]

The quesion, then, is whether man or some outside force is the determiner. If one observes this distinction between description and prescription, man is left free to choose and determine his own existence, but always within the context of his world. His world affects him and he affects his world. Allport illustrates the differences between the descriptive task of the scientist and the acting, choosing person.[27] He pictures the scientist sitting on a hill observing an oarsman on the river below. From his position on the hill the scientist can observe dangerous rapids just around the bend of the river but yet unknown to the man in the boat. The scientist can predict from what to him is present observation that the oarsman will soon portage, which is yet future to the oarsman. Nevertheless, when the oarsman approaches the obstacle, he will choose and act appropriately and experience his choice and action as his own. It is irrelevant to him how the scientist views the matter.

To counselors it is natural that most emphasis is placed upon the actor and his choice and thus necessarily that great stress is placed upon his freedom to decide and to act. It is also natural that the scientist look for causes and patterns for understanding behavior.

It seems that the determinists and the libertarians are recognizing the same phenomena but are viewing it from differing frames of reference, the determinist focusing primarily upon the objective aspects of behavior and possible causality looking backward, the libertarian upon the subjective side and stressing freedom to will different choices looking forward. The determinist views the choice as having been caused by some preceding motive and supposes that error in predictability is due to a lack of knowledge of such causality rather than to pure free choice. The libertarian would generally not disagree that reasons can be found for choices, but he insists as Krutch did that one must recognize the "minimal man"—a man who does have a certain amount of freedom to decide for himself how he will react to his world and also how he will in turn act upon it. This means that man can choose between alternatives and that to make one choice does not mean that he could not have made another. The important fact is that he is free to make his choice; he asserts his individuality in the realm

[26] *Ibid.*, p. 55.
[27] Gordon Allport, *Becoming* (New Haven: Yale University Press, 1955), pp. 83–84.

of possibility—the possibility of changing himself, his environment, or both. To be free in this sense is also to be responsible.

For the determinist the solution to the problem of freedom rests upon deciding which choices are compelled and which are not. In seeking solutions to this problem, the meaning of freedom has been further clarified in several ways. Some determinists have argued that in order for any choice to be free it must exist as a definite physical or psychological possibility.[28] For example, a young married couple can freely choose which one of them will support the family financially if both are capable of doing so. They cannot, however, decide freely which one will have the babies. Thus, one is free to choose what is possible to do but is not free to do what is impossible. It also follows that one cannot be blamed for not doing what is impossible or for doing what he has no opportunity to avoid.

Another distinction between free choice and determined choice and one that narrows the range of freedom a bit more, can be made on the basis of voluntarism.[29] Any choice that comes from within the individual by his own goals, beliefs, feelings, preferences, or desires is a free choice. In such a case, the individual chooses for himself and is responsible for the consequences of the choice. However, if an individual's choices are determined by outside factors beyond the individual's control, they are not free. Fromm[30] discusses such "loss of freedom" as occurring when the individual in a conformist society chooses what he thinks others want him to choose rather than choosing according to his own honest desires. One can recognize a problem here as to when one is really making his own choice or being manipulated by others, for, as Fromm points out, this can be done without one's full realization. However, it would not seem impossible to choose voluntarily to conform. In this sense, the person would be choosing freely to limit his own freedom in Fromm's sense. Buhler gave some evidence to suggest that conformity may be a natural tendency in some children and becomes a pattern of choice.[31]

Another distinction, which narrows the range of freedom even more, involves the question of rationality versus irrationality. Here the

[28]Mothershead, *Ethics*, p. 55.

[29]*Ibid.*, p. 56.

[30]Erich Fromm, *Escape from Freedom* (New York: Farrar and Rinehart, 1941), p. 185ff.

[31]See Charlotte Buhler, *Values in Psychotherapy* (New York: The Free Press of Glencoe, 1962).

choice that involves the whole self would be free, but any choice involving only a part of self would be less free.[32] A man choosing while in a fit of rage would be less free than a man making a choice in calm contemplation.

A final distinction recognizes the importance of unconscious motivation in the making of choices.[33] This is a controversial viewpoint with many opinions as to the degree of unconscious influence, ranging from one extreme of there being little affecting the normal person to the other extreme of viewing all human behavior as being influenced by the unconscious. This latter view would make man a prisoner of his past and would remove the possibility of any responsibility. Although there is evidence that some unconscious influence is a reality, especially in the abnormal personality, there is also a growing body of evidence that individuals can exercise considerable control over such influence or at least limit its effects greatly by living in greater awareness—in neo-Freudian terms, by strengthening the ego. Man can choose to work with it or against it. In such a view man becomes more free as he loses such unconscious deterministic shackles. Bertocci recognizes a minimal amount of free choice even in the disturbed individual, i.e., the homosexual still chooses his partners, etc. The individual retains some freedom even though it may be severely limited.

The libertarian would agree with the foregoing limitations on free choice but would insist that there are choice points in the ongoing process of human development that cannot be sufficiently explained by previous conditioning. Man is not merely pushed and pulled by forces outside of himself toward ends of his choice. He is self-propelling. He can set goals using as raw materials his past experiences and drive himself toward them. He is a tension-producing as well as tension-reducing being. He is cause as well as effect. He is not solely reactive but is also proactive. On such a view rests the whole case of the dignity of man. If man is not free to choose, he is but an automaton, a mere cog in the universe. If man is not free, counseling is a meaningless activity. If man is free to choose his own ends, he is responsible, a creative being of inherent worth, a being in process of development in a never ending struggle for more and more freedom. It is such a view that is the root from which democracy[34] springs,

[32]Fromm, *Escape from Freedom*, p. 57.

[33]*Ibid.*, p. 58.

[34]Democracy is here used simply to mean a system of government that places great value upon the individual and his potential for playing a rational part in self-government, i.e., "of the people, by the people, for the people."

and it is such a view that is needed to make democracy flourish.

> Up to now the "behavioral sciences," including psychology, have not provided us with a picture of man capable of creating or living in a democracy. ... The theory of democracy requires that man possess a measure of rationality, a portion of freedom, a generic conscience, propriate ideals, and unique value.[35]

Although we do not have a completed science of man, it is my belief that there is a sufficient growing body of evidence to warrant the view of man as an active choosing being in the process of becoming. It is within man's existential nature that one discovers the roots of freedom. Man is potentially a free being. Although he lives in a context of determining forces, it is imperative to recognize the "minimal man"—a man that always has some choice in deciding his destiny. Such freedom makes life problematic, but challenging. Counselors must rise to the challenge of helping individuals to become the free and responsible beings that they potentially are.

> Given time it seems probable that psychology will ripen in the direction of democracy's basic assumptions. ...
> Soon, we venture to predict, psychology will offer an image of man more in accord with the democratic ideals by which psychologists as individuals do in fact live.[36]

Life, then, is a struggle between forces that would squeeze man into a determined mold and the free creative processes inherent in man's nature. This is basically what we mean by growth—the on-going process of man becoming more responsible, more autonomous, more creative—the process of becoming more free. But such a battle is not won easily. To assume that man is born free is to avoid the facts of man's existence, for at birth man is one of the most helpless creatures. He must be cared for. He is not free to do as he wishes. He is dependent upon those who care for him, and his struggle for independence is a battle that stretches over many years. Freedom must be earned—it cannot be purchased cheaply. It is a potentiality in man's being that becomes actuality only by the courageous encounter of life itself.[37] Such encounter is not won by taking the easy way. It is a lonely battle that the individual must wage for himself, a battle that involves

[35] Allport, *Becoming*, p. 100.

[36] *Ibid.*, p. 101.

[37] The reader is encouraged to read Paul Tillich, *The Courage to Be* (New Haven: Yale University Press, 1952).

risk—risk of the unknown and a departure from momentary security.[38]

> Freedom is not a reward or a decoration that is celebrated with champagne. Nor yet a gift, a box of dainties designed to make you lick your chops. Oh no! It's a chore ... and a long-distance race, quite solitary and very exhausting. No champagne, no friends raising their glasses as they look at you affectionately. Alone in a forbidding room, alone in the prisoner's box before the judges, and alone to decide in the face of oneself or in the face of other's judgment. At the end of all freedom is a court sentence; that's why freedom is too heavy to bear, especially when you're down with a fever, or are distressed, or love nobody.[39]

There are many who find the cost too great. It is easier to "escape from freedom," but one never does so without losing one's self in the transaction. The cost is the submission to determining forces such as conformity—a momentary bargain that pays dividends of security but also in turn clouds the meaning of life, negates self-worth, and harnesses one to the burden of living as an automaton.

## SOCIOPOLITICAL FREEDOM

We have to this point discussed in passing several types of freedom. Now let us make distinctions among these different types. Reference can be made to a locus of freedom that is external and one that is internal.

In the beginning of this discussion of freedom, reference was made to the Bill of Rights and the Declaration of Independence. In the Declaration of Independence we find:

> All men are created equal, ... are endowed by their Creator with certain inalienable rights. ... Among these are life, liberty, and the pursuit of happiness. ... *To secure these rights, governments are instituted among men, deriving their just powers from the consent of the governed.*[40]

Freedom to speak and act must be protected by the guarantee of the government. The structure of law provides a necessary framework within which the individual as a dignified being can develop and thrive. Freedom demands authority; certain limitations for its best

---

[38]See also Abraham Maslow, *Toward a Psychology of Being* (New Jersey: D. Van Nostrand, 1962), p. 44.

[39]Gardner, *Self-Renewal*, p. 136, quoting A. Camus, *The Fall* (New York: Alfred A. Knopf, 1960), pp. 132–133.

[40]Italics mine.

growth. Government (or structure) is the means and not the end. The dignity of man and his freedom to develop is the supreme value to which the founders of our country submitted themselves. It is imperative that these values be cherished and protected from what seems a never ending tendency of organization to become the end in itself. Jefferson recognized this tendency when he stated the following in the Declaration:

> Whenever any form of government becomes destructive of these ends, it is the right of the people to alter or to abolish it, and to institute new government, laying its foundation on such principles and organizing its powers in such form as to them shall seem most likely to effect their safety and happiness.

Numerous leaders throughout our history as a nation have recognized the constant threat to freedom of the individual and have striven to protect this most cherished value. In an age that seems to be questioning the importance of authority to freedom, it is important to recognize its significance. To derive the proper balance between the individual and what he wants to do on one hand and necessary restrictions placed upon him by society on the other is an old problem. Too frequently it has been viewed as an "either-or" proposition—society as opposed to the individual and the individual as opposed to society. To look more clearly at the problem one finds that the two are mutually interdependent. One could not have a society without individuals, nor could one have an individual without a society.

> Some moderns are so enamored of the ideal of individuality that they would not think of speaking out on behalf of society. They imagine that the only effect a society can have on the individual is a destructive one. But it is by means of the free society that men keep themselves free. If men wish to remain free, they had better look to the health, the vigor, the viability of their free society—and to its capacity for renewal.[41]

Every individual is imposed upon by his society. A particular language, certain ways of behaving, certain rules and regulations, all are imposed upon him and such impositions are necessary to the growth of freedom. One's freedom of development, for example, would be seriously limited by the inability to speak a language. The important question, then, is not whether imposition takes place but rather whether the imposition is restricting or liberating. Societal re-

[41]Gardner, *Self-Renewal*, p. 66.

strictions can be so great that the individual is completely absorbed into the traditions and customs of the group, which set limits on individual fulfillment, or the individual can be so thrown upon a total permissiveness in the release of his impulses that anarchy is the result. "When the individual seeks autonomy he may achieve freedom and moral responsibility or he may achieve only aggrandizement of the self, with all the accompanying disorders of self-regard, cancerous pride, uncontrolled inflation of his self-evaluations, unfulfillable self-expectations."[42] It is necessary that the individual recognize meaning beyond himself, a meaning that itself is liberating.

> A meaningful relationship between the self and values that lie beyond the self is not incompatible with individual freedom. On the contrary, it is an essential ingredient of the inner strength that must characterize the free man. The man who has established emotional, moral, and spiritual ties beyond the self gains the strength needed to endure the rigors of freedom.[43]

It is part of the individual's obligation in a democracy to make certain that the organizational structure within which he moves does increase rather than decrease responsible freedom. Organization that frees the individual for self-fulfillment will require a balance of the extremes of individual and society.

> Pascal maintained that we are made virtuous not by our love of virtue but "by the counterpoise of two opposite vices." It takes a vice to check a vice and virtue is the by-product of a stalemate between opposite vices. The same probably holds true of individual freedom: we are free not by our own power but by the counterpoise of two opposite powers. Individual freedom is the automatic by-product of a drawn-out contest between more or less equal parties, factions, bodies, and so on.[44]

Sorokin, in his examination of our "crisis age," referred to the differences in interpretation of freedom in different value systems.[45] He contrasted what he called "sensate liberty" and "ideational liberty." "Sensate liberty," derived from a naturalistic value orientation, declares a man to be free if his wishes are equal to his means for achieving them. In this system restraint is minimized; wishes are constantly increased, and so are the means for achieving them. Plea-

[42] *Ibid.*, p. 91.
[43] *Ibid.*, p. 93.
[44] Eric Hoffer, *The Ordeal of Change* (New York: Harper and Row, 1952), p. 96.
[45] Pitirim A. Sorokin, *The Crisis of Our Age* (New York: E. P. Dutton and Co., Inc., 1941), pp. 172–176.

sure is the value that freedom in this sense serves. Such an interpretation of freedom "accentuates and intensifies the struggle of individuals
and groups."[46] "Ideational liberty," in contrast to this view, focuses
internally and emphasizes restriction and restraint in control of
desires. Freedom in this view is achieved by reducing one's wishes
rather than by satisfying them. Based primarily upon a strict supernatural value orientation, it is the freedom of the ascetic. Either of these
systems in themselves produces an overbalanced structure. Only
when the basic freedoms (speech, press, etc.) "are not disassociated
from moral and social responsibilities" are they the greatest boon to
man.

> The acid test of successful democratic government is the de-
> gree of effective liberty it makes available to the individual. That
> criterion establishes an order of values. Self-fulfillment is placed at
> the summit. All other goods are relegated to lower orders of prior-
> ity; even personal security and comfort must have less considera-
> tion.[47]

Lee is another who defended the importance of structure to
freedom.

> At one time leaders in the field of interpersonal relations held
> that unlimited freedom *from* would be conducive to freedom *for* or
> *to*. But recently this notion has been questioned. Educational leaders
> now consider that unbounded freedom is chaotic and frightening,
> and they advocate the setting of limits. But the limit, in American
> imagery, is something external; so we have seen the suggested limit
> as a surrounding boundary, a fence around the formless area of
> freedom. But I believe that the trouble is not that the individual is
> frightened by unbounded freedom, but rather that the lack of struc-
> ture leaves him inert. And the introduction of outer boundaries is no
> solution, within the American cultural framework. What incites the
> American individual to an answering engagement in the situation is
> definiteness, caliber, *within* the situation; a strong framework,
> "guts." Unstructured freedom, whether fenced in or not, is still
> namby-pamby. The limits must have the character of a skeleton.
> Randomness, the unplanned and unscheduled, are like the jellyfish,
> and perpetuate or evoke inertia. Modupe's silences, during which he
> became attuned to the rhythm of the earth, do not incite to an
> answering actualization of the capacity to do or feel.[48]

[46]*Ibid.*, p. 174.
[47]Henry M. Wriston, "The Individual," in *Goals for Americans* (New York:
Prentice-Hall, Inc., 1960), p. 48.
[48]Dorothy Lee, *Freedom and Culture* (New York: Prentice-Hall, Inc., 1959),
p. 57.

The individual can move with a sense of direction within a framework of values and goals. Freedom is based upon a balance of individuality with responsibility—a responsibility that derives from a commitment to meaningful social values that transcend the self—a commitment that becomes increasingly more difficult if the society is fragmented or suffering from moral fatigue. In such a time of value crisis it becomes imperative that we examine the structure within which we live and the values inherent within it.

Freedom must also include the right to dissent. The use of freedom as a goal, when interpreted in a narrow sense, can actually become a source of conflict rather than of unity. In such a parochial use of the word freedom, emphasis is given to the idea as belonging to the "in group." Individuals have freedom in this sense only as it agrees with the concept of the in group—any deviation therefrom becomes heresy. With such a narrow view of freedom, the in group feels a sense of responsibility to protect its absolutist view, and so much of its activity is channeled into seeking out and destroying any encroachments that would differ from its view of truth. Conflict is inevitable in such a situation. Consider the many "antigroups" found in our society today.

When freedom incorporates the right to dissent and a protection of that right, it becomes a unifying force. To disallow man's right to dissent is to distrust him, to be in direct opposition to a belief in man as a being of inherent worth. It is to make man earn his equality rather than to recognize equality as an aspect of basic human nature, which includes uniqueness of the individual—his right to be different. To remain parochial in the face of contrary evidence is to cause decay of the "habit of truth."

> The state of mind, the state of society is of a piece. When we discard the test of fact in what a star is, we discard it in what a man is. A society holds together by the respect which man gives to man; it fails in fact, it falls apart into groups of fear and power, when its concept of man is false. We find the drive which makes a society stable at last in the search for what makes us men. This is a search which never ends: to end it is to freeze the concept of man in a caricature beyond correction, as the societies of caste and master-race have done.[49]

It is also important to recognize here that freedom is *not* rebel-

[49]Bronowski, *Science and Human Values*, p. 59.

lion. Rebellion may be a part of the movement toward freedom, but to equate freedom with rebellion is to equate it with license.

> Since the rebel gets his sense of direction and vitality from attacking the existing standards and mores, he does not have to develop standards of his own. Rebellion acts as a substitute for the more difficult process of struggling through to one's own autonomy, to new beliefs, to the state where one can lay new foundations on which to build.[50]

Nor is freedom the same as planlessness, for freedom in the true sense must exist within a liberating structure. It does not come about by sitting around and waiting for it to happen.

To provide freedom in the fullest sense is to follow principles of truth-seeking that are universal.[51] To be a scientist anywhere and at anytime is to self-impose the conditions of rational investigation—an open mind, intellectual honesty, adherance to the laws of logic and scientific method. To be a scientist in this sense is not to be neutral to values, as some would contend, but to explicitly subscribe to human values of which freedom is a vital part. Bronowski has helped to clarify the relationship between values and the scientific method.

> If we are to study conduct, we must follow it in both directions: into the duties of men, which alone hold a society together, and also into the freedom to act personally which the society must still allow its men. The problem of values arises only when men try to fit together their need to be social animals with their need to be free men. There is no problem, and there are no values, until men want to do both. If an anarchist wants only freedom, whatever the cost, he will prefer the jungle of man at war with man. And if a tyrant wants only social order, he will create the totalitarian state.[52]

All of our knowledge has been built up in a social setting, and all questions of *ought* refer to a social context. To be a scientist requires trust of others, and from this "it follows that there is a principle which binds society together, because without it the individual would be helpless to tell true from the false. This principle is truthfulness. If we accept truth as an individual criterion, then we have also to make it the cement to hold society together."[53]

Bronowski examined the society of scientists to uncover the

[50]May, *Man's Search*, p. 135.

[51]Peter Bertocci and Richard Millard, *Personality and the Good* (New York: David McKay Co., 1963), pp. 416–418.

[52]Bronowski, *Science and Human Values*, p. 70.

[53]*Ibid.*, p. 74.

principles that have bound them together into an enduring society, one that has been able to endure change and outlast any modern state. The basic unity derives from the unbiased search for truth and the testing of it in action. From this basic principle grow other values:

> The society of scientists is simple because it has a directing purpose: to explore the truth. Nevertheless, it has to solve the problem of every society, which is to find a compromise between man and men. It must encourage the single scientist to be independent, and the body of scientists to be tolerant. From these basic conditions, which form the prime values, there follows step by step the spectrum of values: dissent, freedom of thought and speech, justice, honor, human dignity and self-respect.[54]

Such values are the mark of a truly free society, and "dissent is the mark of freedom."

It is the society that encourages dissent that is the growing society. The conforming society nourishes the seeds of its own obsolescence. The secret of unity and growth lies in the ability of a society to fuse public and private needs. "It can keep alive and grow only by a constant tension between dissent and respect, between independence from the views of others and tolerance for them."[55] Tolerance must be based upon respect for the individual and belief in his worth, and these are not a product of indifference. They must be self-imposed. Such values are not mechanical but are the products of human nature. "The sense of human dignity ... is the cement of a society of equal men, for it expresses their knowledge that respect for others must be founded in self-respect."[56] It is the society of scientists that is more important than their discoveries.[57] From such a society we can learn much as to the importance of the values inherent in freedom for the larger society.

> The dilemma of today is not that the human values cannot control a mechanical science. It is the other way about: the scientific spirit is more human than the machinery of governments. We have not let either the tolerance or the empiricism of science enter the parochial rules by which we still try to prescribe the behavior of

---

[54] *Ibid.*, p. 88.
[55] *Ibid.*, p. 80.
[56] *Ibid.*, p. 83.
[57] *Ibid.*, p. 93.

nations. Our conduct as states clings to a code of self-interest which science, like humanity, has long left behind.[58]

This foregoing discussion of freedom has focused primarily upon the external aspects—the freedom to act within a context. The context, structure, is important as a means to freedom and to choosing freely one's goals for commitment. It provides the context for effectual choice.[59] A man is free in this sense "in proportion as he *does or thinks what he chooses.*" Let us call this first type of freedom sociopolitical freedom. This leads us to our discussion of the second type of freedom, the one that focuses internally within the individual, which we shall call psychological freedom.

## PSYCHOLOGICAL FREEDOM

A free societal structure does not guarantee free individuals. An individual can live in a free society yet be a prisoner within himself, and without free individuals a social structure cannot long remain free. It takes free individuals to nourish a free society. "The moral for modern man is clear. He has a duty to nourish those qualities within himself that make him a free and morally responsible being. And he has an equally compelling duty to honor values beyond the self."[60] "Every incompetent citizen is a menace to the freedom of all."[61]

It is possible to get caught up with the man on the street's view that freedom is absence of external restraint and that there "just ain't no other kind." We cannot afford to be so easily satisfied. In any individual oriented society the most important natural resource is its people, and it is only logical that the fullest possible development of the potentiality of individuals would be a major goal.

The moment is ripe to remind ourselves once again that ideas come from individuals, that progress stems from ideas. In the same way morals are the exclusive possession of individuals; phrases like group morality cloud the reality rather than helping to clarify it. . . .

There are many legitimate goals for the United States. None of them—literally none—is attainable without the intelligence, courage, and industry of individuals. The central goal, therefore, should

[58]*Ibid.*, p. 90.
[59]Perry, *Humanity of Man*, p. 28.
[60]Gardner, *Self-Renewal*, p. 93.
[61]Wriston, "The Individual," p. 53.

be a renewal of faith in the infinite value and the unlimited possibilities of individual development.[62]

What does it mean to say that one has psychological freedom? The existentialists have helped us to understand more fully this inner type of freedom through their discussions of subject-object dualism. In the proceedings of the value study at Harvard University, Weisskopf discussed this point.[63] All human experience consists of two parts of a dialectic: the subject who experiences and the object that is experienced. These two poles are interdependent, each determines the other, and neither can exist apart from the other. That is, they are ontologically one. This split has important implications in understanding the ontological roots of human freedom.

> The basic source of the split in human existence is *consciousness*. Man can *transcend* any given situation because he is aware of it. Man "is" and, at the same time, he is conscious of his being. This establishes a cleavage between himself as a conscious subject and the objective situation of which he is conscious. Transcendence through consciousness is the basis of human freedom. By transcending the given situation through his consciousness man frees himself within certain limits from the necessities of this situation. This opens up alternatives: the dimension of actuality is left behind and the realm of potentiality is entered, creating the possibility of choice and the necessity of decision based on guiding values. The entire sequence of transcendence through consciousness, grasping of potential alternatives and the exercise of choice based on values, constitutes man's freedom.[64]

There has in recent years been a greater emphasis upon psychological freedom. Men have too often in history secured freedom from external restraints only to succumb to subtle and often perhaps more lethal internal restraints. Frankl has helped us learn that, although man may be under the most severe external restraint, he still retains the freedom to choose his internal state—his attitudes. The reverse of this is perhaps less true, for we can become "fascinated by the growth of freedom from powers outside of ourselves and are blinded to the fact of inner restraints, compulsions, and fears, which tend to undermine the meaning of the victories freedom has won against its traditional enemies."[65] It is imperative not only that we continue to

---

[62] *Ibid.*, p. 57.

[63] Walter A. Weisskopf, "Existence and Values," in A. Maslow (ed.), *New Knowledge in Human Values* (New York: Harper and Row, 1959), pp. 108-109.

[64] *Ibid.*

[65] Fromm, *Escape from Freedom*, p. 105.

increase and preserve our freedom to act externally but that we also "gain a new kind of freedom, one which enables us to realize our own individual self, to have faith in this self and in life."[66]

It is this inner freedom that is the source of creativity. Liberty, or external freedom, has to do with the action of circumstances upon the man. Freedom that is inner has to do with a man's action on circumstances.[67] To be free psychologically is to be able to express one's unique individuality by reasoned choice. It is to be independent and autonomous in an environment of deterministic forces. It is to be fully responsible for one's choices. All expressions of individuality are not free but may be illusory. *"The right to express our thoughts . . . means something only if we are able to have thoughts of our own;* freedom from external authority is a lasting gain only if the inner psychological conditions are such that we are able to establish our own individuality."[68]

It is natural for a child to be curious, to be spontaneous, and this spontaneity is the essence of inner freedom.[69] In the process of socialization, however, he may be taught to suppress his individuality, his spontaneity, for the sake of conformity to some pattern. Fromm has written concerning the prevalence of this in our culture. Children are too frequently taught not to be spontaneous and creative but rather to learn what others expect and to imitate this pattern. Yet such conformity is produced in the name of freedom, with the individual assuming that he is truly free when he is in actuality but a puppet responding only as others pull the strings. He is taught to love all people, to always be friendly and pleasant, to not show hostility, to hide any emotion, to believe anything that comes from an authority. "He has become a part of the machine that his hands have built. He thinks, feels, and wills what he believes he is supposed to think, feel, and will; in this very process he loses his self upon which all genuine security of a free individual must be built."[70]

This also produces a loss of identity. If one has lost his real self, how does he know who he is? This loss makes it even more important to conform, for "it means that one can be more sure of oneself only if one lives up to the expectations of others."[71] The price of giving up

[66]*Ibid.*, p. 106.
[67]Perry, *Humanity of Man*, p. 28.
[68]Fromm, *Escape from Freedom*, p. 241.
[69]Deriving from the Latin root *sponte*, meaning "of one's free will." *Ibid.*, p. 258.
[70]*Ibid.*, pp. 253–254.
[71]*Ibid.*, p. 254.

one's self is high and results in a thwarting of life, unhappiness, and often despair. Such an individual cannot live productively. For Fromm, "positive freedom consists in the spontaneous activity of the total, integrated personality. . . . Only if man does not repress essential parts of his self, only if he has become transparent to himself and only if the different spheres of life have reached a fundamental integration, is spontaneous activity possible."[72] This implies the "full affirmation of the uniqueness of the individual." Only as men become free internally as well as externally is democracy in the fullest sense of the term possible.

> The victory of freedom is possible only if democracy develops into a society in which the individual, his growth and happiness, is the aim and purpose of culture, in which life does not need any justification in success or anything else, and in which the individual is not subordinated to or manipulated by any power outside of himself, be it the State or the economic machine; finally, a society in which his conscience and ideals are not the internalization of external demands, but are really his and express the aims that result from the peculiarity of his self.[73]

In reference to what we are calling psychological freedom, Bertocci made an important distinction between what he called "ethical freedom" and "moral freedom." Most psychologists have defined freedom on the basis of a biological model, describing it as "the fulfillment of potential with a view to optimum fulfillment of potential."[74] This Bertocci called "ethical freedom." This freedom is based upon the biological growth process. A plant when grown in favorable environmental conditions will actualize its potential in interaction with the physical world. Such natural development, however, may be hindered (have its freedom restricted) by such encumbrances as weeds or plant lice. The horticulturist assists the plant to maximize its potential by eliminating the restrictions and thus providing an environment conducive to fullest freedom of growth. Animals, although having greater plasticity and thus complexity of behavior, become all their potential allows within the existing conditions. Humans, to most psychologists, although having even greater plasticity, also follow this pattern.

---

[72] *Ibid.*, pp. 258–259.
[73] *Ibid.*, p. 271.
[74] Bertocci and Millard, *Personality and the Good*, p. 176.

> To be "free" is to fulfill one's own given potential for growth. To become free is to guide growth by understanding one's potential, by knowing the conditions that keep that potential from growing, and by getting rid of the obstacles to growth, so that the individual's needs and abilities may blossom.[75]

Bertocci criticized this popular view for not doing justice to what actually goes on in the human being and detected a deterministic tendency within.

> The terms "freedom" and "creativity" and even "choice" occur frequently, but in the last analysis, the growth, change, or development that they have in mind involves the becoming that a given individual, with his potential, *must* become in the environment that presses in upon him. The change is "free" if some notion of an implicit goal is injected as the "end" of the development.[76]

Such a view of freedom emphasizes the plasticity and opportunity of the individual on one hand and the fulfillment of potential on the other. This view is not incorrect, only partial. It lacks the further element of freedom described by Bertocci as "moral freedom." In his development, the individual soon comes upon alternatives where he must make some choice of direction. Such freedom to choose is "moral freedom" and involves the important question of free will. Man can be a good chooser or a bad chooser and, because he is not bound by time, can create goals. Bertocci focused within individual experience to describe that an individual "can make some difference to the process-in-course by willing an end other than the one that was about to take place."[77]

> Such free will, to use the traditional terminology, has been called "free" to emphasize at least three contentions: (a) such willing is part of the intrinsic capacity of a human being who has matured to the point where he can think alternatives, (b) such willing is an initiating influence in (many) human situations where alternatives seem possible, and (c) such initiating "will" is not *the product* of the rest of the personality's configuration of needs, wants, habits, abilities.[78]

Such willing is different from "wanting" or "desiring." Although it can function only within the range of possibility and is limited by deter-

[75] *Ibid.*
[76] *Ibid.*, p. 177.
[77] *Ibid.*, p. 179.
[78] *Ibid.*, p. 182.

mining forces, its most significant aspect is that, by "willing," the course of the future can be changed to other than what its course appeared to be preceding the act of will. To say that the individual's choice is determined by something of which he is not aware, and if we knew enough could have predicted his choice, is to go beyond actual experience and in its place to assert "an unexperienced state of affairs in order to save the theory."[79]

Bertocci used the terms will-agency and will-power to further explain the process of willing.[80] "Will-agency" refers to the *freedom to initiate* action toward a goal." Will-power" involves the *"freedom to effectuate* that goal in different degrees." A man who chooses to break the smoking habit is utilizing "will-agency." Whether he will be successful or not will depend upon the "will-power" that he can bring to bear upon the elements that resist the goal. The significant points in this discussion are that the individual can direct his own growth within the context of his internal or external limitations,[81] that the decision to think or not to think concerning alternatives regarding further development is of great significance to later judgments and actions, and that "will-agency" and "will-power" have a profound effect upon the course a life will take. Chosen goals and the means to them will influence the direction taken. "It must still be remembered, however, that if a man is free to choose between alternatives (moral freedom) the problem he faces is to choose those ends that do allow him *ethical freedom*, that is, the optimum fulfillment of his potential."[82]

## THE COUNSELOR AND FREEDOM

In summary, we can view the ultimate task of the counselor in the public school as one of helping the individual to become the free person he potentially is. Some may call this "ambiguity reduction," "becoming," "self-actualization," "seeking identity," or a host of other terms. Too frequently the individual learns a pseudo-identity from his culture that is restricting rather than freeing. In our turbulent society there is a danger of great ambiguity in the wake of rapidly changing and conflicting values. Perhaps the easiest way to find an

[79] *Ibid.*, p. 183.
[80] *Ibid.*, p. 184.
[81] *Ibid.*, p. 193.
[82] *Ibid.*, p. 197.

identity is to merely accept the one given, as confusing as it may be, by the culture that surrounds us. This becomes a frustrating route when the messages conflict with the inner being.

> By definition, the thing that an individual should prize most highly is himself. And yet the thoughtful, mature individual secretly, or perhaps even openly despises himself. Why is this so? Can it be that the self which the individual despises is not really his own true self? That it is the self which unreligious religion, immoral morality and unlawful law have made of him.?[83]

The counselor can aid the individual to discover the identity that is his "real self." In so doing, he becomes free from those outside forces that would keep him in bondage to others. Arbuckle states this position well when he says:

> Man basically is free, and any man can come to learn and to grow and to become the free person he is. This is the purpose of counseling—to help the individual to loose himself from his deterministic shackles, and to come to realize and to see what he has always had—choice and freedom.
> Being free is difficult and one cannot be free without continually running the risk of losing one's person. The struggle to be free, too, is often much more intense and complicated, at the inner self level, than the struggle against overt and obvious forces of oppression. If education results in real understanding, it can widen one's horizon of freedom, and the counselor must be concerned about the extent to which the educational experience helps to free each child.[84]

To be truly free is to be able to choose and to own the choices as one's own. To do this is to be responsible. To be free in this sense, the person can experience commitment. Commitment can be defined as the willingness of an individual to give up certain freedoms (such as immediate pleasures) in order to achieve greater freedom (such as enhancement of choice opportunities through the discipline of further education). He can examine the alternatives open to him, can select his own values, and can commit himself to them and use them as a guide for further decisions and as a basis around which to organize his life. It is in such choice and commitment that ultimate meaning will be found if it is to be found. To be free is also to be open to continuing

---

[83]Thomas A. Cowan, "Special Interests and Value," in F. C. Gruber (ed.), *Aspects of Value* (Philadelphia: University of Pennsylvania Press, 1959), p. 63.

[84]Dugald S. Arbuckle, *Counseling: Philosophy, Theory, and Practice* (Boston: Allyn and Bacon, Inc., 1965), p. 275.

examination and modification of such values: Tentativeness and commitment need not be polarities but can rather be unifying principles.[85]

> Here then is that freedom, or exercise of enlightened choice, which I conceive to be that which is variously called "humane," "humanity," "humanistic," "humanism," or "liberal culture." Its specifications are: learning, imagination, sympathy, dignity, and civility. You may recognize them by their opposites. The man who lacks freedom is ignorant, narrow, indoctrinated or dogmatic through lack of learning or imagination; insensible, apathetic, prejudiced, censorious, opportunistic, sordid or self absorbed through lack of sympathy; base, ascetic, trivial or snobbish through lack of dignity; dull, boorish or brutal through lack of civility.[86]

The counselor who is committed to freedom as a goal is not neutral. He is prejudiced for the best and highest goals that freedom can bring and is committed to the worth of the individual and to his fullest development as it unfolds by his own creative choice. To be free in this sense is to be human in the fullest meaning of the term.

## THE COUNSELOR AND THE GROUP

But there is one more aspect of the question that needs emphasis. Because the chief focus in guidance has been placed historically upon the "one-to-one" relationship, the individual has received the greatest amount of attention and the subjective side of individual choosing has been stressed. However, to recognize the subjective and objective as complementary parts of reality is to recognize that the group also plays an important role in any individual's life. An example of such a realization is found in these excerpts from Patterson's discussion of Frankl's ideas:

> Although each individual is unique, he would have no meaning by himself. "The significance of such individuality, the meaning of human personality, is, however, always related to community." In the community each individual, because he is unique, is irreplaceable. This is the difference between the community and the "mass," which is composed of identical units. "The community needs the individual existence in order for itself to have meaning," but also, "the meaning

<hr>

[85] Allport, "Psychological Models for Guidance," *Harvard Educational Review*, XXXII, 4 (Fall 1962), 378.

[86] Perry, *Humanity of Man*, p. 40.

of individuality comes to fulfillment in the community. To this extent, then, the value of the individual is dependent upon the community." The mass, however, submerges the individual: "by escape into the mass, man loses his most intrinsic quality, responsibility." But by becoming a part of the community, which is in itself a choice, man adds to his responsibility.[87]

And, "the intimate community of oneself with another is the area in which experiential values are especially realizable."[88]

The individual is always the "being-*in*-the-world." He is an individual *in* a group. He is basically free, but the group will have an effect upon him, and this effect will be a matter of degree. The more self-actualized the individual, the less he is likely to feel the power of group influence. All individuals, however, would to some degree be influenced by the group to which they belong at any moment. All individuals, for example, want to feel accepted, to be held in esteem. It is also important to remember that the individual is potentially free to interpret his situation and thus choose his response to the group.

The group, therefore, is an important influence upon the individual. Certain norms of behavior grow from it, and what is "normal" behavior is defined in terms of group consensus. It is possible for such norms to be either restricting or liberating. As Fromm[89] has indicated, one can have an entire society that is "sick" as measured in terms of some other standard, for example, freedom.

The group is extremely important to the adolescent. This has been true in the past and has been recognized as a necessary step in the process of becoming a mature adult. It is within the framework of rebellion against adult values that young people try out their wings, establish their autonomy as unique individuals, and then move toward becoming like the adult models who to them form somewhat of an ideal. Today there is question as to whether the process of growing up is still occurring in this fashion, for there have been changes that seem to lead to a different process. First, it appears that more and more young people are finding difficulty in emulating adult models. This may be a product of the vast gap between generations that is so evident today. One would find it difficult to emulate models who are, in the eyes of the young, obsolete. Second, the youth culture has been

[87]C. H. Patterson, *Theories of Counseling and Psychotherapy* (New York: Harper and Row, 1966), pp. 458–459.
[88]*Ibid.*, p. 470.
[89]Fromm, *The Sane Society* (New York: Holt, Rinehart, and Winston, 1955).

pushed by a society that has refused it a meaningful place into forming a society of its own.[90] Much writing exists on this topic, and a full description of this society would be beyond our purposes here. Suffice it to say that the models that youth emulate seem to be more and more chosen from within the youth society itself.[91] The importance of this change rests upon the models chosen as well as upon the direction and power of the group pressure. A major concern for the educational system and also for the counselor arises when the rewards of the social system are in conflict with the kinds of behavior that will lead to greater freedom. It can happen that a particular value orientation of a community may act as a restricting force in the development of individuals. For example, a community may urge a "stay-at-home" policy for its youth when there are no longer economic or psychological resources at home to foster healthy development. Other communities may hold to an "anti-education" attitude when education is vital to the very existence of the community. The traditional answer has been to aid the individual in some way to overcome his conflict or to learn to live within the system in spite of the conflict.

The question now arises as to whether there are ways by which groups as well as individuals can be helped. Can the social system itself be influenced in meaningful ways? A solely individualized approach may now be too narrow for current needs.

> Psychotherapy remains much too constrictive a term, too loaded with dubious assumptions which tempt us to believe that virtually all we need to cure the ailments of our time is to attack them, as it were, from the inside out as though the objective world will become healthy and sound only when the subjective psyche has *first* become healthy and sound. This is the supreme psychotherapeutic fallacy. It is peculiarly dangerous in education because it offers moral sanction for aloofness from the most controversial issues of society and politics. Its bias is correctible only through *the unity of a discipline in which psychotherapy's own theory and practice are amalgamated with the theory and practice of planned sociocultural diagnosis and prognosis.*[92]

It would be a fallacy in the opposite direction to say that one should work solely with groups of people. To view each side as equally important is necessary.

[90]James S. Coleman, *The Adolescent Society* (New York: The Free Press, 1961).
[91]Gary Walz referred to this point in an address at Boston University in 1965.
[92]Brameld, "Anthropotherapy—Toward Theory and Practice," *Human Organization*, XXIV, 4 (Winter 1965), 288–293.

Brameld[93] has expressed the importance of ideology and utopia in the epistemology of any group. The culture is always in process, that is, it is dynamic and changing. He describes this movement on a continuum, with ideology on one end and utopia on the other. Ideology represents a "social consensus about a culture more or less established," whereas utopia represents a "social consensus about a culture not yet established."[94] There exists, then, in any culture, a lag between its future goals or beliefs of what *should be* and its status quo or what *is*. Any group can best move in a positive direction if it is willing to critically examine its ideology and formulate its plans upon carefully thought out and validated goals. It is as this occurs that the cohesiveness of a group can function in a productive way by uniting its members and encouraging action in directions that enhance the process of moving ever closer to the realization of its goals. It is from such consensus that the framework or structure will come that will allow for freedom in the sense described in this chapter. Brameld calls the end that this structure serves "social self-realization."

> It is not to be taken to mean "freedom *from*"; it is not a negative term implying that the best life is one in which the individual is as little as possible responsible to, or controlled by, organized society. Rather, it should be understood to mean "freedom *for*"— freedom for the positive achievement of individual and social values; freedom to attain the widest possible range of goals; freedom to hope that the majority of people throughout the world can satisfy their fundamental wants.[95]

But again this involves value judgments.

Nagel[96] describes two kinds of value judgments that are commonly made by behavioral scientists. The first type he calls "characterizing value judgments," which consist of merely a description of a condition or conditions of whatever happens to be the object of investigation. This kind of judgment is similar to what has been referred to in this study as descriptive value. It represents the position of the "unbiased" and "objective" scientist. The second type of value judgment Nagel referrs to as "appraising value judgments." Similar to what we have called "normative value," such judgments appraise the condition described as being desirable or undesirable and in need or

[93]Brameld, *Toward A Reconstructed Philosophy of Education* (New York: Dryden Press, Inc., 1956).
[94]*Ibid.*, p. 97.
[95]*Ibid.*, pp. 118–119.
[96]Ernest Nagel, *The Structure of Science* (New York: Harcourt, 1961), pp. 482–495.

not in need of treatment based upon some norm.

Counselors, of necessity, make both types of judgments either explicitly or implicitly. In every situation, the counselor decides upon the basis of his ultimate goal; first, whether to enter into or continue a relationship with an individual, and, second, how to proceed. The question here is whether or not he now should begin to focus also upon groups in an appraising sense.

To make appraising judgments of groups can be frightening, for in a pluralistic society one may ask, "Who am I to judge what is best or desirable for any particular group?" But to not make any explicit judgment is to make an implicit judgment frequently based upon indifference. And to make an explicit judgment need not mean an imposition in an indoctrinating or controlling sense. An appraising judgment need not be as intruding as it may sound, for it depends upon the norm upon which it is based. As has been noted in Chapter 2, there are values that are relative, but there are also values that approach universality. Such universal values, as represented here by freedom, operate at a middle level that provides a framework within which both individual and group are enhanced. Although there is much yet to be learned concerning values, as Edel has discovered, there are points of covergence, and these points can be found within the concept of freedom as we have discussed it or in what Brameld has referred to in a perhaps more complete sense as *social self-realization.* Such a goal incorporates both the individual and the group and is, for Brameld, the "supreme value."

Several points are pertinent in consideration of such a norm.

1. It can serve as a criterion upon which appraising value judgments can be based.

2. This need not be a dogmatically imposed standard but rather can serve as a tool by which confrontation (or encounter) can occur and value options can be expressed.

3. The standard itself demands continuing reevaluation and refinement.

4. The subjective aspect of choice-making individuals must always be recognized as necessary to any type of meaningful change (the counselor is merely a "facilitator").

Brameld suggests the following as an example of convergence of goals approaching universality:

1. Most people do not want to be hungry; they cherish the value of sufficient *nourishment.*

2. Most people do not want to be cold or ragged; they cherish the value of *adequate dress.*

3. Most people do not want uncontrolled exposure, either to the elements or to people; they cherish the value of *shelter* and *privacy.*

4. Most people do not want celibacy; they cherish the value of *sexual expression.*

5. Most people do not want illness; they cherish the value of *physiological* and *mental health.*

6. Most people do not want chronic economic insecurity; they cherish the value of *steady work, steady income.*

7. Most people do not want loneliness; they cherish the value of *companionship, mutual devotion, belongingness.*

8. Most people do not want indifference; they cherish the value of *recognition, appreciation, status.*

9. Most people do not want constant monotony, routine, or drudgery; they cherish the value of *novelty, curiosity, variation, recreation, adventure, growth, creativity.*

10. Most people do not want ignorance; they cherish the value of *literacy, skill, information.*

11. Most people do not want to be continually dominated; they cherish the value of *participation, sharing.*

12. Most people do not want bewilderment; they cherish the value of *fairly immediate meaning, significance, order, direction.* [97]

The fields of social psychology and human relations have brought the emphasis of man *in* community and the process of change as it occurs *in* a group to a focus. Although this view is not new to psychology (it was already the major focus of Moreno and Adler during the time of Freud), its popularity as an important means of effecting change is relatively new. The focus is upon interaction between individuals, how they are changed in the process, and, in turn, how they influence and change the social group. The study of group dynamics is a complex area, but one in which knowledge is accumulating rapidly. One can see some of the dynamics of change inherent in these eight principles set forth by Cartwright, which he based upon a summary of research involving techniques of achieving change in human behavior.

(1) If the group is to be used effectively as a medium of change,

[97]Brameld, *Toward a Reconstructed Philosophy*, pp. 115–116.

those people who are to be changed and those who are to exert influence for change must have a strong sense of belonging to the same group; (2) The more attractive the group is to its members the greater is the influence that the group can exert on its members; (3) In attempts to change attitudes, values, or behavior, the more relevant they are to the basis of attraction to the group, the greater will be the influence that the group can exert upon them; (4) the greater the prestige of a group member in the eyes of the other members, the greater the influence he can exert; (5) Efforts to change individuals or subparts of a group which if successful, would have the result of making them deviate from the norms of the group, will encounter strong resistance; (6) Strong pressure for changes in the group can be established by creating a shared perception by members of the need for change, thus making the source of pressure for change lie within the group; (7) Information relating to the need for change, plans for change, and consequences of change must be shared by all relevant people in the group; (8) Changes in one part of a group produce strain in other related parts which can be reduced only by eliminating the change or by bringing about readjustments in the related parts.[98]

Other writers,[99] such as Opler, Kluckhohn, Brameld, Syz, and Burrow, to name a few, have given support to this view, stressing the importance of man *in* his culture, affecting and being affected by it. Based upon the knowledge of group process, the counselor can become an effective facilitator of entire groups toward group goals incorporated within the ultimate goal of social self-realization, which places emphasis upon responsibility—self and other.

New terminology[100] has come into existence that stresses this

[98]Dorwin Cartwright, "Achieving Change in People: Some Applications of Group Dynamics Theory," *Human Relations*, IV, 4 (1951), 388–391, as quoted by Bruce Shertzer and Shelley C. Stone, *Fundamentals of Guidance* (Boston: Houghton Mifflin Co., 1966), pp. 166–167.

[99]See, for example, Marvin K. Opler, *Culture, Psychiatry and Human Values* (Springfield, Ill.: Charles C. Thomas, 1956); Clyde Kluckhohn and others, "Values and Value-Orientations in the Theory of Action," in Talcott Parsons and Edward Shils (eds.), *Toward a General Theory of Action* (New York: Harper and Row, 1962); Theodore Brameld, *Cultural Foundations of Education* (New York: Harper and Brothers, 1957); Hans Syz, "A Summary Note on the Work of Trigant Burrow," *International Journal of Social Psychiatry*," VII, 4 (1961) and "Reflections on Group- or Phylo-Analysis," Supplement to *Acta Psychotherapeutica et Psychosomatica*, XI (1963), 37–88; Trigant Burrow, "Prescriptions for Peace: The Biological Basis of Man's Ideological Conflicts," in Pitirim A. Sorokin (ed.), *Explorations in Altruistic Love and Behavior* (Boston: Beacon Press, 1950).

[100]It is interesting to note that Nietzsche referred to the philosopher as the "physician of culture." See Rollo May, *The Meaning of Anxiety* (New York: The Ronald Press, 1950), p. 12.

point of view. "Phylo-Analysis" was coined in the thirties by Trigant Burrow and has more recently been emphasized by Syz.[101] Brameld has discussed what he calls "anthropotherapy," defined in "preliminary fashion as *the theory and practice of descriptive and prescriptive human roles.* "[102]

In the counseling field there appears to be a trend toward viewing the larger social context as an important medium for effecting change. Stewart and Warnath[103] have emphasized the role of the counselor as a social change agent. Fullmer and Bernard[104] have emphasized the need for working with family groups. Numerous articles and books are now appearing that deal with effecting change through counseling groups. Rogers[105] also has moved in this direction. He has emphasized the importance of the "basic encounter" that occurs between individuals in an intensive group experience and the impact that this could have upon a total educational system.

It is important to work with individuals, for in so doing the counselor is aiding the individual in becoming more free through a fuller experiencing of his own subjectivity in relation to his objective world. But the individual also belongs to a group (or groups), and these groups represent more than the mere sum of individuals. For the individual enhances or hinders the development of other individuals by his interaction with them, and he in turn will be equally affected by them. It is important that the counselor recognize that the group is indeed an important influence on all of us.

We began this chapter with the question, "Is there a value base that can be made explicit and validated that can serve as a guide in counseling and against which practice can be evaluated?" It has been argued that freedom must serve as a major part of such a base. An attempt has been made toward both clarification and validation. It is recognized that much more remains to be done. However, the counselor who understands the various facets of freedom is in a better position to know which road he is traveling in the counseling process and can use this standard to insure that he is working "with" and "for"

[101]Syz, "A Summary Note."

[102]Brameld, "Anthropotherapy."

[103]Lawrence H. Stewart and Charles Warnath, *The Counselor and Society: A Cultural Approach* (Boston: Houghton Mifflin Co., 1965).

[104]Daniel W. Fullmer and Harold W. Bernard, *Counseling: Content and Process* (Chicago: Science Research Associates, Inc., 1964).

[105]Carl R. Rogers, "A Plan for Self-Directed Change in an Educational System," *Freedom to Learn* (Columbus, Ohio: Charles E. Merrill, 1969), pp. 303-323.

the individual rather than "against" him. He will be aware that the client always possesses a minimal amount of freedom of choice, no matter how difficult the situation. He will recognize that he must consider the context within which the client lives so as to best promote a structure which provides socio-political freedom, freedom which allows for maximum self-development. But he will also recognize that there is an inner freedom which must be nourished in individuals and which leads to increased authenticity in living as well as increased moral responsibility.

It now remains, in the final chapter, for us to draw this study of values in the counseling process to a close and to focus upon a summation and some concluding remarks.

# chapter 8

# The Counselor and Values: Where Do We Go from Here?

## SUMMARY

We began this book by citing descriptions of our culture as a crisis culture moving toward a decisive moment, a continual choosing of ends that will lead toward renewal or disintegration. Change has reached drastic proportions today. The alternatives in our society that force choice are beginning to outweigh the commonly agreed upon beliefs, ideas, and ways of acting. This situation requires that individuals be flexible and capable of change, but the bases or criteria for making "good" choices are becoming less tangible. The anxieties of individuals seem to be increasing in quantity and intensity.

We have seen that one of the problems young people face is that they continue to get ambiguous messages concerning who they are as well as what is "good." The school grading system has been made the measure of inner worth. Adolescents learn to hate success in others, for that means defeat for themselves and increased negative self-concept, and they tend to view themselves deterministically in a field of economic forces rather than as autonomous beings. Fear of failure has become a motivating force. Although our generation has unprecedented abundance and the hope of an ever increasing standard of living, which comes more and more to represent our idea of the good life, there is the grim realization that something is amiss, that there must be something more to life than this. Never before has man had in his control the capabilities of total destruction. We may live in what is referred to as a "free society," but many people within themselves are psychologically in chains, for conformity is sought at the cost of one's freedom to be himself.

Such is the cultural setting in which young people today are attempting to discover themselves. The questions of the young ("Who am I?" "What can I do?" "Where am I going?") receive no final answers. In times of confusion when one can see what to him are traditional values on the wane, though they may not seem so to others, there is danger in the tendency to "tell" and to "teach" rather than to listen. The counselor must remember that he is a "helper" of dynamic, self-propelled, and becoming beings with all the dignity and respect entailed, not static and plastic human objects or blank slates. To the counselor who listens, who is able to tune in to the correct wave length of youth, such questions regarding the quest for identity loom large in counseling, are at the very heart of the counseling process itself. Such a search is deeply personal and is a search for values. Therefore it is imperative for the counselor to consider and understand the philosophy of value and recognize the perplexing methodological questions in dealing with values that arise within the counseling relationship.

We have observed that the counselor through his counseling behavior expresses a social philosophy, and his recognition of this should make him aware of his responsibility then to philosophize as effectively as possible. It is of greatest importance for each counselor to look honestly at himself and to be aware of his presuppositions in order to avoid subtly imposing values upon clients.

We have attempted to discover what value is and have found it difficult to define in a short descriptive statement, for axiology—the specific study of values—recognizes the concept as being quite broad. Value is a learned conception, explicit or implicit, of what is desirable. It is a hypothetical construct, a criterion upon which choice either by an individual or a group is justified and which also serves as a motivator to commitment and action. Values are not the same as needs, goals, attitudes, or preferences, though these are related concepts.

We have considered also the question of whether objects possess value because we desire them or whether we desire them because they possess value. I have argued that this subjective-objective controversy may be the result of a dualism that in actuality does not exist. Rather than being viewed as separate and contradictory, they can be viewed as complementary, as two sides of the same coin. Value experience is a dynamic relationship, for in each individual there will be a continuing interaction between the subjective and the objective.

In this book the breakdown of persistent dualisms has been an underlying theme. In pointing up the weaknesses of such dualistic thinking I have argued for a "both-and" over an "either-or" position. Other dualisms related to and growing from the subjective-objective controversy are fact versus value, freedom versus determinism, individual versus society, and universalism versus relativism.

One can view the major conflicts growing from these dualisms in terms of a dialectic. One has a thesis—the individual—and an antithesis—society or the group. To emphasize only the former is to promote anarchic, narcissistic views emphasizing the "I" in an extremely egoistic fashion. To emphasize the latter, however, is to promote a dead, static philosophy that denies the worth and dignity of the individual. This position views the individual as subordinate to and thus in need of being imposed upon by the society. These two points of view clash, the one negating the other, but from this clash there now can arise a synthesis at a higher level and such a synthesis can be found by a breakdown in such dualistic thinking. The new synthesis consists in recognizing the subjective and the objective as complementary. Man is viewed as a being of worth and dignity, but in a world of "others." The emphasis becomes focused upon responsibility. Freedom is vital but always within a world of limits. Some values are relative but others are universal, with a broad spectrum in between. Scientific "facts" are important but cannot be divorced from those subjective judgments that precede or follow from them. From such a synthesis grows a new perspective—a perspective that recognizes the importance of man as a choosing, valuing being and thus responsible for his behavior.

In our review of the literature we have seen that, until recently, values in counseling have remained largely implicit. It is imperative that counselors continually examine and be aware of what values they serve and why. There is general agreement that the counselor should serve the ultimate values of the dignity and worth of the individual and his right to freedom of choice. These values are basic to our democratic society; however, there is danger when these come into conflict with values of a technological society, which are also prevalent today. The counselor must make explicit for himself the values he serves in order to understand the direction of his influence. There exist conflicting loyalties on his part to the client, society, the employing institution, the profession, and to himself. Such conflicts can be resolved only by recourse to a framework of values. Although an ethical code may serve as a guideline, the final judgment rests upon the individual counselor, his values, and his perception of the axiological dilemma.

To make such a judgment requires great moral courage and integrity.

We have found growing agreement that the counselor cannot avoid bringing his values with him to the counseling relationship. He cannot avoid the consideration of ultimate values in counseling nor can he avoid operating according to some philosophical point of view. There is some support for the view that counselor values do influence clients.

If counselors influence their clients, this presents an inescapable responsibility. The counselor is forced to ask the often embarrassing questions: Who wants to be like me? How consistent is my philosophy of life? To what degree do I embody the values to which I give lip service? One might also ask: Why am I a counselor? What sort of meaning do I find in my work?

Is a counselor who is confused about his own commitments likely to be of much assistance to a client who is in search of meaning? In a confused world when counseling and guidance come under fire and counselors become insecure in their role, the identity of the counselor may be difficult to maintain, and it becomes easy for them to develop an apologetic attitude. Only when a counselor can find clear meaning in what he is doing can he commit himself to a firm professional identity.

Although we have gained some tentative answers to the question of how values are actually communicated and how values should be handled within the counseling relationship, the problem still remains open. We have discussed the polarities of a cautious approach on one hand and an active attempt to induce certain values on the other. We have noted that a counselor's view of the nature of man is a part of his philosophy and will influence his counseling behavior. If a counselor believes that man is inherently evil and that his tendency is toward evil, however defined, he is likely to be more active in assisting the client to control his evil impulses and to serve the "right" values. If he views man as inherently good with a basic tendency in a positive direction, he will tend to allow the client to express this positive nature and will seek to help eliminate hindrances to its expression. Impartation of values in this case would not seem necessary. If the counselor views man as neither good nor evil, but neutral, he is likely to view the learning of positive values as an important part of the counseling process. All three views of the nature of man are represented in the literature.

The counselor's view regarding the nature of values is also important. If he believes that values come strictly from within the individual and that there are no external values, he will not actively promote values in the counseling process but will assist the client to search within himself for his own values. If the counselor believes that values are external, he will likely take an active approach in "teaching" values or confronting the client with alternative value orientations, or will even attempt to impose a specific orientation upon the client. Counselors who view values as both external and internal recognize the client as a being who is in the world and is involved in a dynamic relationship between his own perceptions of value and external values.

The question of religious values and their importance is also one that must be considered today by the counselor. Religion has here been broadly defined as a philosophy of life to which one is committed. Religious experience must be recognized as a real part of the whole individual. This has not always been the case. In a pluralistic society the question of religion becomes problematic, for it is necessary to promote the right to dissent as well as tolerance of differences. What is the role of the counselor in relation to the client's religious values? He first must recognize them, for treating them as nonexistent carries with it the connotation that they are not important (and most writers would agree that religious values are important). It has been noted in the literature also that religious value orientations may operate below the level of the counselor's awareness, and therefore it is important for him to become aware of them and realize the part they play in his counseling relationships.

The school should play an important role in confronting students with varying value orientations, both to promote understanding and tolerance as well as to assist the student in the development of his own philosophy of life. The school at present has not been successful in this task. The counselor's role is to assist the student in the discovery of meaning. Therefore the counselor should be able to assist the client to examine his feelings in this area as well as in any other. The counselor must know his own values in order to know when they are interfering. He should be able to state his own religious beliefs without imposing them upon the client, either when asked by the client to state them or when he feels that making his values explicit will help avoid their subtle imposition. It is imperative that the counselor hold the dignity and worth of the individual and his right to free choice, which includes the right to disagree, as a higher value than his own religious beliefs, or impositions are likely to occur. If the reverse of this were true, it would be difficult to avoid imposition.

After examining the literature in the area of values we asked whether or not there is a value base that can serve as a guide in counseling against which practice can be evaluated. The value *freedom* has been offered for serious consideration in serving this purpose. The counselor must, however, recognize the complexity of the term and also take notice of the context in which freedom operates. Freedom and determinism are not always opposites, and the counselor must recognize the relativity of both freedom and authority. The ultimate task of the counselor in the public school is to help the individual to become the free person he potentially is, to discover the identity that is his "authentic" self. To be truly free is to be able to choose and to own the choices as one's own. To do this is to be responsible, and to be free in this sense means that one can experience commitment. It is in such choice that commitment occurs and ultimate meaning will be found. As we stated previously, the counselor who is committed to freedom as a goal is not neutral but is prejudiced for the best and highest goals that freedom can bring and is committed to the worth of the individual and to his fullest development as it unfolds by his own creative choice. To be free in this sense is to be human in the fullest meaning of the term.

We come then to a point of conclusion of this analysis of values in counseling, and at this point, after reviewing and summarizing what we have discussed, it seems appropriate to reiterate the purpose of this study. The intent was not to come up with a list of absolutes to which the counselor can turn and say, "Here is the answer!" It was rather to analyze the various concerns that grow from value issues in counseling, to make them explicit, and to make more evident the questions that need to be asked. Hopefully, as a result, the reader will be stimulated to a self-examination that will help him more clearly recognize his own value involvements within the everyday process of living and, even more so, within the counseling relationship.

It would be premature to pretend closure even in definition. We have discovered some basic meanings within the term value, but the valuing process involves the individual within a dialectic of subject and object. He must come to terms with his own situation. He is the "being-in-the-world" and must come to own his own values, to recognize that he is responsible. The valuing process must be idiosyncratic —unique to each individual. It is through his experiencing that anything will become meaningful. Thus, at the "middle level" of values, the "good" choices may vary from individual to individual. For example, to one individual freedom may be "good" in that he is living in the bondage of compulsive self-protection—in Gardner's words, a "do-it-yourself-jailbird." He needs to learn the freedom of taking risks, of venturing forward in unrestricted growth. Another individual may be so "free" that he is dissatisfied with his own lack of goals and self-discipline. One can thus see that prescription does not lend itself easily to the counselor's role. The counselor must recognize the play of the subjective and the objective within his role. He must recognize that the client is an experiencing being and that values, to be meaningful, must grow from such experiencing. But he must also recognize that the client lives within an objective world of which the counselor also is a part. The client is confronted by the question: "What does life expect from me?" and it is from this dialectic of subject and object that a synthesis of responsibility—a full valuing of "self" and "others"— can emerge. The counselor's task consists in the facilitation of this dialectical process.

This process is similar to the one involved in finding new opinions as described by William James:

> The process here is always the same. The individual has a stock of old opinions already, but he meets a new experience that puts them to a strain. Somebody contradicts them; or in a reflective moment he discovers that they contradict each other; or he hears of facts with which they are incompatible; or desires arise in him which they cease to satisfy. The result is an inward trouble to which his mind until then had been a stranger, and from which he seeks to escape by modifying his previous mass of opinion. He saves as much of it as he can, for in this matter of belief we are all extreme conservatives. So he tries to change first this opinion, and then that . . . until at last some new idea comes up which he can graft upon the ancient stock with a minimum of disturbance of the latter, some idea that mediates between the stock and the new experience and runs them into one another most felicitously and expediently.[1]

This process is not dissimilar to that of the well-known Socratic dialogue, a similarity that also runs through the cultural context. In a culture that was seeking unity, as is ours, Socrates, who has been referred to as the "conscience of Athens,"[2] advocated a confrontation of every individual with himself. He encouraged men to face themselves, to know themselves, and then to go about living honestly and

---

[1] William James, *Essays in Pragmatism* (New York: Hafner Publishing, 1949), pp. 147–148.

[2] Micheline Sauvage, *Socrates and the Conscience of Man* (New York: Harper and Brothers, 1960), p. 100.

courageously. In times of great anxiety, the breakdown of human functioning is likely to incorporate a lack in either or both of these two characteristics. Individuals become dishonest with themselves and thus do not face up to their existence and responsibility. They may fear taking a step or making a choice that might make them vulnerable to failure. The counselor must embody these twin virtues of courage and honesty in himself and then play the midwife in aiding others to be born of themselves. The counselor cannot force growth, but he can encourage it.

> Virtue *cannot be taught,* because it is not a collection of recipes or propositions which can be passed on from master to pupil in exchange for money.
> Virtue *can be taught,* because it consists in a conversation, a movement of the soul which the master helps the student to bring about in himself.[3]

The necessary dialogue demands a sensitivity to the perceptions, values, and meanings of the other person. It demands an intensity that surpasses the superficial and the trivial. As was said of Socrates:

> His brotherly eye seems rather to pierce straight through those outer rinds of human nature which are the realm of idiosyncracies, the external and the accidental, to that deeper region where the person has his roots.[4]

It is within a relationship grounded upon the safety of acceptance and understanding that the individual is able to begin to recognize the deterministic forces affecting him and to begin to emerge through what is sometimes a painful process into the free and responsible being he is.

> Socrates haunts the Athenians like their own conscience . . . he makes men look at themselves (which for most men is the hardest thing in the world) and urges them to a radical transformation.[5]
> Leonard Nelson aptly says: "This method of *forcing* minds to *freedom* constitutes the first secret of the Socratic method."[6]

This need not be as *direct* or manipulative as it may sound. It is rather

---

[3] *Ibid.,* p. 111.
[4] *Ibid.,* p. 90.
[5] *Ibid.,* pp. 90, 101.
[6] Abraham Edel, *Method in Ethical Theory* (New York: Bobbs-Merrill, 1963), p. 104.

a matter of clarification toward the end of inward consistency in one's philosophy of life. Values are not *forced* upon an unwary client; rather, he is forced to face what he already is claiming himself to be. Paul Meehl has recognized this relationship when he states:

> In connection with the shifting of a therapist's role, it should be pointed out that elucidating a contradiction *within* the ethical or value thinking of a patient may not be as drastic and "directive" a step as it appears. Therapists of many persuasions are willing to include certain forms of "reality-confrontation" among the therapeutic agents. . . . Now whatever one's view may be regarding the ultimate source of moral concepts, it is obvious that logic and consistency *within* the moral system which the patient espouses is part of the patient's reality. . . .
>
> In the course of ordinary secular psychotherapy there occur, from time to time, exchanges between patient and therapist which are not defensive intellectualization but which (whatever they may be called within the therapist's preferred theoretical scheme) are, in their actual verbal structure, rather like a segment out of one of the Platonic dialogues. I suspect that one reason why so many therapists are skittish about getting involved in this kind of thing is that they lack talent and training for the Socratic dialogue; and that this deficiency, together with their own personal ambiguity about the value question, makes them feel unsafe if they treat any such material in its own right, rather than as a derivative calling for a psychodynamic interpretation at some other level.[7]

The counselor must also, if he is truly interested in helping his client to unfold, be willing to be changed in the process. He must not only be an innovator in society but he must also innovate in his own life. He must live in a self-transcending manner; he must be a perpetual learner. True learning begins when one can admit his own need to pretend and accept his own need for knowledge (accept his ignorance).

The Socratic method is simply that of dialogue between men in simple interpersonal relations. In it can be recognized the dialectic process, the coming together of subject (thesis) and object (antithesis) from which is born a new synthesis, a step in the process of the slowly but continually emerging free individual. It is the task of the counselor to lead individuals to autonomy.

---

[7]Paul E. Meehl, "Some Technical and Axiological Problems in the Therapeutic Handling of Religious and Valuational Material," *Journal of Counseling Psychology*, VI, 4 (Winter 1959), 257–258.

> Socrates forces the young man to think, to think about that which so far he had been confined, as an obedient child, to living.[8]

Without dialogue there can be no self-awareness.[9] The task of the counselor is not to transmit great words of wisdom but rather to bring the individual into an encounter with himself, to leave him with a hunger for self-fulfillment and to beckon him to self-renewal. The role is well described by May:

> The therapist's aim, with regard to ethical standards, is to help the other person to remove distortions and the various forms of neurotic contradictions within himself that he may arrive at and choose freely the value judgments and ethical standards which are most constructive for him. This ability to be a "midwife," to use Socrates' word, is not easy of attainment, and it can well be a goal toward which a therapist works in his own development year in and year out. As Kierkegaard remarked about Socrates, "how rare the magnanimity" of a helper who can be sufficiently concerned with the other person's self-realization and sufficiently free of his own need to dominate that he is willing to be merely an "occasion" for the other's achievement of his own values.[10]

In conclusion we now turn to the following principles as important considerations for counselors.

## SOME VITAL CONSIDERATIONS FOR COUNSELORS

1. *The counselor should as far as possible attempt to understand the society of which he is a part and especially the value conflicts stemming from it.*

As we have seen, the counselor as well as the client is very much a part of the culture in which he lives. To fail to have some understanding of the forces operating upon individuals in such a culture is to run the risk of becoming what Wrenn called the "culturally encapsulated counselor."[11] One tends to assume that the society and culture with which he is most familiar (his own) is the only "real" one. This may stem either from a general naivete about sociological matters or from

---

[8]Sauvage, *Socrates*, p. 108.

[9]*Ibid.*, p. 109.

[10]Rollo May, "Historical and Philosophical Presuppositions for Understanding Therapy," in O. Hobart Mowrer (ed.), *Psychotherapy: Theory and Research* (New York: The Ronald Press, 1953), p. 43.

[11]C. Gilbert Wrenn, "The Culturally Encapsulated Counselor," *Harvard Educational Review*, XXXII, 4 (Fall 1962), 444–449.

an ever-present tendency to cling to the organized pattern of thinking within which we are most comfortable and so resist facing change. Such a counselor is not likely to eagerly seek out implications of change in society. As Wrenn stated it:

> Like Job of old we protest the inevitable, we argue about it. Even better than Job we protect ourselves from the disturbing reality of change by surrounding ourselves with a cocoon of *pretended* reality—a reality which is based upon the past and known, upon seeing that which is as though it would always be. This is "cultural encapsulation," and encapsulation within our world, within our culture and sub-culture, within a pretense that the present is enduring.[12]

Such a counselor will fail also to recognize the influence of social forces upon development in general as well as in specific behavior.

We have found a recent growing awareness of the importance of cultural and sociological understanding, and texts have recently been published dealing specifically with this area.[13] Lloyd-Jones and Rosenau express in the introduction to their book the need for understanding in this area:

> Those who are members of an institution not only perpetuate it and are acted upon by it, but also inevitably modify it either in random and unexamined or in purposive ways. At some point, if he is competent to do so, a guidance-personnel worker can become an analyst of human problems, not only in the counseling booth, but of human problems in the society that has helped to cause them and that exacerbates them. So he inevitably becomes involved with all kinds of problems for which his professional preparation as it is presently offered in universities, has not necessarily prepared him.
>
> He realizes at about this point that he has no way of really understanding the social-cultural nature of his school or college. He has simply taken it for granted up to this point. It reminds one of Charles Darwin's description of a trip he took to Wales in 1830 to study strata. He studied strata diligently but did not even see the effects of glaciation. It was not until after Agassiz did his work on glaciation that Darwin saw the effects of glaciation and wondered that he could have been so blind before.
>
> We have begun to realize that we have had no way of really understanding the social-cultural nature of our schools and colleges.

[12] *Ibid.*, p. 445.
[13] See Donald A. Hansen, *Explorations in Sociology and Counseling* (Boston: Houghton Mifflin Co., 1969); Esther M. Lloyd-Jones and Norah Rosenau (eds.), *Social and Cultural Foundations of Guidance: A Sourcebook* (New York: Holt, Rinehart, and Winston, 1968); and Carl Weinberg, *Social Foundations of Educational Guidance* (New York: The Free Press, 1969).

> We have simply taken "culture" for granted up to this point.
>     If the guidance-personnel worker were to learn in some depth about social systems and culture, he could understand his students and the context in which they live and grow and could have much more realistic and creative views as to whether and how a school or college can be purposively altered by those who are members of it.[14]

Only when one has an understanding of culture and society can one begin to understand some of the value conflicts that grow therefrom.

    2. *The quest for identity is in reality a search for meaning and significance; the counselor should be mindful that it is a value-laden quest.*

    This we discussed in Chapter 2. Every individual experiences a dialectical relationship between one's own experiencing (of self) and the world of others, including various value options. Counseling, in this regard, is a search for values. As Wheelis has suggested, the quest for identity is a quest for meaning. When achieved minimally it gives one the sense of playing some significant part within his social existence. It is a feeling of organized "constructive intent." We strive to maintain an organized value system that makes sense to us and puts into perspective at least tentative answers to the crucial philosophical questions with which we are confronted. It is in the valuing process that the individual bridges the gap between his own experiencing and the world or the value options "out there." This involves a process of questioning, of being willing to surrender some security when questioning leads in new directions, of "pushing against" some of the traditional values to test their meaning potential, and finally to begin to own certain values as one's own, which includes commitment to them.

    When the counselor recognizes that the nature of such counseling involves him in value quests, he has made the first step toward becoming more effective and being "for" and working "with" the client in such quests.

    3. *Because values play an important part in the counseling process, the counselor should attempt to understand the nature and philosophy of value. Thus, also, the philosophy of value should be recognized as an important part of the curriculum in counselor education.*

    The question arises here as to just how important this is and how much time should be given to the topic in an already overburdened

---

[14]Lloyd-Jones and Roseneau, *Social and Cultural Foundations*, p. 2.

curriculum. The answer must be, as our previous discussion attests, that an understanding of values is indeed very important. This need not mean, however, that a course dealing specifically only with this topic must be offered, although when possible this would be worthwhile. Just as values permeate the counseling process, so they permeate the counselor education process. The study of values can be a meaningful part of every course from the initial foundations and theory courses to the advanced practicums and internships. It is in the latter that one is able to witness, as far as counseling is concerned, values in operation at the action level. But for optimum learning to take place, the counselor educator must also understand theory of value and be sensitive to how values function. For just as the client in counseling is often unaware of values that may be operating, in the same manner the student-counselor will not always be aware of values that come into play in his involvement with others.

4. *The belief in the worth and dignity of the individual and in his right to free choice must be uppermost in the counselor's hierarchy of values. The client must be free to choose his own values.*

As stated previously, every individual has a hierarchy of values. Such a hierarchy is difficult to describe but can be inferred from actions. Such hierarchies are not static (although they are relatively stable) and may change and shift from time to time. The counselor who believes, above all, in the worth of the individual and his sovereign right to make his own choices cannot with a clear conscience indoctrinate another. The counselor who truly respects the individual, even if absolute in his own beliefs, allows the individual the right to reject such beliefs and recognizes as well his right to be responsible (answerable) for himself. The individual who holds beliefs higher than his belief in the right of the individual to make his own choice is likely to impose himself upon the client.

5. *The counselor should work toward enhancing the freedom of his client. Intermediate and immediate goals will derive meaning from this broader framework.*

This means that the counselor accepts as a goal the enhancement of the power of an individual to achieve, to become productive, to choose, to transcend himself. This includes the recognition that the client is responsible for himself and chooses his own goals as he becomes more able to take the risks necessary for growth. This view also recognizes that authority is not the opposite of freedom, but at times may even enhance freedom. As Nash states:

When we examined "authority" and "freedom" in context, we quickly came to realize that we do not want *all* kinds of freedom: nor do we want all kinds of authority. We want, rather, to examine and evaluate these key terms and their relationships in a variety of situations and under diverse influences. The purpose is to judge what *kind* of authority and what *kind* of freedom we want to foster or discourage.[15]

The key is to determine which kinds of authority are restricting and which are freeing to the developmental growth of the individual. The same is true for freedom. Which kinds of freedom enhance the power of becoming and which kinds restrict it? Nash goes on to say that

some forms of authority lead to a loss of freedom. But it would be inappropriate to infer from this that freedom is enhanced by the absence of authority. For we found that some forms of authority, under certain conditions, lead to some of the highest forms of freedom.[16]

The problem, then, is one of distinguishing between what is stifling and what is liberating. Nash found that liberating forms of authority were characterized by being "often rational, personally relevant, just, and individually appropriate."[17]

The counselor who has developed greater depth of understanding of the various meanings of freedom as well as of authority (determinism), is better equipped to judge sensitively the implications of choices and to aid the client to be more sensitive to the logical consequences of his choices. This means that if a counselor is committed to such an ultimate but "middle level" value as freedom, his moment-by-moment choices, even of the words he uses, will be governed by a broader and more justifiable intent. Important subsidiary values that are complementary to freedom are those of acceptance, understanding, and faith in the individual, as well as openness and creativity represented in the fully functioning person.

6. *A counselor cannot avoid influencing the client, and he must be aware of and concerned about the direction of this influence.*

7. *The client both discovers and creates his values through the development of meaning resulting from the interplay between the polarities of subjective experiencing and objective world.*

8. *The counselor should recognize that he is a role model to his*

[15] Paul Nash, *Authority and Freedom in Education* (New York: John Wiley and Sons, Inc., 1966), pp. 325–326.

[16] *Ibid.*, p. 326.

[17] *Ibid.*

*clients and should consider the responsibility that this entails.*

Being an "occasion" for another's achievement of values is likely to involve the counselor as a role model. If Rosenthal's findings are correct,[18] changes in values following counseling are likely to be in the direction of the values of the counselor. This adds to the burden of responsibility and to the demand for humility. As Carkhuff and Berenson have stressed, the entire system and process of counseling can be only as effective as the counselor is a "whole" person.[19] A "whole" person can play an important part in the individual's conceptualization of his "constructive intent."

> Young people . . . do not learn ethical principles; they emulate ethical (or unethical) people. They do not analyze or list the attributes they wish to develop; they identify with people who seem to them to have these attributes. That is why young people need models, both in their imaginative life and in their environment, models of what man at his best can be.[20]

The counselor may serve as a role model both in the kind of person he is as well as in his own philosophy of life. It is in this last respect that he must be certain that the client is free to reject his values if he so desires. Although the counselor's purpose is not to indoctrinate the client in a fixed set of beliefs, his own values will at one time or another enter the process. This can be healthy, for, providing that the freedom to reject values is present, it gives the client something to push against in testing objective alternatives open to him. The entire educational system should be one that continually confronts students with objective value alternatives. The main focus in counseling, however, must remain on the *client's* perceptions and not on those of the counselor. In counseling the increase of awareness must remain a key focal point. Speaking once again from the viewpoint of ethical theory, Edel states:

> In ethical theory, I think we are approaching the point where we will reinstate as the primary context in which one receives guidance that in which one *learns* or *comes to see clearly*. For it is a simple fact that when men are helped to see clearly what they want and what activities will bring what they want, and what the consequences of their action will be and what they will want in the subse-

---

[18]David Rosenthal, "Changes in Some Moral Values Following Psychotherapy," *Journal of Consulting Psychology*, XIX, 6 (1955), 431–436.

[19]Robert R. Carkhuff and Bernard G. Berenson, *Beyond Counseling and Therapy* (New York: Holt, Rinehart, and Winston, 1967).

[20]John Gardner, *Self-Renewal* (New York: Harper and Row, 1963), p. 124.

quent conditions, then they have received guidance. . . . To guide is not to determine, nor is to commend to force. There is a gap not only between decision and action, but also between judgment and decision-as-act. Moral judgment is no more (and no less) practical than science is perceptive; science uses and learns from each fresh perception, and moral judgment uses and learns from each fresh decision.[21]

The role of the counselor is that of assisting the client to see more widely and broadly his whole experiential field so that the whole spectrum of values and meanings become open and visible to him. The client does not always discover value and meaning solely on his own. As Frondizi states:

> Esthetic and moral education does not consist in calling the young man's attention to certain questions of fact, or consequences produced by certain actions, but also in focusing his very eyes upon the presence of values which his inexperienced observations have not as yet discovered.[22]

9. *The counselor must make his own values explicit to himself, and when appropriate, to his client.*

As has been previously stated, the counselor's values need not be imposed when presented in an atmosphere of acceptance in which the client is free to reject them. The appropriateness of making them explicit should be decided on the basis of when such values are implicitly hindering the counseling process by limiting the client's freedom of choice.

10. *The counselor should think of vocation in terms of the whole person within the context of total life goals.*

In the core meaning of the term vocation, "a calling," one finds inherent the concept of commitment. One finds meaning through commitment, and thus the whole quest for vocation is a value quest. In times of rapid technological change with the accompaniment of automation, meaningful jobs will become harder to find. This is likely to be so, even in the midst of task enlargement (adding extraneous or subsidiary tasks to one's main function to keep him busy as well as to give him a greater feeling of significance) and other attempts at preventing the meaningless. In such a world it means that individuals must seek meaning and commitment in a broader context, within the whole of their activities. It means that many may not find much gratification in their work, but that after doing rather routine work for

[21]Edel, *Method in Ethical theory,* p. 153.
[22]Risieri Frondizi, *What Is Value?* (LaSalle, Ill.: Open Court, 1963), p. 108.

monetary purposes they can seek meaningful pursuits during their leisure time. Leisure, thus, also becomes a value-involved pursuit, a pursuit that is also likely to continue to become more and more of a focus for discussion within counseling. A vocational sense, in this broader context, is closely related to the sense of identity and of significance. As an individual commits himself to what he feels are worthwhile purposes, he gains a sense of vocation, of identity, of significance.

11. *The counselor should recognize the importance of group influence upon individuals.*

There is a growing need to diagnose group and institutional restrictions upon the freedom of individuals to grow and become, and then to seek means by which needed change can be facilitated. The emphasis upon intensive group experiences as a means to institutional change is especially exciting and appears to offer great potential along these lines.[23]

12. *The value, freedom, should be considered a major part of an evaluational base for counseling, and against which effectiveness in counseling can be judged.*

·    ·    ·    ·    ·

Of all the things that have been said, it needs to be reemphasized that the individual is a free being. Though he lives in a world of objects —that is, of things as well as persons outside of himself—it is he who discovers values outside of himself and "creates" them in the sense that he gives them meaning by his experiencing of them. It is to this that I think Frankl was referring when he stated:

> "Meaning" is not only an emergence from existence itself but rather something confronting existence. ... The meaning of our existence is not invented by ourselves, but rather detected. ... Values, however, do not drive a man; they do not *push* him, but rather pull him. ... Now, if ... man is *pulled* by values, what is implicitly referred to is the fact that there is always freedom involved; the freedom of man to make his choice between accepting or rejecting an offer, i.e., to fulfill a meaning potentiality or else to forfeit it.[24]

The challenges that individuals face in our world today are not small ones. Without a vision of what they can become as well as a

[23]See Carl Rogers, *Freedom to Learn* (Columbus, Ohio: Charles E. Merrill, 1969), especially Part V and the epilogue, pp. 327–342.

[24]Viktor Frankl, *Man's Search for Meaning* (New York: Washington Square Press, 1959), pp. 156–158.

responsibility to bring it about, it will be easy for many to join the cult of despair. In the words of John Gardner:

> Thanks to our prosperity, we don't have to put out great effort for physical survival; and a free people has no taskmasters.
>
> With such an unprecedented release from outward pressures, free men fall easily into the error of thinking that no effort is required of them. It is easy for them to believe that freedom and justice are inexpensive commodities, always there, like the air they breathe, and not things they have to earn, be worthy of, fight for and cherish.
>
> Nothing could be more dangerous to the future of our society.
>
> Free men must set their own goals. There is no one to tell them what to do; they must do it for themselves. They must be quick to apprehend the kinds of effort and performance their society needs, and they must demand that kind of effort and performance of themselves and of their fellows. They must cherish what Whitehead called the "habitual vision of greatness." If they have the wisdom and courage to demand much of themselves—as individuals and as a society—they may look forward to long-continued vitality. But a free society that is passive, inert, and preoccupied with its own diversions and comforts will not last long. And freedom won't save it.[25]

Counselors in our society today face a great challenge and a great responsibility. The task will require free men in the fullest meaning of the term who must dare to cultivate the "habitual vision of greatness."

[25] John Gardner, *Excellence* (New York: Harper and Row, 1961), pp. 160–161.

# Bibliography

## BOOKS

Adams, James F., ed. *Understanding Adolescence: Current Developments in Adolescent Psychology.* Boston: Allyn and Bacon, Inc., 1968.

Adler, Alfred. *Social Interest: A Challenge to Mankind.* New York: Putnam, 1939.

Allport, Gordon. *Becoming.* New Haven: Yale University Press, 1955.

———. *Personality and Social Encounter.* Boston: Beacon Press, 1960.

American Personnel and Guidance Association. *Counseling, A Growing Profession.* Edited by John W. Loughary. Washington, D.C.: American Personnel and Guidance Association, 1965.

Arbuckle, Dugald S. *Counseling: Philosophy, Theory, and Practice.* Boston: Allyn and Bacon, Inc., 1965.

Association for Supervision and Curriculum Development. *Perceiving, Behaving, Becoming.* Yearbook chairman, Arthur W. Combs. Washington, D.C.: National Education Association, 1962.

Axline, Virginia. *Dibs: In Search of Self.* Boston: Houghton Mifflin Co., 1964.

Barclay, James R. *Testing for Higher Education.* Student Personnel Series No. 6. Washington, D. C.: The American College Personnel Association, 1965.

Barry, Ruth, and Beverly Wolf. *Epitaph for Vocational Guidance.* New York: Bureau of Publications, Teachers College, Columbia University, 1962.

———. *Modern Issues in Guidance-Personnel Work.* New York:

Bureau of Publications, Teachers College, Columbia University, 1957.

————. *Motives, Values, and Realities.* New York: Bureau of Publications, Teachers College, Columbia University, 1965.

Barzun, Jacques, and Henry F. Graff. *The Modern Researcher.* New York: Harcourt, Brace and World, 1957.

Beck, Carlton E. *Guidelines for Guidance.* Dubuque: William C. Brown, 1966.

————. *Philosophical Foundations of Guidance.* New York: Prentice-Hall, Inc., 1963.

Bentley, Joseph, ed. *The Counselor's Role: Commentary and Readings.* Boston: Houghton Mifflin Co., 1968.

Bertocci, Peter A., and Richard M. Millard. *Personality and the Good.* New York: David McKay Co., 1963.

Blocher, Donald M. *Developmental Counseling.* New York: The Ronald Press, 1966.

Bode, Boyd H. *Progressive Education at the Crossroads.* New York: Newson and Co., 1938.

Bonner, Hubert. *On Being Mindful of Man.* Boston: Houghton Mifflin Co., 1965.

Borow, Henry, ed. *Man in a World at Work.* Boston: Houghton Mifflin Co., 1964.

Boy, Angelo V., and Gerald J. Pine. *The Counselor in the Schools: A Reconceptualization.* Boston: Houghton Mifflin Co., 1968.

Brameld, Theodore. *Cultural Foundations of Education.* New York: Harper and Brothers, 1957.

————. *Education as Power.* New York: Holt, Rinehart, and Winston, 1965.

————. *Education for the Emerging Age.* New York: Harper and Brothers, 1961.

————. *Philosophies of Education in Cultural Perspective.* New York: Dryden Press, 1958.

————. *Toward a Reconstructed Philosophy of Education.* New York: Dryden Press, 1956.

Brameld, Theodore, and Stanley Elam, eds. *Values in American Education.* Bloomington: Phi Delta Kappa, 1964.

Bredemeier, Harry C., and Jackson Toby. *Social Problems in America.* New York: John Wiley and Sons, Inc., 1960.

Brightman, E. S. *An Introduction to Philosophy.* Revised by Robert Beck. New York: Holt, Rinehart, and Winston, 1963.

———. *Moral Laws*. New York: Abingdon Press, 1933.

———. *Nature and Values*. New York: Abingdon-Cokesbury Press, 1945.

Bronowski, Jacob. *Science and Human Values*. New York: Harper and Row, 1956.

Buhler, Charlotte. *Values in Psychotherapy*. New York: The Free Press of Glencoe, 1962.

Byrne, Richard H. *The School Counselor*. Boston: Houghton Mifflin Co., 1963.

Carkhuff, Robert R., and Bernard G. Berenson. *Beyond Counseling and Therapy*. New York: Holt, Rinehart, and Winston, 1967.

Carpenter, Marjorie, ed. *The Larger Learning*. Dubuque: William C. Brown, 1960.

Coleman, James S. *The Adolescent Society*. New York: The Free Press, 1961.

Conant, James B. *The American High School Today*. New York: McGraw-Hill, 1959.

Dewey, John. *Democracy and Education*. New York: The Macmillan Co., 1963.

———. *Human Nature and Conduct*. New York: Henry Holt and Co., 1957.

———. *Individualism Old and New*. New York: Capricorn Books, 1962.

———. *Moral Principles in Education*. New York: Philosophical Library, Inc., 1959.

Dreikurs, Rudolf. *Psychodynamics, Psychotherapy, and Counseling*. Chicago: Alfred Adler Institute, 1967.

Dugan, Willis E., ed. *Counseling Points of View*. Minneapolis: University of Minnesota Press, 1959.

Edel, Abraham. *Ethical Judgment*. New York: The Free Press of Glencoe, 1955.

———. *Method in Ethical Theory*. Indianapolis: Bobbs-Merrill, 1963.

Edel, May, and Abraham Edel. *Anthropology and Ethics*. Springfield, Ill.: Charles C. Thomas, 1959.

Educational Policies Commission. *Moral and Spiritual Values in the Public Schools*. Washington, D. C.: National Education Association, 1951.

Ellis, Albert. *Reason and Emotion in Psychotherapy*. New York: Lyle Stuart, 1962.

Farwell, Gail F., and Herman J. Peters, eds. *Guidance Readings for*

*Counselors.* Chicago: Rand McNally and Co., 1960.

Feigel, Herbert. *Aims of Education for Our Age of Science: Reflectings of a Logical Empiricist.* Fifty-fourth Yearbook of the National Association for the Study of Education, 1955.

Frankl, Viktor. *Man's Search for Meaning.* New York: Washington Square Press, 1959.

Fromm, Erich. *Escape from Freedom.* New York: Farrar and Rinehart, 1941.

––––––. *The Art of Loving.* New York: Harper and Row, 1962.

––––––. *The Sane Society.* New York: Holt, Rinehart and Winston, 1955.

Frondizi, Risieri. *What Is Value?* LaSalle, Ill.: Open Court, 1963.

Fullmer, Daniel W., and Harold W. Bernard. *Counseling: Content and Process.* Chicago: Science Research Associates, Inc., 1964.

Gardner, John W. *Excellence.* New York: Harper and Row, 1961.

––––––. *Self-Renewal.* New York: Harper and Row, 1963.

Gendlin, Eugene. *Experiencing and the Creation of Meaning.* New York: The Free Press of Glencoe, 1962.

Girvetz, Harry K. *The Evolution of Liberalism.* New York: Collier Books, 1963.

Glasser, William. *Reality Therapy: A New Approach to Psychiatry.* New York: Harper and Row, 1965.

Goodman, Paul. *Growing Up Absurd.* New York: Random House, 1956.

Griswold, A. W. *Liberal Education and the Democratic Ideal.* New Haven: Yale University Press, 1959.

Gross, Ronald. *The Teacher and the Taught.* New York: Dell Publishing Co., 1963.

Gruber, Frederick C., ed. *Aspects of Value.* Philadelphia: University of Pennsylvania Press, 1959.

Hansen, Donald A. *Explorations in Sociology and Counseling.* Boston: Houghton Mifflin Co., 1969.

Hartman, Heinz. *Psychoanalysis and Moral Values.* New York: International Universities Press, Inc., 1960.

Henry, Jules. *Culture Against Man.* New York: Random House, 1963.

Hoffer, Eric. *The Ordeal of Change.* New York: Harper and Row, 1952.

––––––. *The Temper of Our Time.* New York: Harper and Row, 1969.

Hook, Sidney, ed. *Determinism and Freedom.* New York: Collier Books, 1961.

James, William. *Essays in Pragmatism.* New York: Hafner Publishing, 1949.

Jersild, Arthur T. *In Search of Self.* New York: Bureau of Publications, Teachers College, Columbia University, 1952.

———. *When Teachers Face Themselves.* New York : Bureau of Publications, Teachers College, Columbia University, 1955.

Jones, W. T. *A History of Western Philosophy.* Volumes I and II. New York: Harcourt, Brace and World, 1952.

Josephson, Eric, and Mary Josephson, eds. *Man Alone.* New York: Dell, 1962.

Kell, Bill L., and William J. Mueller. *Impact and Change: A Study of Counseling Relationships.* New York: Appleton-Century-Crofts, 1966.

Kemp, C. G. *Intangibles in Counseling.* Boston: Houghton Mifflin Co., 1967.

Kluckhohn, Clyde. *Mirror for Man.* Fifth Premier Printing. New York: McGraw-Hill, 1963.

Krasner, L., and L. P. Ullman, eds. *Case Studies in Behavior Modification.* New York: Holt, Rinehart, and Winston, 1965.

Krumboltz, John D., ed. *Revolution in Counseling.* Boston: Houghton Mifflin Co., 1966.

Krutch, Joseph W. *Human Nature and the Human Condition.* New York: Random House, 1959.

———. *The Measure of Man.* Indianapolis: Bobbs-Merrill, 1954.

———. *The Modern Temper.* New York: Harcourt, Brace and Co., 1929.

Kubie, Laurence S. *Neurotic Distortion of the Creative Process.* New York: The Noonday Press, 1958.

Lamont, Corliss. *Freedom of Choice Affirmed.* New York: Horizon Press, 1967.

Lee, Dorothy. *Freedom and Culture.* New York: Prentice-Hall, 1959.

Lepley, Ray. *The Language of Value.* New York: Columbia University Press, 1956.

———. *Value: A Cooperative Inquiry.* New York: Columbia University Press, 1949.

———. *Verifiability of Value.* New York: Columbia University Press, 1944.

Lewis, C. S. *Mere Christianity.* New York: The Macmillan Co., 1952.

———. *The Abolition of Man.* New York: Collier Books, 1962.

*Foundations of Guidance: A Sourcebook.* New York: Holt, Rinehart, and Winston, 1968.

Lloyd-Jones, Esther M., and Esther Westervelt, eds. *Behavioral Science and Guidance: Proposals and Perspectives.* New York: Bureau of Publications, Teachers College, Columbia University, 1963.

London, Perry. *The Modes and Morals of Psychotherapy.* New York: Holt, Rinehart, and Winston, 1964.

Mahrer, Alvin R., ed. *The Goals of Psychotherapy.* New York: Appleton-Century-Crofts, 1967.

Mannheim, Karl. *Ideology and Utopia.* New York: Harcourt, Brace and Co., 1936.

Maslow, Abraham H., ed. *New Knowledge in Human Values.* New York: Harper and Row, 1959.

―――. *Toward a Psychology of Being.* New Jersey: D. Van Nostrand, 1962.

Mathewson, R. H. *Guidance Policy and Practice.* Third Edition. New York: Harper and Row, 1962.

May, Rollo, Ernest Angel, and Henri F. Ellenberger, eds. *Existence.* New York: Basic Books, 1958.

―――, ed. *Existential Psychology.* New York: Random House, 1961.

―――. *Man's Search for Himself.* New York: The New American Library, Inc., 1967.

―――. *Psychology and the Human Dilemma.* Princeton: D. Van Nostrand, 1967.

―――. *The Meaning of Anxiety.* New York: The Ronald Press, 1950.

Mercer, Blaine E. *The Study of Society.* New York: Harcourt, Brace and World, 1958.

Miller, Carroll H. *Foundations of Guidance.* New York: Harper and Brothers, 1961.

Morris, Charles. *Varieties of Human Value.* Chicago: University of Chicago Press, 1956.

Morris, Van Cleve. *Existentialism in Education.* New York: Harper and Row, 1966.

Mothershead, John, Jr. *Ethics.* New York: Henry Holt and Co., 1955.

Mowrer, O. Hobart, ed. *Psychotherapy: Theory and Research.* New York: The Ronald Press, 1953.

Nagel, Ernest. *The Structure of Science.* New York: Harcourt, Brace and World, 1961.

Nash, Paul. *Authority and Freedom in Education.* New York: John Wiley and Sons, Inc., 1966.

National Education Association. *Education in a Changing Society.* Project on the Instructional Program of the Public Schools. Washington, D.C.: National Education Association, 1963.

Olmsted, Michael S. *The Small Group.* New York: Random House, 1959.

Opler, Marvin K. *Culture, Psychiatry and Human Values.* Springfield, Ill.: Charles C. Thomas, 1956.

Packard, Vance. *The Hidden Persuaders.* New York: David McKay Co., 1957.

Parker, De Witt H. *The Philosophy of Value.* Ann Arbor: University of Michigan Press, 1957.

Parsons, Frank. *Choosing a Vocation.* Boston: Houghton Mifflin Co., 1908.

Parsons, Talcott, and Edward A. Shils, eds. *Toward a General Theory of Action.* New York: Harper and Row, 1962. ©Harvard University, 1951.

Patterson, C. H. *Counseling and Psychotherapy: Theory and Practice.* New York: Harper and Brothers, 1959.

————. *Theories of Counseling and Psychotherapy.* New York: Harper and Row, 1966.

Perry, Ralph B. *The Humanity of Man.* New York: George Braziller, Inc., 1956.

————. *Realms of Value.* Cambridge: Harvard University Press, 1954.

Personnel Services in Education. Fifty-eighth Yearbook of the National Society for the Study of Education. Part II. Chicago: University of Chicago Press, 1959.

Peters, Herman J., and others, eds. *Counseling: Selected Readings.* Columbus, Ohio: Charles E. Merrill, 1962.

Riesman, David. *The Lonely Crowd.* New Haven: Yale University Press, 1950.

Rogers, Carl R. *Client-Centered Therapy.* Boston: Houghton Mifflin Co., 1951.

————. *Counseling and Psychotherapy.* Boston: Houghton Mifflin Co., 1942.

————. *Freedom to Learn.* Columbus, Ohio: Charles E. Merrill, 1969.

————. *On Becoming a Person.* Boston: Houghton Mifflin Co., 1961.

Rosenthal, Robert, and Lenore Jacobson. *Pygmalion in the Classroom.* New York: Holt, Rinehart, and Winston, 1968.

Rossiter, Clinton. *Conservatism in America*. New York: Random House, 1962.

Runes, Dagobert D., ed. *Dictionary of Philosophy*. Patterson, N.J.: Littlefield, Adams, and Co., 1962.

Salter, A. *Conditioned Reflex Therapy*. New York: Creative Age Press, 1949.

Sauvage, Micheline. *Socrates and the Conscience of Man*. New York: Harper and Brothers, 1960.

Shertzer, Bruce, and Shelley C. Stone. *Fundamentals of Guidance*. Boston: Houghton Mifflin Co., 1966.

Skinner, B. F. *Science and Human Behavior*. New York: The Macmillan Co., 1953.

Smith, B. O., W. O. Stanley, and J. H. Shores. *Social Diagnosis for Education*. New York: World Book Co., 1950.

Smith, C. E., and O. G. Mink. *Foundations of Guidance and Counseling: Multidisciplinary Readings*. New York: J. B. Lippincott Co., 1969.

Sorokin, Pitirim A., ed. *Explorations in Altruistic Love and Behavior*. Boston: Beacon Press, 1950.

————. *The Crisis of Our Age*. New York: E. P. Dutton and Co., Inc., 1941.

Stein, Morris. *Contemporary Psychotherapies*. New York: The Free Press, 1961.

Stevenson, Charles L. *Ethics and Language*. New Haven: Yale University Press, 1944.

Stewart, Lawrence H., and Charles F. Warnath. *The Counselor and Society: A Cultural Approach*. Boston: Houghton Mifflin Co., 1965.

Tillich, Paul. *The Courage to Be*. New Haven: Yale University Press, 1952.

Ulrich, R., T. Stachnik, and J. Mabry, eds. *Control of Human Behavior*. Glenview: Scott, Foresman and Co., 1966.

Weinberg, Carl. *Social Foundations of Educational Guidance*. New York: The Free Press, 1969.

Wheelis, Allen. *The Quest for Identity*. New York: W. W. Norton and Co., Inc., 1958.

Wolpe, J. *Psychotherapy by Reciprocal Inhibition*. Stanford: Stanford University Press, 1958.

Wolpe, J., and A. A. Lazarus. *Behavior Therapy Techniques*. New York: Pergamon Press, 1966.

Wrenn, C. Gilbert. *The Counselor in a Changing World.* Washington, D.C.: The American Personnel and Guidance Association, 1962.

Wriston, Henry M., and others. *Goals for Americans.* New York: Prentice-Hall, Inc., 1960.

## PERIODICALS

Albert, Ethel M. "Conflict and Change in American Values," *Ethics,* LXXIV, 2 (October 1963), 19–33.

Allport, Gordon. "Psychological Models for Guidance," *Harvard Educational Review,* XXXII, 4 (Fall 1962), 373–381.

——. "The Psychological Nature of Personality," *Personalist,* XXIV (1953), 347.

American Personnel and Guidance Association. "A Statement of Policy Concerning the Nation's Human Resources Problems," *Personnel and Guidance Journal,* XXXVI, 7 (March 1958), 454–455.

Arbuckle, Dugald S. "Counseling: Philosophy or Science." *Personnel and Guidance Journal,* XXXIX, 1 (September 1960), 11–14.

——. "Existentialism in Counseling: The Humanist View," *Personnel and Guidance Journal,* XLIII, 6 (February 1965), 558–567.

——. "Five Philosophical Issues in Counseling," *Journal of Counseling Psychology,* V, 3 (Fall 1958), 211–215.

——. "The Learning of Counseling: Process Not Product," *Journal of Counseling Psychology,* X, 2 (Summer 1963), 163–168.

——. "The Self of the Counselor," *Personnel and Guidance Journal,* XLIV, 8 (April 1966), 807–812.

——. "The Various Faces of Freedom," *Counselor Education and Supervision,* III, 3 (Spring 1964), 115–121.

Astor, Martin H. "Counselors Seek to Understand Themselves: A Philosophical Inquiry," *Personnel and Guidance Journal,* XLIII, 10 (June 1965), 1029–1033.

Barclay, James R. "The Attack on Testing and Counseling: An Examination and Reappraisal," *Personnel and Guidance Journal,* XLIII, 1 (September 1964), 6–16.

Barry, Ruth, and Beverly Wolf, "Five Years of the Personnel and Guidance Journal," *Personnel and Guidance Journal,* XXXVI, 8 (April 1958), 549–555.

————. "Should Vocational Guidance Be Junked?" *National Education Association Journal*, LII, 9 (December 1963), 31.

Berdie, Ralph J. "Counseling Principles and Presumptions," *Journal of Counseling Psychology*, VI, 3 (Fall 1959), 175–182.

————. "The Counselor and His Manpower Responsibilities," *Personnel and Guidance Journal*, XXXVIII, 6 (February 1960), 458–463.

Berger, Emanual M. "Zen Buddhism, General Psychology, and Counseling Psychology," *Journal of Counseling Psychology*, IX, 2 (Summer 1962), 122–127.

Bixler, Ray H. "The Changing World of the Counselor II: Training for the Unknown," *Counselor Education and Supervision*, II, 4 (Summer 1963), 168–175.

Blocher, Donald H. "Issues in Counseling: Elusive and Illusional," *Personnel and Guidance Journal*, XLIII, 8 (April 1965), 796–800.

————. "Wanted: A Science of Human Effectiveness," *Personnel and Guidance Journal*, XLIV, 7 (March 1966), 729–733.

Brameld, Theodore. "Anthropotherapy—Toward Theory and Practice," *Human Organization*, XXIV, 4 (Winter 1965), 288–293.

————. Book Review, *The Philosophical Forum*, XXI (1963–1964), 112.

Bray, Douglas W. "Vocational Guidance in National Manpower Policy," *Personnel and Guidance Journal*, XXXIV, 3 (November 1955), 194–199.

Brigante, Thomas R. "Fromm's Marketing Orientation and the Values of the Counselor," *Journal of Counseling Psychology*, V, 2 (Summer 1958), 83–87.

Cartwright, Dorwin. "Achieving Change in People: Some Applications of Group Dynamics Theory," *Human Relations*, IV, 4 (1951), 388–391.

Chenault, Joann. "Counseling Theory: The Problem of Definition," *Personnel and Guidance Journal*, XLVII, 2 (October 1968), 110–113.

————. "Professional Standards and Philosophical Freedom: A Peaceful Coexistence," *Counselor Education and Supervision*, III, 1 (Fall 1963), 8–12.

Collins, Charles C. "Junior College Counseling: A Critical View," *Personnel and Guidance Journal*, XLIII, 6 (February 1965), 546–550.

Cottingham, Harold F. "The Challenge of Authentic Behavior," *Personnel and Guidance Journal*, XLV, 4 (December 1966), 328–336.

Crawford, Claud C. "Commitment," *Personnel and Guidance Journal*, XLIV, 9 (May 1966), 907–909.

————. "The School Counselor and Religious Liberty," *Counselor Education and Supervision*, VI, 3 (Spring 1967), 208–209.

Curran, Charles A. "The Counseling Relationship and Some Religious Factors," *Journal of Counseling Psychology*, VI, 4 (Winter 1959), 266–270.

————. "Some Ethical and Scientific Values in the Counseling Psychotherapeutic Process," *Personnel and Guidance Journal*, XXXIX, 1 (September 1960), 15–20.

Dewal, Onkar Singh. "Philosophy of Guidance: View from the East," *Personnel and Guidance Journal*, XLVII, 2 (October 1968), 116–119.

Dey, Glen R. "Philosophers, Counselor Educators, and Relevant Questions," *Counselor Education and Supervision*, VIII, 2 (Winter 1969), 135–142.

Dilley, Josiah S. "Decision-Making: A Dilemma and a Purpose for Counseling," *Personnel and Guidance Journal*, XLV, 6 (February 1967), 547–551.

Dinkmeyer, Don. "Contributions of Teleoanalytic Theory and Techniques to School Counseling," *Personnel and Guidance Journal*, XLVI, 9 (May 1968), 898–902.

————. "Developmental Counseling in the Elementary School," *Personnel and Guidance Journal*, XLV, 3 (November 1966), 262–266.

Dreyfus, Edward A. "The Counselor and Existentialism," *Personnel and Guidance Journal*, XLIII, 2 (October 1964), 114–117.

————. "Humanness: A Therapeutic Variable," *Personnel and Guidance Journal*, XLV, 6 (February 1967), 573–578.

Edel, Abraham. "Education and the Quest for Values," *The Philosophical Forum*, XX (1962–1963), 17–34.

————. "Science and the Structure of Ethics," *International Encyclopedia of Unified Science*, II, 3 (1961), 1–101.

Edgar, Thomas E. "Wistful Wish: Evaluation Without Values," *Personnel and Guidance Journal*, XLIV, 10 (June 1966), 1025–1029.

Farson, Richard E. "Introjection in the Psychotherapeutic Relationship," *Journal of Counseling Psychology*, VIII, 4 (Winter 1961), 337–343.

Feder, Daniel D. "Perspectives and Challenges," *Personnel and Guidance Journal*, XL, 1 (September 1961), 6–10.

Ferree, George. "Psychological Freedom as a Counseling Objective," *Counselor Education and Supervision*, III, 1 (Fall 1963), 13–18.

Froehlich, Clifford. "Bedrock for Vocational Guidance," *Journal of Counseling Psychology*, II, 3 (1955), 170–175.

Ginzberg, Eli. "Guidance: Limited or Unlimited," *Personnel and Guidance Journal*, XXXVIII, 9 (May 1960), 707–712.

Grater, Harry A. "When Counseling Success Is Failure," *Personnel and Guidance Journal*, XXXVII, 3 (November 1958), 323–325.

Green, Arnold W. "Social Values and Psychotherapy," *Journal of Personality*, XIV, 3 (March 1946), 199–228.

Hadley, Robert G. "Letter to the Editor," *Journal of Counseling Psychology*, V, 2 (Summer 1958), 152.

Hansen, Donald A. "The Indifferent Intercourse of Counseling and Sociology," *Journal of Counseling Psychology*, X, 1 (Spring 1963), 3–13.

Harris, Philip R. "Guidance and Counseling: Where It's Been—Where It's Going," *The School Counselor*, XV, 1 (September 1967), 10–15.

Hart, Dale J., and Walter M. Lifton. "Of Things to Come—Automation and Counseling," *Personnel and Guidance Journal*, XXXVII, 4 (December 1958), 282–286.

Hipple, John. "Development of a Personal Philosophy and Theory of Counseling," *The School Counselor*, XVI, 2 (November 1968), 86–89.

Horst, Paul. "Educational and Vocational Counseling from the Actuarial Point of View," *Personnel and Guidance Journal*, XXXV, 3 (November 1956), 164–170.

Hummel, Dean L. "The Other Counselor," *Counselor Education and Supervision*, IV, 4 (Summer 1965), 171–179.

Isaacs, W., J. Thomas, and I. Goldiamond. "Application of Operant Conditioning to Reinstate Verbal Behavior in Psychotics," *Journal of Speech and Hearing Disorders*, XXV (1960), 8–12.

Jessor, Richard. "Social Values and Psychotherapy," *Journal of Consulting Psychology*, XX, 4 (1956), 264–266.

Johnson, Ernest L. "Existentialism, Self-Theory and the Existential

Self," *Personnel and Guidance Journal*, XLVI, 1 (September 1967), 53–58.

Jones, A. A. "Proposed Change of Name of the National Vocational Guidance Association," *The Vocational Guidance Magazine*, 8 (1929–1930), 103–105.

Kagan, Henry E. "Psychotherapy as a Religious Value," *Journal of Counseling Psychology*, VI, 4 (Winter 1959), 263–266.

Kagan, Norman. "Three Dimensions of Counselor Encapsulation," *Journal of Counseling Psychology*, XI, 4 (Winter 1964), 361–365.

Kemp, C. Gratton. "Another Note on Counseling and the Nature of Man," Comments and Letters, *Journal of Counseling Psychology*, VIII, 2 (Summer 1961), 186–188.

Krumboltz, John D. "Behavioral Counseling: Rationale and Research," *Personnel and Guidance Journal*, XLIV, 4 (December 1965), 383–387.

———. "Behavioral Goals for Counseling," *Journal of Counseling Psychology*, XIII, 2 (Summer 1966), 153–159.

———. "Parable of the Good Counselor," *Personnel and Guidance Journal*, XLIII, 2 (October 1964), 118–124.

Landfield, A. W., and M. M. Nawas. "Psychotherapeutic Improvement as a Function of Communication and Adoption of Therapist's Values," *Journal of Counseling Psychology*, XI, 4 (Winter 1964), 336–341.

Landsman, Ted. "Existentialism in Counseling: The Scientific View," *Personnel and Guidance Journal*, XLIII, 6 (February 1965), 568–573.

Lowe, C. Marshall. "Value Orientations—An Ethical Dilemma," *The American Psychologist*, XIV (1959), 687–693.

McCully, C. Harold. "Conceptions of Man and the Helping Professions," *Personnel and Guidance Journal*, XLIV, 9 (May 1966), 911–918.

Maes, Wayne R. "Human Freedom and the Counselor," *Personnel and Guidance Journal*, XLVI, 8 (April 1968), 777–781.

Mann, Kenneth W. "Religious Factors and Values in Counseling: Their Relationship to Ego Organization," *Journal of Counseling Psychology*, VI, 4 (Winter 1959), 259–262.

Mathewson, Robert H. "School Guidance: A Four-Dimensional Model," *Personnel and Guidance Journal*, XXIX, 8 (April 1961), 645–649.

Meehl, Paul E. "Some Technical and Axiological Problems in the

Therapeutic Handling of Religious and Valuational Material," *Journal of Counseling Psychology*, VI, 4 (Winter 1959), 255–259.

Morris, Charles, and Phyllis Meek. "Comment," *Personnel and Guidance Journal*, XLV, 3 (November 1966), 217–218.

Mowrer, O. Hobart. "Science, Sex, and Values," *Personnel and Guidance Journal*, XLII, 8 (April 1964), 746–753.

———. "Some Philosophical Problems in Psychological Counseling," *Journal of Counseling Psychology*, IV, 2 (Summer 1957), 103–111.

Moynihan, James F. "The Philosophical Aspects of Guidance," *Review of Educational Research*, XXVII, 2 (April 1957), 186–191.

Murphy, Gardner. "The Cultural Context of Guidance," *Personnel and Guidance Journal*, XXXIV, 1 (September 1955), 4–9.

Nash, Paul. "Some Notes Toward a Philosophy of School Counseling," *Personnel and Guidance Journal*, XLIII, 3 (November 1964), 243–248.

Nelson, Marven O. "Individual Psychology as a Basis for the Counseling of Low Achieving Students," *Personnel and Guidance Journal*, XLVI, 3 (November 1967), 283–287.

Nordberg, Robert B. "Persons and Praxis—A Reply to Rogers," Letters and Comments, *Personnel and Guidance Journal*, XL, 1 (September 1961), 58–59.

Nosal, Walter S. "Letters to the Editor," *Journal of Counseling Psychology*, III, 4 (Winter 1956), 299–302.

Patterson, C. H. "Comment," *Personnel and Guidance Journal*, XLIII, 2 (October 1964), 124–126.

———. "Control, Conditioning, and Counseling," *Personnel and Guidance Journal*, XLI, 8 (April 1963), 680–686.

———. "The Place of Values in Counseling and Psychology," *Journal of Counseling Psychology*, V, 3 (Fall 1958), 216–223.

Peters, Herman J. "The Nature of the Guidance Function," *Counselor Education and Supervision*, III, 3 (Spring 1964), 122–128.

Pohlman, Edward. "Counseling Without Assuming Free Will," *Personnel and Guidance Journal*, XLV, 3 (November 1966), 212–216.

"Religious Factors and Values in Counseling: A Symposium," *Journal of Counseling Psychology*, VI, 4 (Winter 1959), 255–274.

Robb, J. Wesley. "Self-Discovery and the Role of the Counselor," *Personnel and Guidance Journal,* XLV, 10 (June 1967), 1009–1011.

Robert, M., B. Klinger, and Joseph Veroff. "Cross-Cultural Dimensions in Expressed Moral Values," *Personnel and Guidance Journal,* XLII, 9 (May 1964), 899–903.

Rockwell, Perry J., and John W. Rothney. "Some Social Ideas of Pioneers in the Guidance Movement," *Personnel and Guidance Journal,* XL, 4 (December 1961), 349–354.

Rogers, Carl R. "A Note on 'The Nature of Man,' " *Journal of Counseling Psychology,* IV, 3 (Fall 1957), 199–203.

———. "The Place of the Person in the New World of the Behavioral Sciences," *Personnel and Guidance Journal,* XXXIX, 6 (February 1961), 442–451.

Rosenthal, David. "Changes in Some Moral Values Following Psychotherapy," *Journal of Consulting Psychology,* XIX, 6 (1955), 431–436.

Roskens, Ronald W. "Pry Loose Old Walls," *The School Counselor,* XI, 2 (December 1963), 69–84.

Rousseve, Ronald J. "Counselor, Know Thyself!," *Personnel and Guidance Journal,* XLVII, 7 (March 1969), 628–633.

Rudikoff, Lynn C., and Barbara A. Kirk. "Goals of Counseling: Mobilizing the Counselee," *Journal of Counseling Psychology,* VIII, 3 (Fall 1961), 243–249.

Samler, Joseph. "Change in Values: A Goal in Counseling," *Journal of Counseling Psychology,* VII, 1 (Spring 1960), 32–39.

———. Editorial, *Personnel and Guidance Journal,* XXXIV, 1 (September 1955), 41.

Schell, Edith, and Edward Daubner. "Epistemology and School Counseling," *Personnel and Guidance Journal,* XLVII, 6 (February 1969), 506–513.

Schrier, H. "The Significance of Identification in Therapy," *American Journal of Orthopsychiatry,* XXIII (1953), 585–604.

Schwebel, Milton, "Ideology and Counselor Encapsulation," *Journal of Counseling Psychology,* XI, 4 (Winter 1964), 366–369.

Seeley, John R. "Guidance: A Plea for Abandonment," *Personnel and Guidance Journal,* XXXIV, 9 (May 1956), 528–535.

———. "Guidance and the Youth Culture," *Personnel and Guidance Journal,* XLI, 4 (December 1962), 302–310.

Segal, Stanley J. "The Role of the Counselor's Religious Values in Counseling," *Journal of Counseling Psychology*, VI, 4 (Winter 1959), 270–274.

Shoben, Edward J., Jr. "The Counseling Experience as Personal Development," *Personnel and Guidance Journal*, XLIV, 3 (November 1965), 224–230.

———. "Personal Responsibility, Determinism, and the Burden of Understanding," *Personnel and Guidance Journal*, XXXIX, 5 (January 1961), 342–348.

———. "The Therapeutic Object: Men or Machines?," *Journal of Counseling Psychology*, X, 3 (Fall 1963), 264–268.

Sorenson, Garth. "Pterodactyls, Passenger Pigeons, and Personnel Workers," *Personnel and Guidance Journal*, XLIII, 5 (January 1965), 420–437.

Stern, Herbert J. "The Immediate Task of School Counselors," *Counselor Education and Supervision*, IV, 2 (Winter 1965), 93–96.

Stone, Shelley C., and Bruce Shertzer. "The Militant Counselor," *Personnel and Guidance Journal*, XLII, 4 (December 1963), 342–347.

———. "Ten Years of the Personnel and Guidance Journal," *Personnel and Guidance Journal*, XLII, 10 (June 1964), 958–969.

Street, Paul. "Guidance: The Century's Educational Necessity," *Personnel and Guidance Journal*, XXXV, 7 (March 1957), 460–462.

Strickland, Ben. "Kierkegaard and Counseling for Individuality," *Personnel and Guidance Journal*, XLIV, 5 (January 1966), 470–474.

———. "The Philosophy-Theory-Practice Continuum: A Point of View," *Counselor Education and Supervision*, VIII, 3 (Spring 1969), 165–175.

Stroup, Herbert. "Philosophic Aspects of Counseling Communication," *Personnel and Guidance Journal*, XLIV, 10 (June 1966), 1020–1024.

———. "Theoretical Constructs in Student Personnel Work," *Journal of Higher Education*, XXVIII (June 1957), 319–326.

Syz, Hans. "Reflections on Group- or Phylo-Analysis," Supplement to *Acta Psychotherapeutic et Psychosomatica*, XI (1963), 37–88.

———. "A Summary Note on the Work of Trigant Burrow," *International Journal of Social Psychiatry*, VII, 4 (1961), 283–291.

Taylor, Charlotte P. "Social and Moral Aspects of Counseling," Letters from Readers," *Personnel and Guidance Journal*, XXXV, 3 (November 1956), 181.

Vance, Barbara. "The Counselor—An Agent of *What* Change?" *Personnel and Guidance Journal*, XLV, 10 (June 1967), 1012–1016.

Vaughan, Richard P. "Existentialism in Counseling: The Religious View," *Personnel and Guidance Journal*, XLIII, 6 (February 1965), 553–557.

Walker, Donald E. "Carl Rogers and the Nature of Man," *Journal of Counseling Psychology*, III, 2 (Summer 1956), 89–91.

Walker, Donald E., and Herbert C. Peiffer, Jr. "Description, Not Evaluation: A Logical Confusion in Counseling," *Journal of Counseling Psychology*, IV, 2 (Summer 1957), 111–112.

———. "The Goals of Counseling," *Journal of Counseling Psychology*, IV, 3 (Fall 1957), 204–209.

Walters, Orville S. "Metaphysics, Religion, and Psychotherapy?" *Journal of Counseling Psychology*, V, 4 (Winter 1958), 243–252.

Wilkins, William D., and Barbara J. Perlmutter "The Philosophical Foundations of Guidance and Personnel Work," *Review of Educational Research*, XXX, 2 (April 1960), 97–104.

Williamson, E. G. "Counseling in Developing Self-Confidence," *Personnel and Guidance Journal*, XXXIV, 7 (March 1956), 398–404.

———. "The Counselor as Technique," *Personnel and Guidance Journal*, XLI, 2 (October 1962), 108–111.

———. "The Fusion of Discipline and Counseling in the Educative Process," *Personnel and Guidance Journal*, XXXIV, 2 (October 1955), 74–79.

———. "The Meaning of Communication in Counseling," *Personnel and Guidance Journal*, XXXVIII, 1 (September 1959), 6–14.

———. "Value Options and the Counseling Relationship," *Personnel and Guidance Journal*, XLIV, 6 (February 1966), 617–623.

———. "Value Orientation in Counseling," *Personnel and Guidance Journal*, XXXVI, 8 (April 1958), 520–528.

———. "Youths' Dilemma: To Be or To Become," *Personnel and Guidance Journal*, XLVI, 2 (October 1967), 173–177.

Willis, Benjamin C. "The Contribution of Guidance to the High School Educational Program," *Personnel and Guidance Journal*, XXXV, 8 (April 1957), 489–494.

Winborn, Bob. "Comment on Crawford," *Personnel and Guidance Journal,* XLIV, 9 (May 1966), 910.

Wolfle, Dael. "Guidance and Educational Strategy," *Personnel and Guidance Journal,* XXXVII, 1 (September 1958), 17–25.

Wrenn, C. Gilbert. "The Culturally Encapsulated Counselor," *Harvard Educational Review,* XXXII, 4 (Fall 1962), 444–449.

————. "The Ethics of Counseling," *Education and Psychological Measurement,* XII, 2 (Summer 1952), 161–177.

————. "Psychology, Religion, and Values for the Counselor," *Personnel and Guidance Journal,* XXXVI, 5 (January 1958), 331–334.

————. "Status and Role of the School Counselor," *Personnel and Guidance Journal,* XXXVI, 3 (November 1957), 175–183.

Zaccaria, Joseph S. "Developmental Tasks: Implications for the Goals of Guidance," *Personnel and Guidance Journal,* XLIV, 4 (December 1965), 372–375.

## OTHER SOURCES

*Chicago Tribune.* Editorial, "Protest! Keep the Slobs Out of the Schools," August 4, 1963.

Commission on the Reorganization of Secondary Education, Cardinal Principles of Secondary Education, Bulletin No. 35, Washington, D.C.: U.S. Government Printing Office, 1918.

Cribbin, James J. "An Analysis of the Theological, Philosophical, Psychological, and Sociological Principles of Guidance Presented in Textbooks Published Since 1935." Unpublished doctoral dissertation, Fordham University, 1951.

Knowles, Malcolm. An Address at Boston University in May, 1965.

Kohak, Irizim. Notes of lectures given in social philosophy at Boston University in 1965.

Lowe, C. Marshall. "Value Orientations in Counseling: An Ethical Dilemma." Master of Art's thesis, Ohio State University, 1958.

Michael, Donald N. *Cybernation and Social Change: Seminar on Manpower Policy and Program.* Washington D.C.: U.S. Department of Labor, Manpower Administration, 1964.

Mowrer, O. Hobart. "Christianity and/or Psychoanalysis?" Unpublished paper presented at the American Personnel and Guidance Association Convention, Boston, Massachusetts, 1963.

National Defense Education Act, 1958. Washington, D.C.: Congress of the United States.

Ratigan, William. "Conflicts Within Counseling and Guidance in Broad Historical Perspective and in Contemporary Professional Focus." Unpublished doctoral dissertation, College of Education, Michigan State University, 1963.

Richmond, Bert O. "A Concept of Freedom Related to Recent Pronouncements in Counseling and Guidance." Unpublished doctoral dissertation, Indiana University, 1964.

*This Week Magazine,* April 7, 1968.

United States Congressional Labor Committee hearings, televised in March, 1967, regarding the revision of the draft.

Walz, Gary. An address at Boston University to the NDEA Guidance and Counseling Institute in 1965.

# Index

## SUBJECT INDEX